First published in the United States of America in 1991 by

RIZZOLI INTERNATIONAL PUBLICATIONS, INC.
300 Park Avenue South, New York, NY 10010

LC 91-52792
ISBN 0-8478-1413-0

Color separations by Reprocolor Llovet, S. A., Barcelona
Printed and bound by La Polígrafa, S. A.
Parets del Vallès (Barcelona)
Dep. Leg. B. 15.501 - 1991 (Printed in Spain)

Richard Armstrong

AL HELD

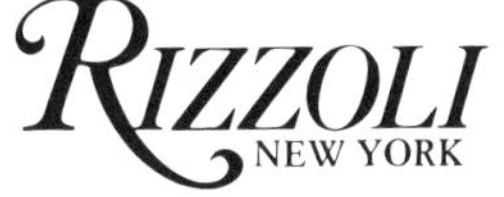

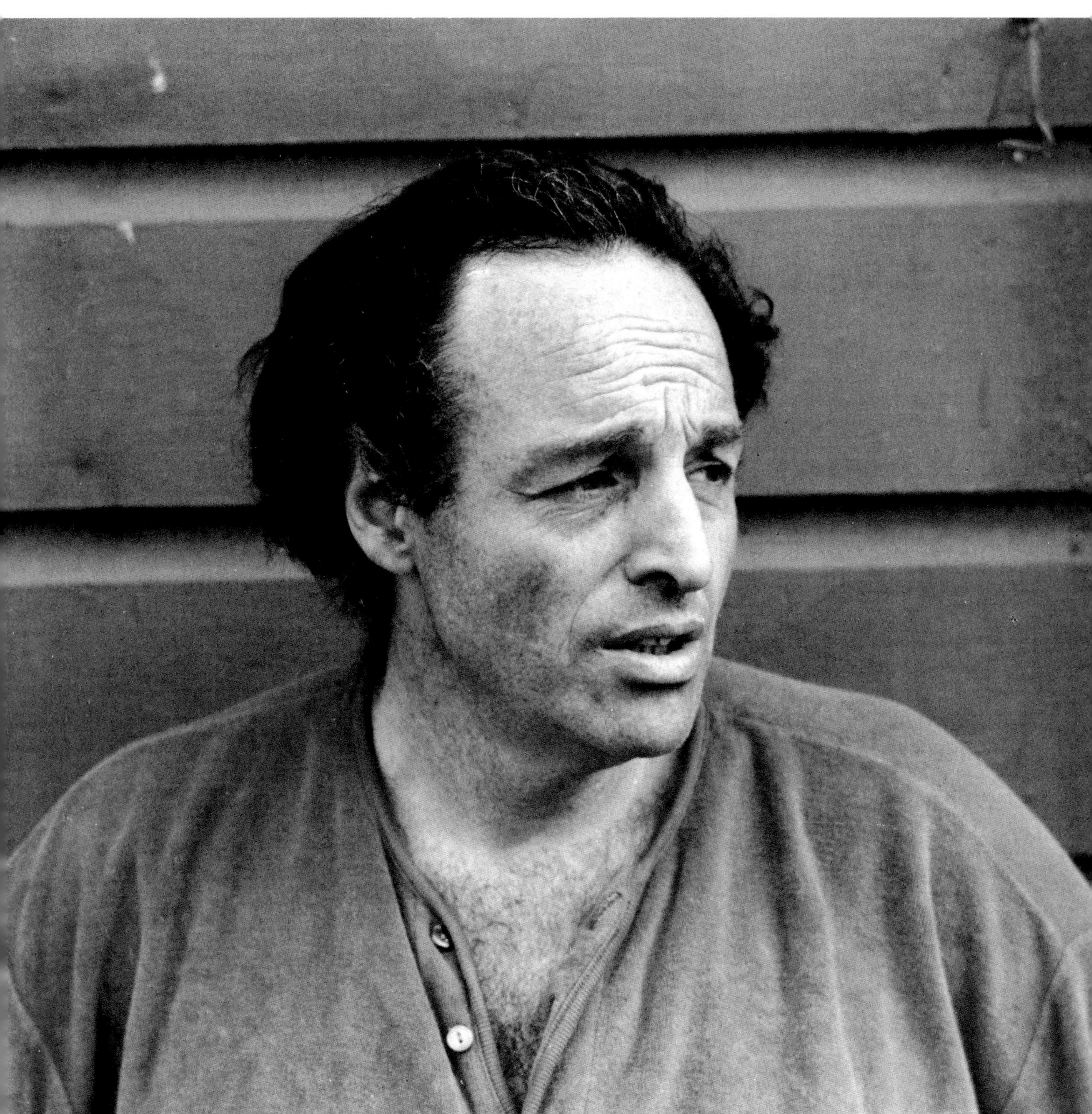

Al Held, 1967.

When they first appeared nearly thirty-five years ago, Al Held's paintings were out of the mainstream of contemporary art. Today his work is even more of an anomaly. Since his decisive turn from Greenbergian formalism in the mid-1960s, Held has sought to revive nonobjective painting. A dedicated abstractionist, he has reconciled himself to theoretical isolation. Lacking context, he found support first in New York School modernism, more recently in the art of the Italian Renaissance. Held's quest to renew abstraction is not unique in his generation, but his continued development of an uncompromisingly geometric vocabulary, illusionistically presented, marks him as exceptional among his peers.

Likewise, a gradual smoothing of the finish and a simultaneous move toward greater clarity of image sets his work apart. The visual language that Held has developed is not always familiar. It is antithetical to the programmatic origins and the product of conceptualism, though it values ideas. It does not employ the vernacular appropriations of pop art or its recent revivals, although it values social dialogue. Nor does it participate in the ambiguous poetics of abstraction as practiced by color-field painters and their reductivist kin, both of whom use treatment as subject. Bereft of irony, his work remains rooted in the heroics of abstract expressionism. Held seems deeply attracted to its use of universal symbols and tendency toward large scale. Avoiding, however, the abstract expressionist's public revelations of ego in their paintings, he has substituted the construct of illusionistic space: its composition and perception, as well as its significance.

In her introduction to the catalogue for the Held retrospective at the Whitney Museum of American Art in 1974, Marcia Tucker noted the parallel between his evolution as an artist and a child's developing spatial perception as described by the Swiss psychologist Jean Piaget. First there is a topological phase, when perceptions of surface are paramount. Held's impastoed paintings of the 1950s recall this stage. Second, a comprehension of space in perspective arises as the individual develops a point of view. Held's simplified pictures of the 1960s come to mind here because of their frontal composition and shallow, layered space. Finally there comes an abstract understanding of space in three dimensions. Held's paintings after 1967 conform to this stage. At first they were exclusively black and white; since 1978 they have been realized in color. In the colored paintings of the last decade or so, Held distorts and greatly dramatizes Euclidian spaces with a characteristic bravado that has made their acceptance even more difficult. At regular intervals in all three stages, Held has worked on grand horizontal paintings (often as commissioned murals) that summarized his evolving ambitions. These pictures constitute one of the most compelling bodies of work in postwar American art. If their premises can be accepted, their conclusions are at once as logical as they are inspired.

As Al Held remembers it, he was expelled from high school in the Bronx on his sixteenth birthday in 1944. A poor reader (today he would be diagnosed as dyslexic), he had lost interest in schoolwork long before. For most of the previous two years, he had taken the subway each morning to New York's Times Square and spent the day going from one movie house to another and watching whatever was playing. The children of Polish immigrants, Held and his younger sister were brought up as cultural rather than religious Jews. Although trained as a jeweler, their father operated a small pickle and herring-vending business that often required his son's help. Like many other Eastern Europeans in New York, the elder Held clung to a belief in Marxism, championing the Soviet system throughout the dark hours of Stalinism. Disputatious political discussions were common in the household; the rest of Held's education took place largely on the streets of Brooklyn and the Bronx. Times Square was an escape from the misery of school and wartime life in New York. Held's apprenticeship in fantasy at the movies obliged him to learn to look. Watching countless hours of film, he became an acutely visual person, one who ingested information looking up at a grand silver rectangle on which larger-than-life images in black-and-white sped before his eyes. After leaving high school, he supported himself with a series of odd jobs until he joined the Navy in 1945.

During two years in the Navy, Held came into contact with all kinds of people and for the first time experienced life outside the confines of the struggling existence of a first-generation New York Jew. In his free time as his ship cruised the Caribbean, Held discovered the joy of reading for pleasure. He devoured whatever books came into his hands and became transfixed by the world of ideas. Like his earlier exposure to films, his reading was random.

Mustered out of the Navy in 1947, Held returned to New York and again took odd jobs while pondering what he wanted to do. His enthusiasm for Henry Wallace's presidential candidacy on the Progressive ticket led him to a group of activists known as Folksay. Members included writers, musicians such as Pete Seeger, and a number of artists, including two young painters, the brothers John and Nicholas Krushenick. Nicholas was especially influential in showing Held that art could be a good medium to express both himself and his Leftist sympathies. Thus, with the assistance of a stipend under the G. I. Bill, Held enrolled in classes at the Art Students League in the summer of 1948. He studied drawing with Kimon Nicolaides and anatomy with Robert Beverly Hale.

Despite the emergence by this time of such avant-garde artists as Jackson Pollock, Clyfford Still, and Robert Motherwell, Held's political ideas fed his initial taste for social-realist art, an orientation reinforced by classes with Harry Sternberg during 1949. With government assistance still available (ninety dollars monthly allowance, of which fifteen was earmarked for supplies), Held made plans to study in Mexico City with the muralist David Siqueiros. When Siqueiros's school suddenly lost its G. I. Bill accreditation, Held quickly decided to go to Paris instead. Henry Wallace's defeat had soured him on American politics, and he had been stunned by a show of Jackson Pollock's work that made him realize the power of abstraction. Thus he wanted not only to get out of the country but also to get away from the two influences on his student work — the Lower East Side and the Art Students League.

Late in 1949, Held sailed for France. To qualify for his monthly government check, he enrolled in the Académie de la Grande Chaumière on the edge of the Latin Quarter in Paris. There he sporadically attended classes of the sculptor Ossip Zadkine. The Left Bank was filled with other young American war veterans trying to forget the war, immersing themselves in the twilight of School of Paris art, and talking big about art. Their contact with the remaining titans of French art — Pablo Picasso, Henri Matisse, Fernand Léger — was largely incidental. Instead the Yanks made friends among themselves. At the Grand Chaumière, Held recalls that critiques in the life class were were conducted by an artist from New York, Earl Kerkham, and half of the students were American. Held saw a great deal of Sam Francis, Salvatore Romano, and George Sugarman; his acquaintances included Ellsworth Kelly, Kenneth Noland, Jules Olitski, and Milton Resnick.

In Paris, Held abandoned his preference for figurative art. Although his first self-appointed exercise had been to cover long lengths of paper with huge, grappling figures, abstraction now absorbed him. The works of Jackson Pollock were distant sirens, especially in contrast to the generally poor abstract paintings on view in Paris. Held soon began a series of small abstractions. He later characterized them as abbreviations of Pollock's grand gestures amalgamated with rectilinear forms derived from Piet Mondrian. These small abstractions constituted his first solo show, held in 1952 at the artist-run Galerie Huit in the Latin Quarter. Obliged to sit with the work during the show's three-week run, Held came away resolved to search again for abstraction via organic subjects. Over the succeeding six months, he made hundreds of drawings of spherical shapes based on small stones he gathered while walking around Paris. Executed in various media on paper, the rock drawings were his first concerted attempt at analyzing form. However modest in scale and skill, they were sufficient to free Held from any lingering interest in representational art.

When he returned to painting in 1953, vestiges of the rock forms were quickly subsumed under an all-over impasto. In their somber colors and dependence on the mark to confer meaning, these pictures seem empathetic with the *tachisme* then in vogue in Paris. The nuanced sophistication that distinguishes the best of the tachistes, Pierre Soulages, Hans Hartung, or even Jean-Paul Riopelle, is largely absent from Held's work of this period. Instead his paintings exhibit a labored opacity. As he adopted the compositional device of a light-colored band of interrelated horizontal and vertical strokes — something like a line of text or a beam of light — the work gained interest.

By the early 1950s the motivating ideas of the abstract expressionists had been discussed at length by both its principal and secondary practitioners. American art was well on the way to dominating the aesthetic dialogue of the Western world. When his G. I. Bill stipend ended in 1953 and Held was obliged to come home, he entered the most advanced, biggest, and best informed art community in the world.

Held's intense attraction to Jackson Pollock's work was shared by many young artists who flocked to New York in the late 1940s and early 1950s. Partisans of Pollock and those of Willem de Kooning constituted the two major poles of the 1950s, with the de Kooning crowd more numerous and better connected to the art press of the day.

Held found a loft in Chinatown hard by the Manhattan Bridge and took a carpentry job at a furniture store. Seeking the advice of older artists, he visited the studios of men like Franz Kline and Mark Rothko. The restrained and basically geometric paintings of the latter artist made him something of an odd man out amongst the freewheeling calligraphy of his peers. Rothko welcomed Held into his studio and shared his works in progress, took the younger artist to lunch, and gently admonished him to find artists his own age as friends. At later times, Held would again turn to Rothko as a sympathetic mentor.

In an effort to approximate the impasto of his recent Paris work, Held took up encaustic as a medium (Kline also suggested it). These colored wax paintings quickly assumed greater vibrancy as his palette expanded, lush darkness giving way to a tertiary melange of yellows and reds, highlighted by undiluted whites. After a fire caused by the highly flammable heated wax destroyed his studio and most of its contents, Held began grinding pigment into linseed oil and other carriers to make his own paint. This permitted the luxury of applying paint thickly and repainting at will. As his strokes became more distinct in color, the inherently rough geometry of their arrangement assumed greater clarity. In such early work as *Untitled No. 60* (1954), Held's ambitions for his work become more evident. Eight by six feet, the encrusted picture implies an architectural scale. From this earliest moment of his mature work, the artist's taste for large and highly tactile paintings makes itself felt. The reality that he was seeking to articulate was an externalized one, as big and visually assertive as the city environment he had returned to. In his gradual envolution toward a more conspicuously geometric image, Held parted company with all but a few of his contemporaries. Ellsworth Kelly was one of his few peers pursuing a related goal. So-called second-generation abstract expressionists struggled to extend the vocabulary derived from the automatic writing and biomorphism of their predecessors. Held, in contrast, wished to order and classicize the vocabulary of abstract expressionism.

The studio fire and a soured marriage compelled Held to find studio space outside New York for financial reasons, and he spent the last months of 1954 in Hoboken, New Jersey. Early in 1955 (after the birth of his daughter Mara), Held decided to leave New York again, this time moving to San Francisco. The artistic climate that he was expecting — the one that Sam Francis and other Bay Area painters had described to him in Paris — had disappeared. Although Held experienced little of its mounting attraction, San Francisco was on the verge of a powerful conversion to figurative painting, led by David Park. Held found a carpentry job making concrete forms for building roads. This physical work and the, to him, unsympathetic glare of San Francisco's light slowed Held's development as a painter. Although assembling the elementary shapes required of form-building may have subliminally reinforced his skills in composing abstract two-dimensional images, the salient benefit of Held's one-year stay in San Francisco was his exposure to its vibrant Beat culture. While there he befriended the young artist Ron Bladen and a young actress, Yvonne Rainer, and came to know two of Clyfford Still's most promising followers, Ernie Briggs and Edward Dugmore. The San Francisco museums and galleries made little impression on him, accustomed as he was to the authoritative collection and exhibitions of the Museum of Modern Art in New York. He found the northern California art world to be fragmented, defensive, and poorly informed.

Returning to New York with Rainer the following year, Held sought out old friends such as the Krushenick brothers. During his absence they had insisted that one of his paintings be shown at a small collective gallery, and Held was only too glad to reciprocate by helping them organize a cooperative gallery, the Brata, on Tenth Street. His work (and eventually that of George Sugarman and other friends) would be shown there in group exhibitions over the next five years.

Held found a studio on West Twenty-first Street off Fifth Avenue and resumed painting. More large and heavily impastoed paintings resulted, beginning a series that lasted for the rest of the 1950s. In both horizontal and vertical formats as large as 6′ by 9′, Held's slow accumulations of thick, distinct marks assumed a consistent character. His understanding of "action painting" was instinctual. Perhaps in some ways it was overly literal and deliberate. Typical of his self-imposed rigor, however, was his ability to infuse vitality into presumably exhausted concepts. Held vigorously sought "to give gesture structure" at a time of increasing doubt among the gesturalists themselves. His ambition was conceptually paradoxical because "gesture" as promulgated by the abstract expressionists was inherently at odds with notions of structure and logic.

Held's attitude and his work ran so counter to received ideas of action painting that he gained relatively little exposure during the last part of the 1950s. His work was not included in any of the Stable Gallery annuals or in either of the "Young American" shows at the Whitney Museum (1957 and 1960). It was in none of curator Dorothy Miller's group shows of emerging artists at the Museum of Modern Art (particularly the 1959 show "Sixteen Americans" that included, among others, Ellsworth Kelly and Alfred Leslie); nor was there any mention in the survey book of eleven artists *School of New York: Some Younger Artists*, put together in 1959 by B. H. Friedman. Held's work only gradually attracted partisans, the most important of whom was Irving Sandler. Nonetheless, through regular shows at the Brata and because of his daily presence in the neighborhood, Held became a familiar part of a downtown scene still centered on Tenth Street, the Club, and the Cedar Tavern.

Perhaps because of his position outside the mainstream, Held's efforts to rationalize the gestures in his work took on a startling assertiveness. Though the forms remained somewhat crude, his palette clarified. Black and white are the constants that reinforce the viewer's scanning pace. Interwoven into the lengths, directions, and thicknesses of other over-all strokes, they play against a limited range of clear reds, greens, and yellows, with occasional dark blue, even pink. The more successful of these pictures, such as *Untitled* (1956) and *Untitled No. 57* (1956), present an impenetrable battery of marks that imply elemental geometries — most frequently, triangles. Unapologetically nonobjective, these paintings allude finally to their own manifestly physical construction. Depicting neither landscape nor figure, they imply both. The subject is the struggle to make sense out of the act of painting.

In this regard, it is interesting to recall Held's visits a few years earlier to Franz Kline and Mark Rothko. Some of Held's subsequent work combines Kline's starkly gestural iconography with Rothko's saturated color. His seeking the counsel of these two very different painters is a sign of Held's self-awareness. Furthermore, his ability to build on their achievements towards a synthesis of impulse and order is an impressive testament to his seriousness.

During the late 1950s, Held's personal circumstances changed. His marriage to Yvonne Rainer dissolved after one year together in New York. His friendships with George Sugarman and Ronald Bladen became central. He argued aesthetics with the two sculptors as the Club became less and less vital. Still working in his studio on West Twenty-first Street, he became friends with other artists living nearby, such as Alfred Leslie and Alex Katz, as well as a young sculptor, Sylvia Stone, who later became his wife.

When the Museum of Modern Art's exhibition "The New American Painting" was presented in New York in the summer of 1959, Held analyzed the work of the abstract expressionists from the viewpoint of his developing disenchantment with action painting. Unimpressed by the luminous amorphism that he felt characterized the more recent paintings in the Modern's influential show, he resolved to work toward more precise form and greater clarity.

As he had done earlier in Paris, Held turned to works on paper to experiment. In three large *Untitled* works he made collages of pages from popular magazines and painted over them. More loosely executed than anything that came before, these collages show a determined will to order the tumult of images associated with postwar living. Beneath a boisterous calligraphy of circles, squares, and triangles, Held allows a crazy quilt of found illustrations to establish a real space conjoined with his fabricated one. This incorporation of extraneous imagery is unique in Held's oeuvre. The collages show him grappling with the disjunction of art versus life that would shortly propel many of his contemporaries into a new kind of representationalism dubbed "pop art." By contrast, Held was still trying to classicize gesture and yet retain the authenticity of feeling he so cherished in abstract expressionism.

In 1959, Sam Francis, away in Europe, offered Held the use of this studio at 940 Broadway, near Twenty-third Street. Covered with skylights, with higher ceilings, and larger that the Twenty-first Street studio, this borrowed space afforded Held the perfect opportunity to redirect his work. Soon after taking possession, he covered the walls with paper and began a painting exercise that extended the spatial implications of the 1959 collages. Several months of catharsis ensued, with Held adopting acrylic paint and reveling in his new technical fluency. The rudimentary geometry of the 1959 work grew to occupy long stretches of paper. Celebrating his taste for bright, primary colors, he tagged these pictures the "taxicab series." Their evolution through 1959 and 1960 was largely one of adjusting form, color, and gesture toward a goal of balanced yet highly active iconography. Relatively flat, the work nonetheless exploits the all-over topology of the impasto paintings of the early 1950s. The diffused forms continue, but not the tactile primacy of the impasto. That was superseded by a flatter, yet more illusionistic, treatment. Forms are compounded and superimposed on one another, as in *Taxicab IV* (1959). An implied depth, albeit shallow, is created to accommodate them. The tremendous scale of these paintings (*Taxicab IV* is 107" by 268") underscores their monumentality and reasserts the artist's basic taste for the urban scale of New York. The paintings embody jumbled forms that suggest frenetic New York street scenes. As more black was introduced into these works throughout 1960, the imagery settled a bit. The resulting paintings imply a more recessive space, though still a discernibly planar one.

The taxicab series culminated in a large, three-panel piece called *House of Cards* (1960). The crowded colonies of rough-hewn geometric forms of its precursors give way here to a stark, elegant assembly of bigger, distinctly colored shapes. As the title suggests, they coexist tentatively; planes of color repeatedly seem about to fall across neighboring planes. Held's color sense shows an increasingly idiosyncratic bent. He successfully forces purples and reds, oranges and yellows, greens and whites to share the same sharply outlined areas. Compositionally the picture reads fluently from either left or right. The bluntly rendered, slightly projecting space developed in the impasto paintings has been superseded by a discursive, lateral space. It leads the viewer across the picture plane with only secondary hints of stacked depth. The gigantic whole (the total size of the three panels being 9'6" by 21'1 ¼") overwhelms any sense of its precarious formal arrangement, it is a brash and noisy homage to the structure and motion of city living.

House of Cards represents the apogee of Held's impastoed and empirically geometric style. The paintings of the next four years reflect efforts on his part to admit more eccentric, somewhat biomorphic imagery into his work, while refining its overall finish and iconic impact. *Ivan the Terrible* (1961) was the next milestone in Held's evolving style. It's vertical format, 12' by 9'6", is somewhat anomalous in a body of square and rectangular horizontals. In it a giant orange cross torques into flat blue and yellow space, partially revealing a rotating white cross like one that animated the left side of *House of Cards*. The maroon band bordering the vertical and horizontal arms of the *Ivan the Terrible* painting are among Held's first declarations of indisputable volume. Though visually complicated almost to the point of contradiction, they insist on the third dimension of the cross. In this version an upper panel (the painting is a stacked diptych) sits atop an optical black-and-white T shape that serves as a kind of socle for the flexing shape above. The painting contains Held's most forceful symbols to date. The title comes from his continuing fascination with films. It alludes to Serge Eisenstein's imposition of a single color scene in his black-and-white movie of the same title.

Ivan the Terrible and a companion painting done months before, *Y and I* (1961), exemplify Held's mastery of his newfound medium, acrylic paint. Each accumulated many coats of paint as Held freely changed both imagery and color. Their lushly opaque surfaces evince multiple underlayers, showing vestiges of previous shapes as well as traces of brush marks and knotted imperfections in the supporting canvas. The paintings share iconographic origins in the alphabet as elaborations of the letters Y and I, I and T. In their assertively frontal compositions, accomplished with a new precision of gesture, *You and I* and *Ivan the Terrible* are harbingers.

As Held's emphasis on gesture waned, his tolerance for more eccentric forms increased. Inspiration came, in part, from the example of Henry Matisse's paper cutouts, presented en masse in the Museum of Modern Art exhibition ''The Last Works of Henri Matisse, Large Cut Gouaches'' (October – December, 1961). Held began to incorporate such biomorphic devices as wavy lines into his paintings. *I-Beam* (1961–62), for example, reprises the form of the capital I found in earlier works, such as *House of Cards*. In *I-Beam* the columnar shape of the I is juxtaposed to a sinuous four-color wave that curves over a field of bright blue. The painting echoes plate XIX of the ''Jazz'' series, ''The Lagoon,'' itself a recollection of Matisse's trip to Tahiti, just as the decoupée origins of ''The Wolf'' (pl. VI) or ''Destiny'' (pl. XVI) must have reinforced Held's growing appetite for a shallow, stacked space and their brillance, his growing confidence in high color.

Held's work developed quickly during the next five years. He had joined the prestigious Poindexter Gallery in 1959 and had his first solo show there the same year. Besides offering him steady financial support, the gallery made his work available to the uptown art world. In 1962, Held accepted an associate professorship at Yale University, and his weekly contact with its ambitious students took the place of the largely disbanded Tenth Street scene. Held's friendships and conversations about art continued with the sculptors Bladen and Sugarman, as well as the painters Alex Katz and Philip Pearlstein. For a few years in the early 1960s, Held spent time with the maverick artist Alfred Jensen. If he heard varying points of view about illusory space and appropriate imagery from his other artist friends, he certainly found in Jensen a visionary color sense that conformed in some ways to his own.

Held returned to the architecture of letters of the alphabet in such works as *The Big A* (1962). The painting measures 10′ by 14′. Its vast white field is compressed by a truncated black A. The related painting *The Big D* (1964) is made more abstract and specific by drawing the D backwards. At this point, the ancient calligraphic significance of Held's favored circles and triangles (the Greek letters *omicron* and *delta* respectively) must have become obvious to him, but his interest in the alphabet superseded symbolic meaning — he used it principally as a concrete, formal exercise. He featured them first in the large four-color painting *Circle and Triangle* (1964). A cropped circle and triangle fill its 12 by 28-foot surface. They appear again in

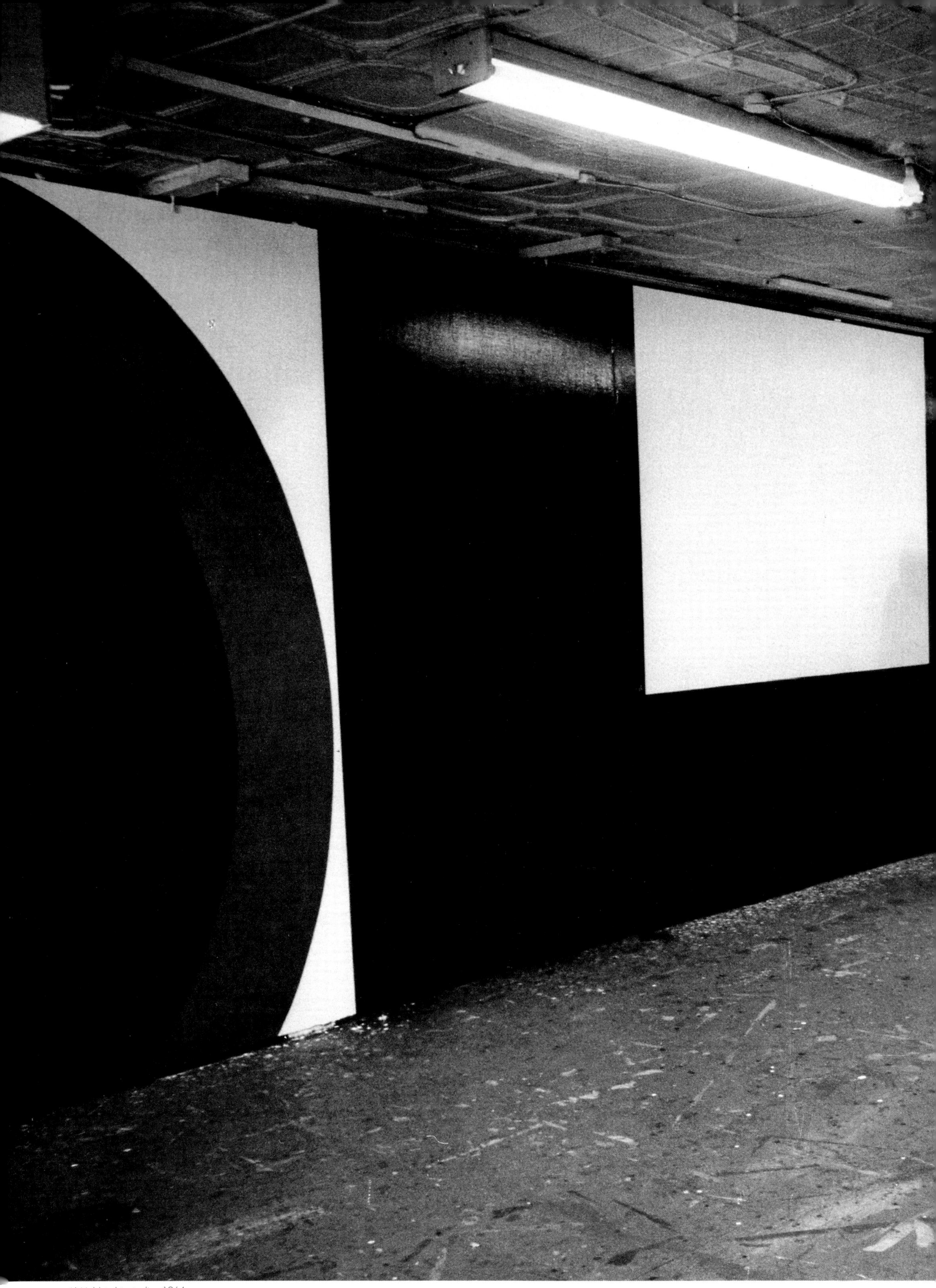

Al Held in his studio, 1964.

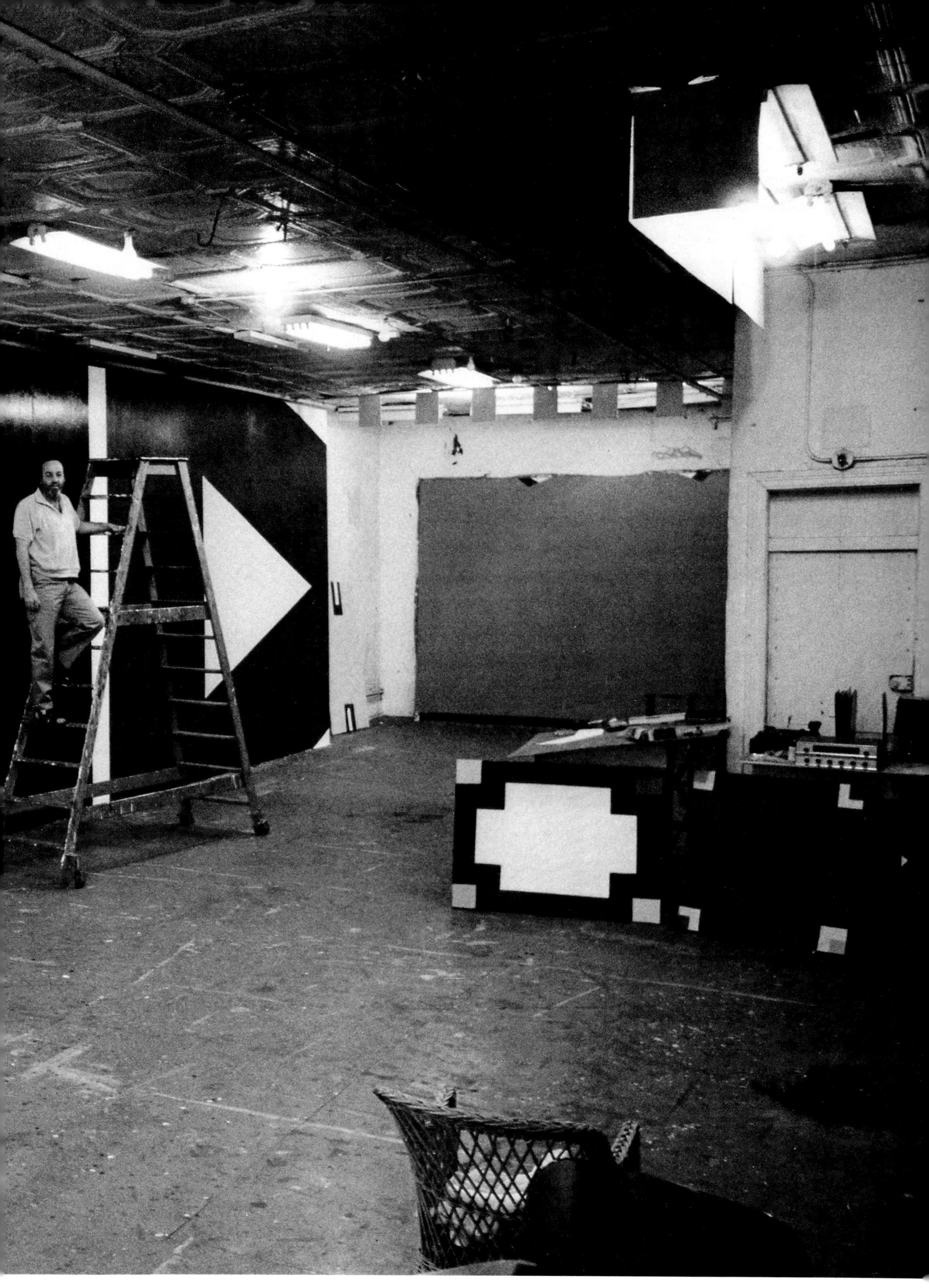

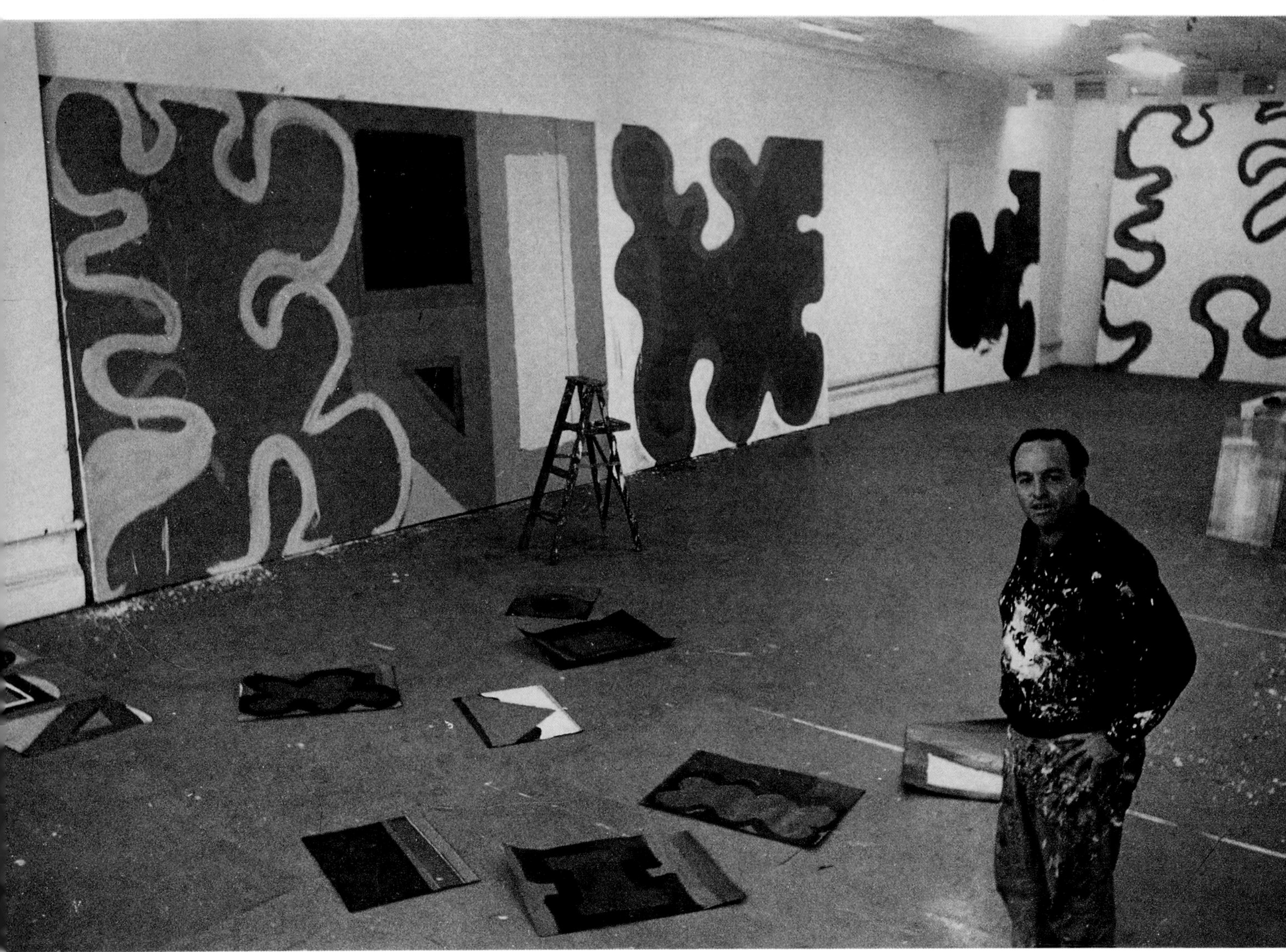

Al Held in studio, 1963. Photo by Rudolph Burckhardt.

the enormous *Greek Garden* (1966); the stark composition consists of a brilliant green field on which an ochre-bordered red circle, a white square overmatted with black, and a yellow triangle stretch side by side across 56 feet of canvas. *Greek Garden* is a summation of his early linguistic-architectural fantasy. By name a landscape and by scale a mural, *Greek Garden* is a synthesis of Held's ambition and his growing powers of articulation.

The origins of the huge images in *Greek Garden* lie in the aptly titled *Genesis*, painted three years earlier. As chronicled by the critic Irving Sandler and the photographer Rudy Burchhardt for one of *Art News* magazine's series on works in progress (''Al Held Paints a Picture,'' May 1964), Held's method of composing by improvisation required a long gestation for each of his paintings. The photographs of the 9'6'' by 28' *Genesis* show it in more than twenty stages of transformation. What begins as a fluid recapitulation of the wave-against-vertical theme of *I-Beam* (with the addition of an oddly anthropormorphic blob that gets covered over, then reappears midway through the sequence, only to be covered over again) is transformed and simplified over months into its final configuration and color scheme. An edge-to-edge orange Maltese cross, framed in dark green on a white field, projects from the picture plane in the left third of the painting, while a giant sinuous black line thrusts leftward from the opposite side. The unifying white field and the pared-down form and color of the work allowed Held to combine both the frontal and lateral spatial effects he was working with at the time.

After his move to the Poindexter Gallery and after the demise of abstract expressionism, Held found new acceptance in the art establishment. His paintings were chose by H. H. Arnason for the ''American Abstract Expressionists and Imagists'' show at the Solomon R. Guggenheim Museum in New York in 1961. They were also included in an important show at the Jewish Museum, ''Toward a New Abstraction,'' in 1963. Furthermore, Clement Greenberg chose them for his eclectic show ''Post-Painterly Abstraction'' in 1964 at the Los Angeles County Museum of Art. In all three instances as well as the Guggenheim show ''Systemic Painting'' in 1966, polemical claims were made for Held's work that were somewhat inaccurate. Despite the wide welcome his work received, Held was already moving away from the concept of total flatness mandated by Greenbergian formalism. His paintings, however slightly, were now obliged to employ illusion in order to properly situate their greatly magnified imagery. Two of his best paintings of 1965 demonstrate this transition. *The Yellow X*, with the familiar form of a distorted cross, is configured as an unmodulated expanse of yellow punctured at each edge by two banded triangles in which separate colors make dimensional and ambient space. The most exaggerated example from this period is *The Big N* which is 9′ high. In it two tiny yellow triangles — one at the top, the other at the bottom of the painting — are butted against small green wedges. These patches of color simultaneously anchor and inflate a blistered white field.

At the same time that he was reducing form in such works as *The Big N*, Held created another body of paintings that presented his familiar images — geometric shapes and letters of the alphabet — in a more illusionistic way. In contrast to the flatness of such rigidly symmetrical works as *Maltese Cross* and *The Red Gull* (both 1964), his subsequent paintings, convey a suggestion of depth in compositions made more complex by the reintroduction if the circles and arcs that form a recurring theme in Held's work. Continuing to use the bright palette that characterized the taxicab paintings, he reordered their eccentrically stacked shapes. For example, a weighty, opaque circle, sliced off by the bottom edge of the stretched canvas, anchors the picture plane in both *The Dowager Empress* (1965) and *Echo* (1966). Each of these large paintings has a thick concentric ring of contrasting color that further fixes the potentially buoyant circle. *The Dowager Empress* recalls *Ivan the Terrible* in the vertical tension of the composition except that the implied activity is now situated in the painting's lower half. A rectangular field of yellow sits atop a red band. Beneath red and green circles, the corners of a black square push into a white border, making an indisputable layered space. Forcing the red band beyond the sides of the canvas reinforces its visual and tensile supremacy. Its point of contact with the yellow further shows Held's insistence on the central role of color in his growing acceptance of illusionism and reiterates the crucial role optical tension would play in all subsequent work.

Paintings like *The Dowager Empress* were increasingly clear expositions of Held's intellectual antipathy to the nonrelational color of Frank Stella's work. Or even more obviously, they reveal Held's rejection of attempts at physical disembodiment, such as those that occupied color-field painters like Noland. In Stella's *Gran Cairo* (1962), concentric squares reflect the shape of the canvas. Stella uses bright unmodulated colors to contradict any sense of depth provoked by single-point perspective. The concentric shapes were an organizing device that Stella had used since his famous black paintings of 1959, although he remained unwilling to contravene modernist taboos against illusionist space until the late 1970s. Similarly, Noland's work from 1958 to 1964 is characterized by a concentric motif: thinly painted circular bands of color, like targets. Centered on square, unprimed canvases, these images are intended to look flat. By contrast, Held's pictures seem, if not labored, then laboriously constructed. Their imagery is obviously the result of trial and error, and in this they differ from the flat abstractions of both Stella and Noland. Moreover, Held's paintings consciously address the role of illusionism in advanced abstraction.

Two works, a large single panel and a two-part mural, typify Held's evolution in the late 1960s. The former, *Mao* (1967), reprises the circles-on-square motif of *The Dowager Empress*. This time, however, Held painted a white circle in the center of the canvas, framing it with an orange-gold concentric band pushed to the edges of the painting. The four corners of a red square peek from under the circle and band. All the three are fitted within a larger, deep blue square. This arrangement reverses the chromatic darkening of *The Dowager Empress*, thereby constructing a spatially recessive image. Beneath the dominant blue square, Held incorporates two planes of color: bands of maroon at the top and bottom and, under their rounded corners, the remnants of a yellow plane. Form and color lock together, making *Mao* an especially confident picture. In its layering of planar space, Held has pushed limitations of this favored arrangement to their limits.

With his first commissioned mural, *I and We*, painted during the summer of 1967, the spatial constraints and possibilities of Held's imagery became even more apparent. When he acquired several barns formerly part of a dairy farm in upstate New York he gained an enormous vaulted studio that facilitated this mural and subsequent large-scale work. Intended for a building designed in Cleveland by Walter Gropius, *I and We* was named in honor of Gropius's book of the same title. There are two parts to the mural; each measures 9′ by 21′. Working in relation to its eventual architectural site, Held set out once again to engage the viewer in the projecting volume of his work. He returned to torqued, notched forms and to spatial disjunctions. Here they are produced by a palette of yellow, blue, and red-orange. At the interstices, black and/or white triangular notches twist and contradict the supposedly layered relationships, as they did in such predecessors as *Ivan the Terrible*. Visually complex and monumental, the *We* half of this work brings together Held's experience in deliberate space-making. In the *I* section, he reconsiders a frontal and more static format, both enlarging and simplifying it. A giant maroon arc glides across a white ground. Optically and logically puzzling, its two fragments slice through the white field, layering whatever space exists inside its circumference from that outside. Installed above eye-level at opposite ends of a large room, the ensemble *I and We* fused Held's frontal and his contorted images, grandly stating the concerns implicit in his 1960s paintings.

Held often took up smaller paintings (mostly 3′ by 2′) during the mid-1960s to explore systematically the iconographic value of letters of the alphabet and similar shapes. Besides his search for nonobjective yet metaphorical form, he resented the constraints against spatial illusion still harbored in his style. Partly in reaction, he made hundreds of drawings in India ink on paper during 1966 and 1967 in which he isolated the gestures of his paintings. Sometimes a single horizontal or vertical line, they are more frequently spare arrangements of circles, squares, and triangles. As usual, drawing hastened Held's conceptual evolution and he resolved to proceed resolutely into illusionism.

With an exhilaration reminiscent of his mood in making his first large-scale paintings in Sam Francis's loft in 1960, Held plunged into the new style. Using charcoal and white acrylic, he drew and painted big colonies of interlocking shapes that, with their curving arrows and fractured arcs, seemed to emerge from the picture plane.

In the early *Untitled* (1967), Held still surrounded his white images with a colored ground (green, in this case). Quickly, however, he eliminated all color and regularized his drawing by using tape for guidelines. In many instances these new pictures show a kinship with formal aspects of the paintings of Fernand Léger. Held used a similar cloisonné-like drawing method. He also created crowded compositions, such as *Four Columns* (1967), that recall the packed clusters of figures characteristic of Léger's late work. Shortly, as if in reaction to this kind of representational inference, Held invented an all-over structure. It appeared in his first fully realized black-and-white paintings, the *B/W* series, begun in late 1967. In these large, squarish pictures, he filled each canvas with both complete and incomplete geometric shapes, predominantly cubes and rhomboids. Their uniform black outlines — the edges made palpable by Held's new technique of first putting down a masking-tape guideline — form a second picture plane parallel to the white field on which they are located. These bold diagrams created highly defined abstract imagery, ultimately revealing the painting's sought-after illusion of depth. The anonometric *B/W* paintings signaled Held's new intentions. Some of them were featured in his second solo exhibition in 1967 at the André Emmerich Gallery and also in 1968.

Though his work shared little or nothing with such dominant 1960s art movements as color-field painting, minimalist sculpture, and pop art, Held attracted important critical and public support. In 1966 the Stedelijk Museum, Amsterdam, gave him a one-man exhibition, and during 1968 two separate solo shows were presented in the United States. The larger exhibition was shown at the San Francisco Museum of Modern Art and the Corcoran Gallery of Art, Washington, D.C. It surveyed almost ten years of Held's paintings, thus affording a rare overview of his work. The smaller show, consisting exclusively of the black-and-white paintings from 1967–68, was presented first at the Institute of Contemporary Art, Philadelphia, and then in the lobby of a Houston skyscraper under the auspices of the Contemporary Arts Museum. Confronted in this show with the results of his previous two years of work, Held redouble his energy. During 1969 he complicated his new imagery and changed its format. In certain canvases, such as *B/W XII* (1968) and *B/W XV* (1968), he successfully introduced vanishing points into the severe black-and-white paintings, varying their internal scale. At the same time, in related works such as *B/W XIII*, a relatively constant internal scale is maintained, but forms are arranged in quirky and intellectually engaging perspectival relationships. Though less crowded than their immediate forebears, these paintings gain strength by their eccentric logic. In his previous color paintings, Held seemed obliged to make theoretically incompatible forms coexist; in the black-and-whites, on the other hand, he accepted the flexible meanings that allowed many simultaneous readings of his imagery. These etherealized black-and-white diagrams leave behind the constraints of gravity, which so often dominated his work of the 1960s.

Intrigued by the infinite permutations that seemed available, Held indulged his taste for epic scale by adopting an enlarged horizontal format. Both his New York loft and his upstate summer studio could accommodate big work. The canvases in the *Phoenicia* series (1969), generally 8′ by 11′, reprise Held's densely packed,

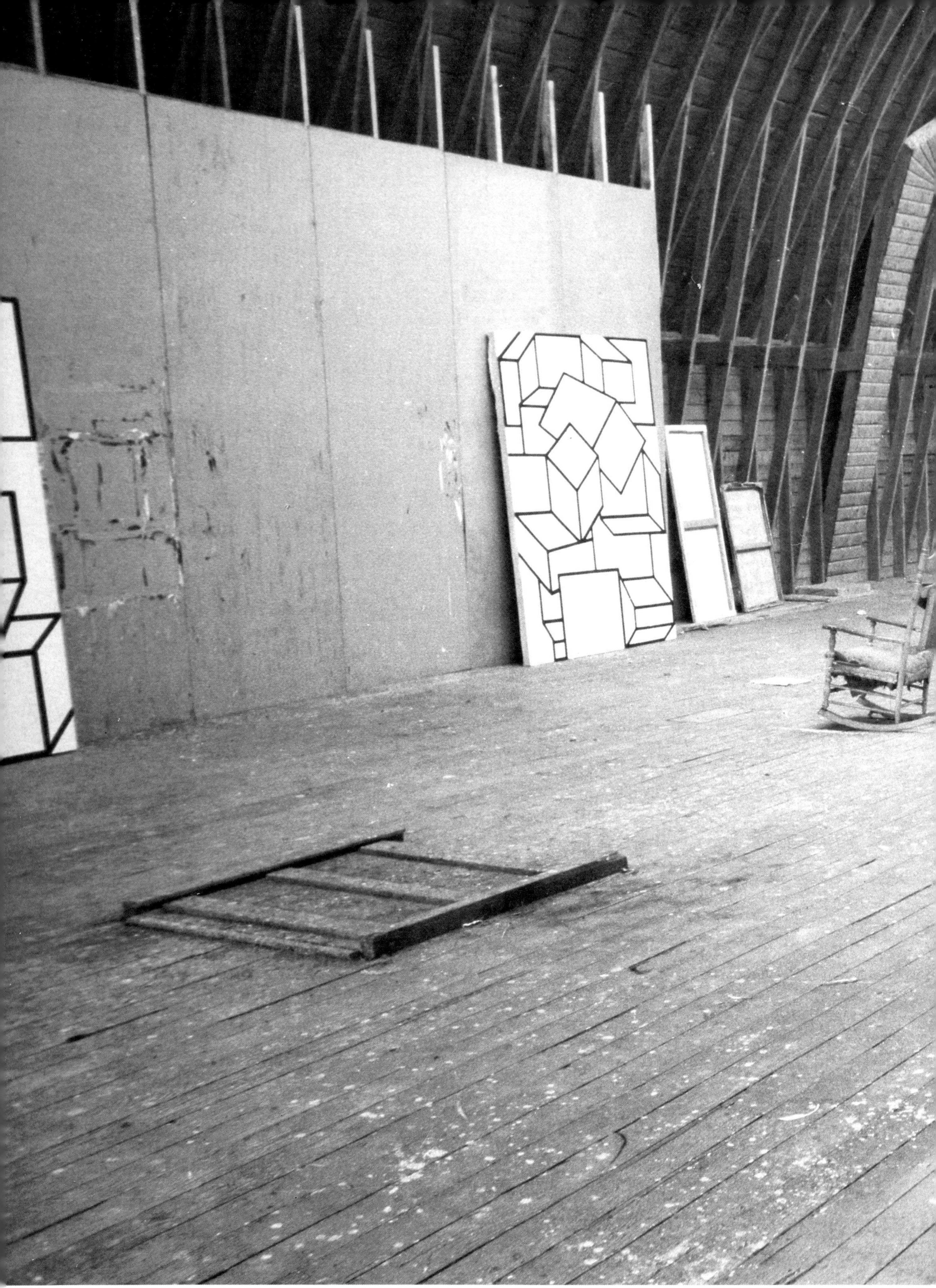

Al Held in his studio, 1967.

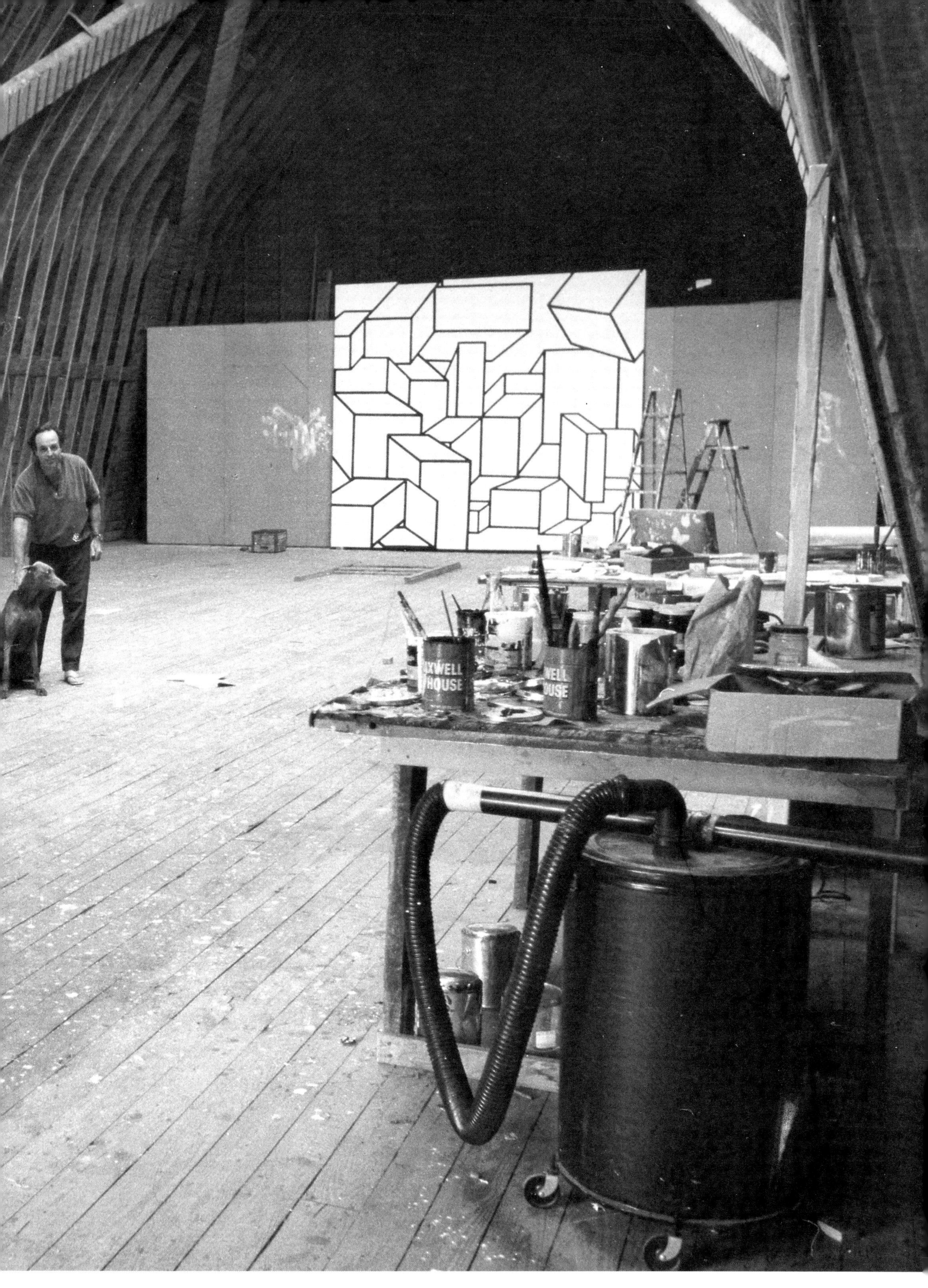

XWELL
HOUSE
WELL
HOUSE

all-over arrangements. Comprised mostly of cubes and rhomboids, these paintings can be read in contradictory ways, as implied volumes alternately pop forward and recede. We are invited to test various readings that allow for discontinuity, random access, and multiple and simultaneous points of view. Elaborate interconnections to different layers of space are thus revealed. In paintings like the *Phoenicia* series, Held turns the canvas into an expanded horizon on which images hover in a suspended yet animated state.

In refining his working method, Held began a few years earlier to use a rotary sander to eliminate the painted-over ghosts of earlier forms. The sanding created a more neutral field but one that admitted its hand-crafted status. Still, roughly parallel strokes of broadly applied white paint are evident on close inspection, and they help energize the field. Held composed empirically on full-size canvases; he used black tape pulled taut to show how linear elements could be arranged and rearranged. Once the composition had been decided (though still subject to countless revisions), black lines were roughly painted and then covered with tape. A coat of white paint was added, and when the tape was peeled away, precise, incised edges bounded the black lines. This depersonalized treatment, which Held continued to refine, amplified the purely visual aspect of his increasingly sophisticated vocabulary. As their tactility was reduced, these structures gained a sense of agravitational solidity that, ironically, rendered them more engaging. Held's decision to remove the traces of his hand is his only connection to either the minimalists or the pop artists that dominated the American avant-garde at that time. His old-fashioned insistence on the transformation of materials put him at odds with the minimalists, while the pop artists' quotations from popular media were utterly foreign to his invented language. The disregard for illusory space of both groups further distanced him from them and the majority of advanced artists.

Held's move to a large-scale rectangular format during 1969 and 1970 was prompted in part by a mural commission for the state capitol building complex in Albany, New York. Because of its extreme length (the canvas is 10′ by 90′) Held composed the Albany mural to be read in motion. The device of a repeated and fragmented arc underscores the internal composition while pacing the rate at which the eye and body digest the total imagery of the piece. A full repertoire of free-floating geometric volumes moves across the picture's surface. Entitled *Rothko's Canvas* in homage to the New York School master, the kinesthetic vibrancy of the work attests to Held's natural affinity for such large scale. It also marks his transition from projective spatial simulations to Euclidean models.

In the painting *Promised Land* (1969–70) and the related *Noah's Focus* series (1970–71), Held reconsidered the elongated composition of *Rothko's Canvas*. Gradually he confounded the seamless sweep of the mural with a variety of spatial nuances. Dramatic and dynamic confluences of volumes coexist with smaller shapes. The steady tumble of forms in the mural is replaced in these later works with a more turbulent and localized sense of space. It is as if major and minor keys are mixed for the first time, as if Held is giving up the harmony of his compositional technique. Likewise, in the somewhat smaller paintings of the *Stratus* series (1971), Held emphasizes these spatial discords, emphatically varying both the thickness of his line, or drawing, and the internal scale of the thing drawn. A related sense of exploration prompted other changes. For example, Held used the tondo format for his *Skywatch* series of 1971–72. The shape of the canvases is often echoed by cylindrical fragments drawn in the works.

More profound, perhaps, was his reversal in 1971 of the role of black and white. Employing the same technique, Held made black paintings in a long series called *Black Nile*. They are devoid of the associative, completely imagined tonalities seen in the white pictures. Any possibility of ambient light coloring Held's forms disappears in a matte, opaque black field. The result is a new emphasis on drawing. The schematized system of white lines must define and activate form on a visually obdurate surface. In the later, large *Black Nile* paintings and their more complex successors, such as *Flemish VIII* (1979), Held's drawing becomes increasingly flat and fragmentary, the imagery less physically plausible. The unabashedly intellectual nature of his abstraction asserts itself most clearly in these black paintings.

During 1973 and 1974, Held's white paintings assumed a classical assurance. Named for points of the compass as if to reinforce their logic and formal specificity, they are grand and concrete. Rectilinear grids subdivide the large canvases (8′ by 12′) and help make them more visually logical. *South-Southwest* (1973), for example, features triangles, circles, rhomboids, and cubes of various sizes outlined in varying thicknesses of black, in front of and behind a slightly skewed and elongated horizontal grid. An elegant weightlessness makes these paintings particularly handsome examples of Held's mature period.

One-man exhibitions at the André Emmerich Gallery in New York in 1968, 1970, 1972, and 1974 brought new converts to Held's work. In the autumn of 1974, a large exhibition of paintings of the previous twenty-five years was presented at the Whitney Museum of American Art. There the evolutionary logic of Held's work became apparent, and both new and old paintings were seen to great advantage.

The Whitney Museum show substantiated Held's theoretical import as an alternative to the abstract painting that followed abstract expressionism. Almost alone among his peers (with the notable exception of Frank Stella), Held decisively rejected reductivist aesthetics. He eschewed the practice of both his color-field painting peers and that of the somewhat younger painters allied with minimalist sculpture. So compelling was Held's desire to construct the most accommodating painting possible that in 1973 he again felt constrained by the limits of imagery. In the *Solar Wind* series (1973–74) of four paintings, each 5′ by 6′, he introduced a new device. Small, opaque circles and squares, taken from his contemporaneous drawings, punctured the skin of his paintings. These small black punctuation marks played havoc with the airy space of the white fields. Although inarguably located on the surface, they establish a picture plane, pictorial space, and scale of their own. By insisting, as they do, on the spatial fiction of the larger environment around them, they indicate the artist's urge to move beyond the synthetic order he had by now achieved in his work.

This development in Held's paintings was serendipitously interrupted during 1975 and part of 1976 while he carried out a commission from the Government Services Administration for an enormous mural for a new Social Security building in downtown Philadelphia. Held conceived two paintings, each 90′ long for the building's ground floor. Separated by a large passageway, they were meant to be read at a distance (optimally from the street) through floor-to-ceiling windows. Entitled *Order/Disorder/Ascension/Descension*, the two parts of the work recapitulate the preceding seven years' work in black and white. The 30′ width of the corridor that houses the mural forces the viewer to read the piece laterally, while walking along its length. Viewed from right to left or left to right, the power of the works is equally affecting. This is a panorama seen up close not unlike the magnified and greatly foreshortened view from the front row of the cinema. From afar the two giant paintings fill the eye.

Held's consistently productive work habits were altered first by helping to organize the museum show and then by the demands of the Philadelphia mural. His drawings during this period, from 1974 to 1976, were an outlet and an experimental forum. The *Solar Wind* paintings, for instance, are peppered with dots, dashes, ellipses, and small squares and rectangles. They outnumber Held's typical volumetric images. Principal among other devices was a doubling and tripling of the familiar parallel lines of varying width that bounded these. Further signaling his appetite for change, Held reintroduced limited color into his works on paper. This radical revision would not appear in his paintings until 1978.

Held's new taste for echoing certain lines bore immediate fruit. In the *Mercury Zone* series of 1976, a grid of parallel lines emphasized the overall field of each painting, subordinating the other imagery, including the ''punctuation marks.'' In the series of black *Volta* paintings made during 1976 and 1977, Held applied the doubling technique to all his forms. The underlying grid thus had a shallow depth that recalled the effect of the triangular wedges in paintings like *The Yellow X*. The doubling of forms also created a torque comparable to that in the earlier pictures. The slightly curved grid in *Volta IV* (1977) makes it look concave, while *Volta VI* (1978) seems convex. Both paintings and larger companion works, such as *Volta V* (1977), are filled with action because of Held's new illusionism.

In white paintings from this period, optical effects are especially pronounced. Doubled and/or curving grids rip through *Inversion X* (1977), for example. Their dynamism is interrupted in turn by a triangle in the center with a smaller triangle on one side and a pair of circles on the other. In the tangle of overlapping shapes that appear, dissolve, and reappear Held has shattered the picture plane into multi-faceted relief, albeit completely illusionistically. Related, if somewhat more subdued, breaks in the picture characterize his 1978 paintings. They are Held's most aggressive works, in terms of optical effect. Sometimes the picture plane is so disrupted as to distort, almost negate, the composition.

Taking up color again in 1978, Held employed shattered, bright, illusionistic compositions, directly related to such precedents as the *Inversion* series. The structures with double and triple outlines that had looked starkly three-dimensional in the black-and-white work assumed different meanings in color. The light of the black-and-whites was evenly dispersed, whereas contrasts of color entailed questions of light sources and modeling. Characteristically, Held brought back color with gusto, seemingly in a great hurry to try out as many (and as many supposedly incompatible) hues as possible. His substantial body of work from the 1960s naturally informed these successor paintings. Interestingly, the earlier work seems to have exhausted his taste for variations on primary colors. Instead Held turned to an unabashedly artificial spectrum with a special fondness, at least initially, for pinks and rose-based browns, as exemplified in such paintings as *B-G-1* and *C-P-1* (both 1978). No doubt concerned to maintain the intellectual integrity of his structures by contradicting any figure/ground readings with their inferences of landscape, Held pursued his unique color sense throughout 1979. In using yellow to direct the spatial dynamics of paintings like *C-Y-1* (1978) and *D-C* (1979), he moved closer to naturalist implications. Perhaps the most successful of the early color paintings are those constructed around a floating, horizontal grid, such as *D-C*, *P-P* (1979), and *M-M* (1979). At 8′ by 14′, *D-C* is the largest of these works and one of the best. The red horizontal grid sets up a tilted plane at variance with the violet-blue ground of the picture plane. Arching over it is a giant brown grid twisted into an eccentric configuration that seems simultaneously concave and convex in relation to the red-laced plane. A bevy of smaller, lightly outlined cubes and triangles floats across the picture plane, passing through three blue and green circles. The ensemble is tied together by a yellow rectangular frame of triple thickness that bends in jagged folds as it weaves through the densely populated composition. A convincing and forceful exposition of the coexistence of a variety of spatial denominators, *D-C* shows Held in full control of the new balance between color and form.

The rectangular bands that bind together *D-C* are converted into L-shaped wickets in other paintings from 1979, such as *S-L*. A dominant yellow-blue band lopes through *S-L*. The painting borrows shapes from *D-C*, but structures and colors them to suggest a vantage point beneath the painting. Related partial views in other 1979 paintings evince the artist's ability to position, and often subsequently refute, the viewer's stance. Cropping and lighting images in particular ways, Held repeatedly demonstrates the accommodating reality of pictorial illusion. With *S-L* he fully activates the space between viewer and painting, suggesting its transformation and conclusion in the art object.

The dialogue with his students that he had once enjoyed no longer satisfied him, so Held resigned his Yale professorship in 1980. That summer he completed the grandest and most portentious of the early color paintings, *M's Passage*. A reprise of the floating grid device, this work benefits from a large format (9'6'' by 16') and a corresponding enlargement of its internal scale. For the first time, the artist also butts together large horizontal planes of color, tacitly providing a horizontal line. An upright grid pierces and suppresses a free-floating grid of light green. A giant curved grid, composed of two closely related blues, swoops behind the other two. A fourth grid, impossibly drawn, seemingly peaked, winds through the whole composition. In paintings like this, the sense of specific location is especially pronounced. Curiously, it may be a presentiment of Held's fate. By the end of 1980, he was in Rome for a six-month residency at the American Academy. Although Held is a relatively well-traveled man, this was his first sustained contact with Italy. Rome's rich melange of urban styles from historical to modern intrigued and instructed him. His January–June sojourn also was timed for him to witness an Italian spring and the change of light. The trove of Renaissance paintings in Rome and its environs was an even richer experience. He could look unhurriedly at early and High Renaissance masterpieces and return to see them in different lights. Outside the centrifugal logic of New York, he could easily identify the enduring values that he had been seeking in his own very different, nonobjective art.

As a result, Held's color paintings assumed a new sureness. In the *Herculaneum* and *Hadrian's Court* series (both, 1982), for instance, he for once constructs what seem to be interior spaces. The vertical and horizontal planes of the *Herculaneum* paintings read as floors and walls, while the fragmentary and angular blue and red ribbons that probe its recesses and protrude from its picture plane are like parts of a mosaic. In the *Hadrian's Court* paintings, by contrast, enclosure is all: a spherical void (perhaps representing the mind) is doubly, then triply encased in a gridded, rectangular structure. The red fields of these paintings add to their ominous mood of entrapment. The manipulated external vantage point of earlier, predominantly horizontal, gridded paintings like *M-M* is forced back into the interior of this work, tacitly becoming its subject.

More familiar, like an urban landscape, is *Piero's Piazza* (1982), in which Held stations upright cubes at the end of a long, forced vista, perhaps in homage to Renaissance architecture. Grids lie horizontally across the bottom of the painting. A light-colored grid, hovering at the top, compresses the painting's atmosphere. A giant grid of fluorescent green recedes from the right side down the center. A high-key conglomeration of orange, yellow, green, pink, and scarlet — Held's salute to his favorite Renaissance artist, Piero della Francesca — exudes a brilliant and inviting light. In the *Rome* paintings that followed, Held maintained the sharply contrasting palette of his Italian series. The largest of these paintings, *Rome II* (1982), is majestically scaled at 9′ by 18′. It is composed as a celebration — an abstract ascension, as it were. A vertical column marks the painting's center. Its radiating spokes turn downward into a blue-green circle and an underlying yellow grid. Above the far perimeter of the circle, three bands of color — orange, maroon, and scarlet — arch up as a kind of rainbow. Floating before this circular gateway (reminiscent of such works as *Dowager Empress* and *Mao*) are seven reddish bands. Rising into the atmosphere, they leaven the painting and impart a gentle motion.

The following year brought another commission for a large mural, this time for the lobby of a Dallas office building. It demanded the grand scale that Held relishes. *Mantegna's Edge* (1983) is enormous: 14′6″ by 52′10″. Filling the space from floor to ceiling, the mural responds to the upward drift of *Rome II*. *Mantegna's Edge* diffuses weightlessness across a broader expanse and does so less explicitly. Densely packed, it is most active at the sides and bottom: large rhomboids project outwards above a stack of parallel grids. The six parallel rhomboidal columns recede into the center of the painting, measuring its depth at three regularly gridded interstices. A light gridlike skein covers the distant, powder-blue sky. This mist further negates the ascension also denied by the single-point perspective that orders at least the middle third of the mural. In *Mantegna's Edge* Held has turned upside down the world considered earlier in *Rome II*. He reconsiders its expansive space and invites the informed viewer to realize the adaptive logic of his imagery.

Other works from the same time exhibit similar attempts to reactivate static space. They range from the looping encirclement of the *Thalassa* series (1982–83) to the implied spinning of *Pisa II* (1983).

The motif of compression that was first suggested in *Piero's Piazza* became more fully developed in the series *Pan North* begun in 1984. A jagged beam strides across the crowded landscape of many of the early paintings in this series. Frequently orange, as in *Pan North IV* (1985), the beam's peaked shape recalls Held's long use of triangles. Like triangles, these shapes boldly insist that all sides (specifically here, the top and bottom of the rectangular paintings) are of comparable value; that is, the composition can be inverted. Enormous expanded grids recede with equal ease from either top or bottom. The neighboring shapes look similarly invertible. In all cases, they interlock in a dense but penetrable way.

None of the *Pan North* paintings evince these qualities more emphatically than the largest, *Pan North XII* (1988). A darker palette, redolent of dusk, distinguishes the work. Its 25′ length is thickly populated with somber circles, cylinders, and a dark, massive, overhead grid. Two bright red V's bounce obliquely through the painting, and distant patches of light green and pink glimmer through the darkness.

This preoccupation with dusky light also characterizes the *Vaporium* paintings of 1987–88. Again, barely distinguishable forms occupy the canvas. Because cylinders most often frame a distant light, the series metaphorically resembles oppressive and constrained movement through a tunnel. Vision is limited by opaque color and form; its only caprice is to seek out the bright patches of color that gleam from the recesses implied in each work.

Concurrently, but on an opposite note, Held elaborated the ascending motion of the *Rome* works in a series of *Circle* paintings begun in 1985. In *The First Circle* from 1985, he positioned two yellow rings above one another. They float in a light green atmosphere that also houses smaller circles, grids, a rhomboid, and a pyramid. The exaggerated length of the painting — it is 5′ by 16′6″ — further heightens the artist's skilful distortions of perspective. Unlike the exclusionary *Vaporiums*, we are immediately insinuated into the lateral expanse of the painting, a sensation Held emphasizes in its companion *The Second Circle* (1987). Six bands of varying scales now fill the canvas, their upward progress held in check by three interstices of a rotated grid that skewers them. No such impediment restrains the ascending concentric bands of *The Third Circle* (1988). Its rectangular format, 14′ by 25′, lifts the painting upwards.

The directed and active visual narrative of *The Second Circle* and *The Third Circle* continues in succeeding paintings. Rather than direct the eye upward, in certain recent paintings such as the *Fathom Mark* series, Held composes subjects to force a deep penetration of the pictorial space. This is first introduced in *Fathom Mark XVI* (1989) and *Vaporium VII* (1989) as a lighted and distant spot framed by dark foreground shapes that beckon the eye through the painting. Given the generally dark palettes of these paintings, Held's light in the distance device appears a forced conjunction of night and day light in one synthesized format. The radically different spatial perceptions of those ambient conditions are contrasted and meld together. The brilliant cerises and oranges of the subsequent *Quattro Centric* paintings evince Held's continuing fascination with the nuances of mass and spatial configuration in various lights.

In the twenty odd years since its maturation, Held's work has come to occupy an uncrowded, if portentious intellectual place within modernist culture. An early and complete refutation of the formalist insistence on flatness, it is nonetheless profoundly attached to the ambitions of abstraction. Complex and patently illusionistic, his paintings stand apart from their peers. He imparts grand meaning to a universe of essentially linear motifs that, in his hands, suggest both the order and the disorder of consciousness itself.

CHRONOLOGY

1928 Born October 12 in Brooklyn, New York, son of Harry and Clara Held. Family (including younger sister, Roberta) lives in Brooklyn and the Bronx where Held attends public schools, leaving high school in 1944.

1945–47 Serves in United States Navy.

1948 Makes friends with artists, poets, and musicians in Folksay, a political activist group, who encourage his nascent interest in painting. Enrolls at Art Students League.

1949 Continues classes at League, studying with Harry Sternberg. Makes plans to study with the muralist David Siqueiros in Mexico but changes his mind when Siqueiros' school loses its G.I. Bill accreditation. Instead he applies to the Académie de la Grande Chaumière and leaves for Paris.

1950–53 Studies with Zadkine at the Académie, concentrating on drawing. Away from New York, Held gains greater appreciation for the School of Paris work on view at The Museum of Modern Art. Living on the Left Bank, Held comes to know the large community of American expatriate G.I.s. His first solo exhibition at Galerie Huit (1952).

1953 Returns to New York, finds temporary work, and marries. A studio fire destroys most of his work.

1954 Daughter Mara born. Moves to Hoboken, New Jersey.

1955 Moves to San Francisco, working as a rough-in carpenter. Meets artists Yvonne Rainer and Ronald Bladen.

1956 Returns to New York. With Folksay friends John and Nicholas Krushenick, founds cooperative Brata Gallery. Frequents The Artists Club and Cedar Tavern, shows work in New York for the first time at Camino Gallery on Tenth Street.

1957 Work included in group show at Tanager Gallery.

1959 First solo show in New York at Poindexter Gallery. Sam Francis lends his large studio at 940 Broadway to Held for two years.

1962 Appointed Associate Professor of Art at Yale University.

1964 Joins André Emmerich Gallery.
Wins Frank G. Logan Medal from Art Institute of Chicago.

1965 Buys farm in the Catskill mountains with large dairy barns which becomes summer residence and studio.

1966 Awarded John Simon Guggenheim Fellowship in painting. Solo exhibition at the Stedelijk Museum, Amsterdam.

1967 Completes mural *I and We* for Tower East, Cleveland.

1968 Solo exhibition presented at the San Francisco Museum of Art, subsequently shown at the Corcoran Gallery of Art, Washington, D.C.
First black and white paintings featured in solo exhibition at the Institute of Contemporary Art, Philadelphia, subsequently shown at Contemporary Arts Museum, Houston.

1969 Moves to loft on West Broadway, Soho.

1970 Completes mural *Rothko's Canvas* for Governor Nelson A. Rockefeller Empire State Plaza, Albany, New York.

1974 Retrospective exhibition presented at the Whitney Museum of American Art, New York.

1976 Completes mural *Order/Disorder/Ascension/Descension* for Social Security Administration's Mid-Atlantic Program Center, Philadelphia.

1978 Paintings and drawings of the previous five years comprise a solo exhibition at the Institute of Contemporary Art, Boston.

1980 Resigns Yale professorship.

1981 Six month residency at American Academy in Rome.

1983 Completes mural *Mantegna's Edge* for Southland Center, Dallas, Texas.
Awarded Poses Creative Arts Award, Brandeis University.

1984 Elected to American Institute of Arts and Letters.

1985 Completes mural *Roberta's House* for Government Building, Akron, Ohio.

1988 Restores farm house as residence and studio near Todi, Italy.
Three large scale paintings presented at 7 World Trade Center lobby, New York.

ONE-MAN EXHIBITIONS

Where an exhibition bore only the artist's name, it is listed without a title.

1952. Paris, Galerie Huit.

1959 New York, Poindexter Gallery.

1960 New York, Poindexter Gallery.

1961 New York, Poindexter Gallery.
Buenos Aires, Bonino Galeria.

1962 New York, Poindexter Gallery.

1964 Zurich, Galerie Renée Ziegler. Catalogue text in German by Harald Szeemann.
Düsseldorf, Galerie Gunar. Catalogue with text by Albert Schulze Vellinhhausen, in German and English, translated by Herbert Kurnitzki; essay by Irving Sandler, reprinted from *Toward a New Abstraction*.

1965 New York, André Emmerich Gallery.

1966 Amsterdam, Stedelijk Museum. Catalogue text in Dutch by W.A.L. Beeren.
Stuttgart, Galerie Müller.

1967 New York, André Emmerich Gallery.
Zurich, Galerie Renée Ziegler.

1968 New York, André Emmerich Gallery.
Philadelphia, Institute of Contemporary Art of the University of Pennsylvania. *Al Held. Recent Paintings*. Catalogue text by John W. McCoubrey. Also shown at the Contemporary Arts Museum, Houston.
San Francisco Museum of Art. Catalogue text by Eleanor Green. Also shown at the Corcoran Gallery of Art, Washington, D.C.

1970 New York, André Emmerich Gallery. *Al Held: New Paintings*.
Zurich, Galerie Renée Ziegler.

1971 Detroit, Donald Morris Gallery. *Al Held: Recent Paintings*.

1972 New York, André Emmerich Gallery. *Al Held: New Paintings*.

1973 New York, André Emmerich Gallery. *Al Held: New Paintings*.

1974 Zurich, Galerie André Emmerich.
Detroit, Donald Morris Gallery. *Al Held: Recent Paintings and Drawings*.
Cologne, Galerie Müller.
New York, Whitney Museum of American Art. Catalogue text by Marcia Tucker.

1975 New York, André Emmerich Gallery.
Toronto, Jared Sable Gallery.
Caracas, Venezuela, Adler Castillo Gallery.

1976 New York, André Emmerich Gallery.

1977 Zurich, Galerie André Emmerich. *Al Held: Neue Bilder und Zeichnungen/Recent Paintings and Drawings*. Commentary by Held in English and German translation.
Zurich, Galerie Renée Ziegler. *Al Held: Frühe Werke/Early Works*. Same catalogue as exhibition at André Emmerich cited above.
Paris, Galerie Roger d'Amecourt. Catalogue introduction in French by Roger d'Amecourt.
London, Annely Juda Fine Art.
Birmingham, Mich., Donald Morris Gallery.

1978 New York, André Emmerich Gallery.
Boston, Institute of Contemporary Art. *Al Held: Paintings and Drawings 1973–1978*. Texts by Elisabeth Sussman and Leon G. Shiman.
Toronto, Marianne Friedland Gallery.
Venice, Calif., Janus Gallery.

1979 New York, André Emmerich Gallery.

1980 Zurich, Gimpel-Hanover & André Emmerich Galerien. *Al Held: Neue Bilder/Recent Paintings*. Texts by Willy Rotzler, in German, and Andrew Forge, in English. Also shown at Annely Juda Fine Art, London; and Quadrat Bottrop Moderne Galerie, Bottrop, Germany.
New York, Robert Miller Gallery. *Al Held 1959–1961*. Text by Irving Sandler.
New York, André Emmerich Gallery. *Al Held: New Paintings 1980*. Text by Andrew Forge.

1981 Paris, Grand Palais. FIAC (Foire Internationale d'Art Contemporain) exhibition with André Emmerich Gallery.
Zurich, Gimpel-Hanover & André Emmerich Galerien.

1982 London, Juda Rowan Gallery.
New York, Robert Miller Gallery. *Al Held: 1954–1959*. Text by Irving Sandler.
New York, André Emmerich Gallery.

1983. Birmingham, Mich., Donald Morris Gallery.

1984. Zurich, Gimpel-Hanover und André Emmerich Galerien. *Al Held: Zeichnungen von 1976*.
Chicago, Richard Gray Gallery.
New York, André Emmerich Gallery. *Al Held: Drawings from 1976*.
Toronto, Marianne Friedland Gallery.

1985. New York, André Emmerich Gallery.

1986. San Francisco, Calif., John Berggruen Gallery.
New York, André Emmerich Gallery.

1987. London, Juda Rowan Gallery.
New York, André Emmerich Gallery.

1988. Birmingham, Mich., Donald Morris Gallery.
New York, Robert Miller Gallery.
New York, André Emmerich Gallery.

1989. New York, André Emmerich Gallery.
Toronto, Marianne Friedland Gallery.
San Francisco, Calif., John Berggruen Gallery.
Zurich, Galerie Renée Ziegler.
Dusseldorf, Hans Meyer Gallery.

1990. New York, André Emmerich Gallery.
New York, Crown Point Press. *Al Held: Prints*.

BIBLIOGRAPHY

Statements, Writings, Interviews by the Artist

It Is, Autumn 1958, p. 78.

Kulcher, Winter 1964/65, pp. 33–36.

Glaser, Bruce. ''The New Abstraction [Discussion with Paul Brach, Al Held, and Ray Parker].'' *Art International*, February 20, 1966, pp. 41–45.

''On art and Architecture.'' *Perspecta II: The Yale Architectural Journal*, 1967, p. 169.

Statement. In ''Sensibility of the Sixties.'' Barbara Rose and Irving Sandler, eds. *Art in America*, January–February 1967, p. 53.

''Jackson Pollock: An Artists' Symposium, Part I.'' *Art News*, April 1967, p. 32.

Interview with Paul Cummings. November 19, December 12, 19, 30, 1975, January 8, 1976. Transcript in Archives of American Art.

Walker, James Faure. ''Al Held, Interview.'' *Artscribe*, July 1977, pp. 5–9.

Cummings, Paul. ''Interview: Al Held Talks with Paul Cummings.'' *Drawing* (New York), July–August 1980, pp. 34–37.

Cooke, C. ''Al Held [Interview].'' *Arts Review* (United Kingdom), February 1982, p. 81.

Statement. In ''The '60s in Abstract: 13 Statements and an Essay.'' Maurice Poirier and Jane Necol, eds. *Art in America*, October 1983, pp. 124–26.

Books

Action/Precision: The New Direction in New York, 1955–60. Exhibition catalogue, Newport Harbor Art Museum, CA, 1984, pp. 90–101, with six color reproductions, essays by Paul Schimmel, B. H. Friedman, John Bernard Myers, Robert Rosenblum.

Dabrowski, Magdalena. *Contrast of Form: Geometric Abstract Art 1910–1980*. Exhibition catalogue, New York: Museum of Modern Art, 1985, p. 223.

Hunter, Sam. *An American Renaissance–Painting and Sculpture Since 1940*. Fort Lauderdale: Museum of Art and New York: Abbeville Press, 1986.

Kuspit, Donald. *Al Held Taxi Cabs*. Exhibition catalogue, New York: Robert Miller Gallery, 1987.

Lewallen, Constance. ''Al Held.'' Interview with the artist, *View*. San Francisco: Crown Point Press, 1989.

Sandler, Irving. *Al Held*. New York: Hudson Hills Press, Inc., 1984.

Articles and Reviews

''Al Held.'' *The Print Collector's Newsletter*, January–February 1987, p. 215.

Ashton, Dore. ''Al Held: New Spatial Experiences.'' *Studio International*, November 1964, pp. 210–13.

Baker, Kenneth. ''Reviews.'' *Artforum*, June 1972, p. 87.

Brach, Paul. ''Review of Exhibitions: Al Held at Emmerich.'' *Art in America*, January 1983, pp. 116–17.

Brenson, Michael. ''Art: Al Held's Taxis, A Watershed from '59.'' *The New York Times*, March 13, 1987, p. C30.

——. ''Al Held.'' *The New York Times*, March 10, 1989, p. 20.

Burton, Scott. ''Reviews and Previews: Al Held.'' *Art News*, April 1967, pp. 9, 12.

——. ''Big H.'' *Art News*, March 1968, pp. 50–53, 70–72.

Coplans, John. ''Post Painterly Abstraction.'' *Artforum*, Summer 1964, pp. 4–9.

Finkelstein, Louis. ''Al Held: Structure and the Intuition of Theme.'' *Art in America*, November–December 1974, pp. 83–88.

Foster, Hal. ''Reviews: Al Held, André Emmerich Gallery.'' *Artforum*, February 1981, p. 75.

Judd, Donald. ''In the Galleries: Al Held.'' *Arts Magazine*, January 1963, p. 47.

Kramer, Hilton. ''Assimilation of the Modern Movement.'' *The New York Times*, April 22, 1967.

——. ''Al Held.'' *The New York Times*, October 12, 1968.

——. ''Forms Filled with Fantasy and Energy.'' *The New York Times*, October 20, 1973.

——. ''Art: An Esthetic Smorgasbord in Chicago.'' *The New York Times*, July 6, 1974.

——. ''Al Held Leaves Us Uneasy and Disturbed.'' *The New York Times*, October 20, 1974.

——. ''Art: Al Held Adds Color to Geometry.'' *The New York Times*, February 23, 1979.

——. ''What Abstract Art Achieved.'' *The New York Times Magazine*, September 19, 1985, pp. 36–41, 82, 86.

Larson, Kay. ''Ecstacy Without Agony.'' *New York Magazine*, December 17, 1984, pp. 88–90.

——. Review, ''Al Held.'' *New York Magazine*, October 18, 1985, p. 141.

Lippard, Lucy R. ''New York Letter.'' *Art International*, Summer 1965, p. 51.

Masheck, Joseph. ''Reviews.'' *Artforum*, December 1973, pp. 78–81.

McCoubrey, John W. ''Al Held: Recent Paintings.'' *Art Journal*, Spring 1969, pp. 322–24.

Perrone, Jeff. ''Reviews: New York.'' *Artforum*, September 1978, p. 87.

Pincus-Witten, Robert. ''Systemic Painting.'' *Artforum*, November 1966, pp. 42–45.

Ratcliff, Carter. ''Reviews and Previews: Al Held.'' *Art News*, April 1970, p. 68.

Rose, Barbara. ''The Second Generation: Academy and Breakthrough.'' *Artforum*, September 1965, pp. 53–63.

——. ''Al Held. Long-Distance Runner.'' *New York Magazine*, April 17, 1972, p. 89.

Russell, John. "Reviews: Monsters: The Phenomena of Dispassion." *The New York Times*, January 30, 1987, p. C22.

Sandler, Irving. "Reviews and Previews: Al Held." *Art News*, May 1961, p. 15.

——. "Reviews and Previews: Al Held." *Art News*, December 1962, p. 14.

——. "Al Held Paints a Picture." *Art News*, May 1964, pp. 42–45, 51.

——. "Al Held and Philip Pearlstein." *Art in America*, September–October 1972, p. 114.

——. "Individual Character and Presence: Al Held's Paintings, 1959–1961." *Arts Magazine*, April 1980, pp. 186–87.

Staniszewski, Mary Anne. "New York Reviews: Al Held." *Art News*, April 1981, pp. 191–92.

Stevens, Mark. "The Dizzy Decade." *Newsweek*, March 26, 1979, p. 89.

Tillim, Sidney. "Scale and the Future of Modernism." *Artforum*, October 1967, pp. 14–18.

Westfall, Steven. "Then and Now: Six of the New York School Look Back." *Art in America*, June 1985, pp. 112–21.

1. **Pollock-Mondrian,** c. 1952.
Oil on canvas mounted on board, 7³/₈×9³/₈ in. (18.7×23.8 cm).
Collection of the artist.

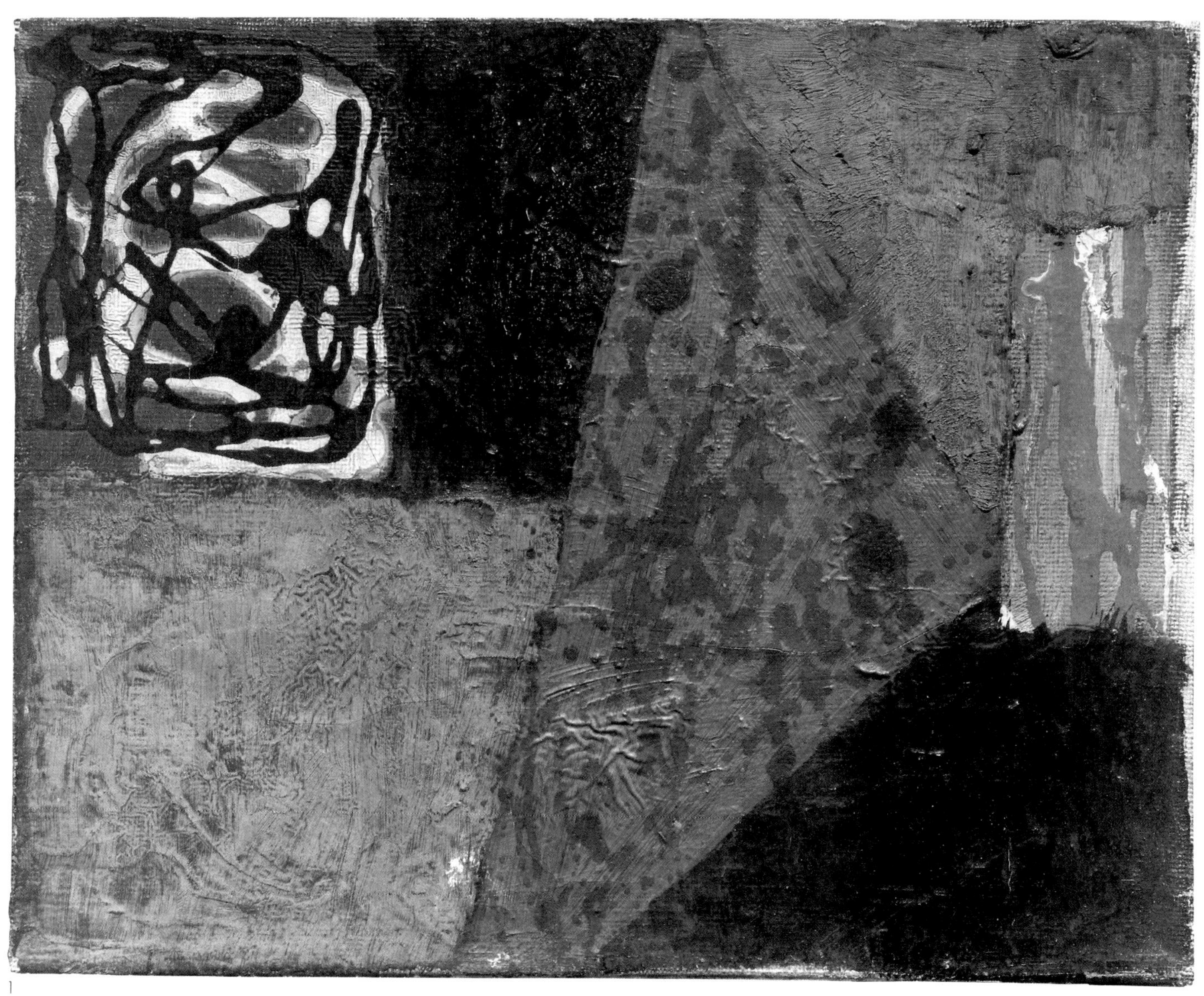

1

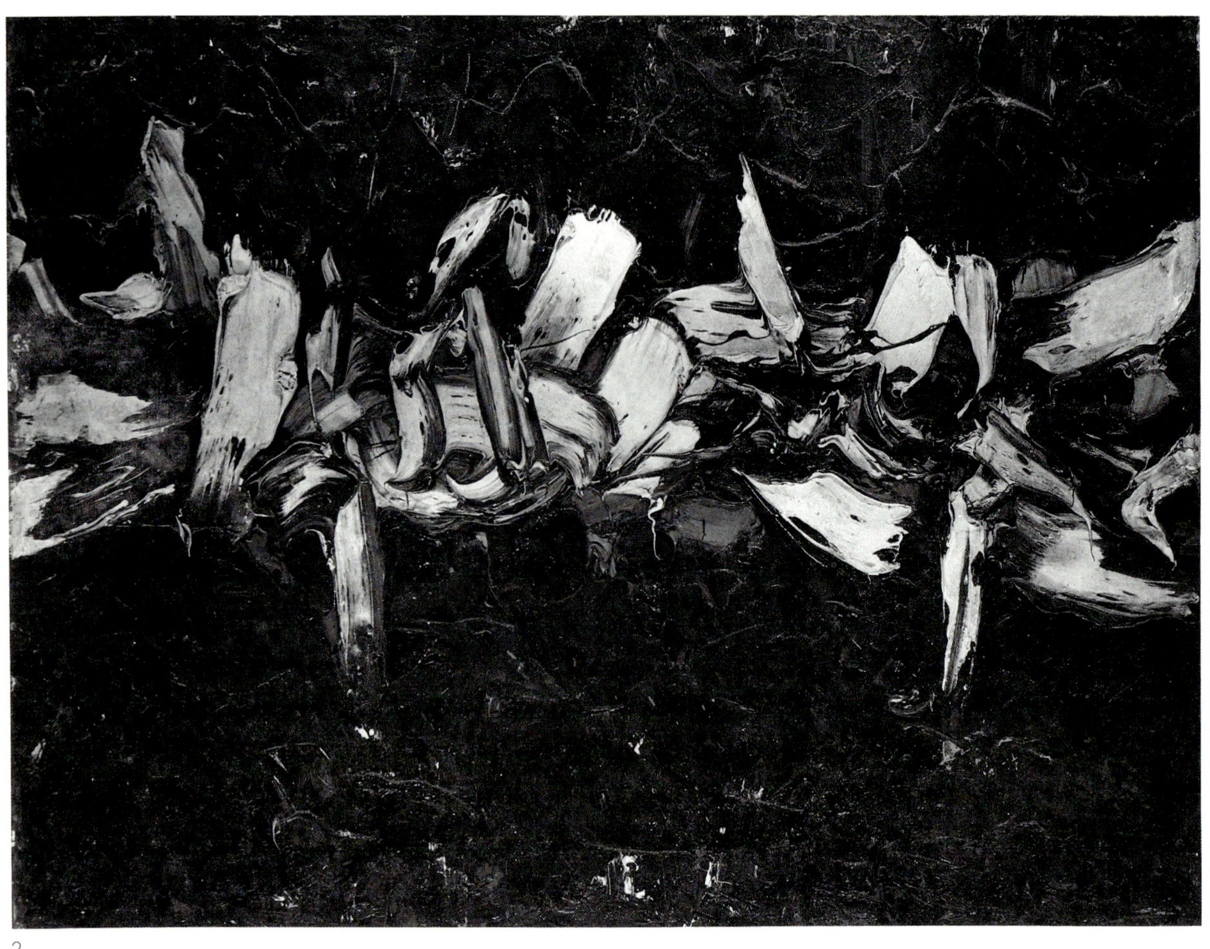

2

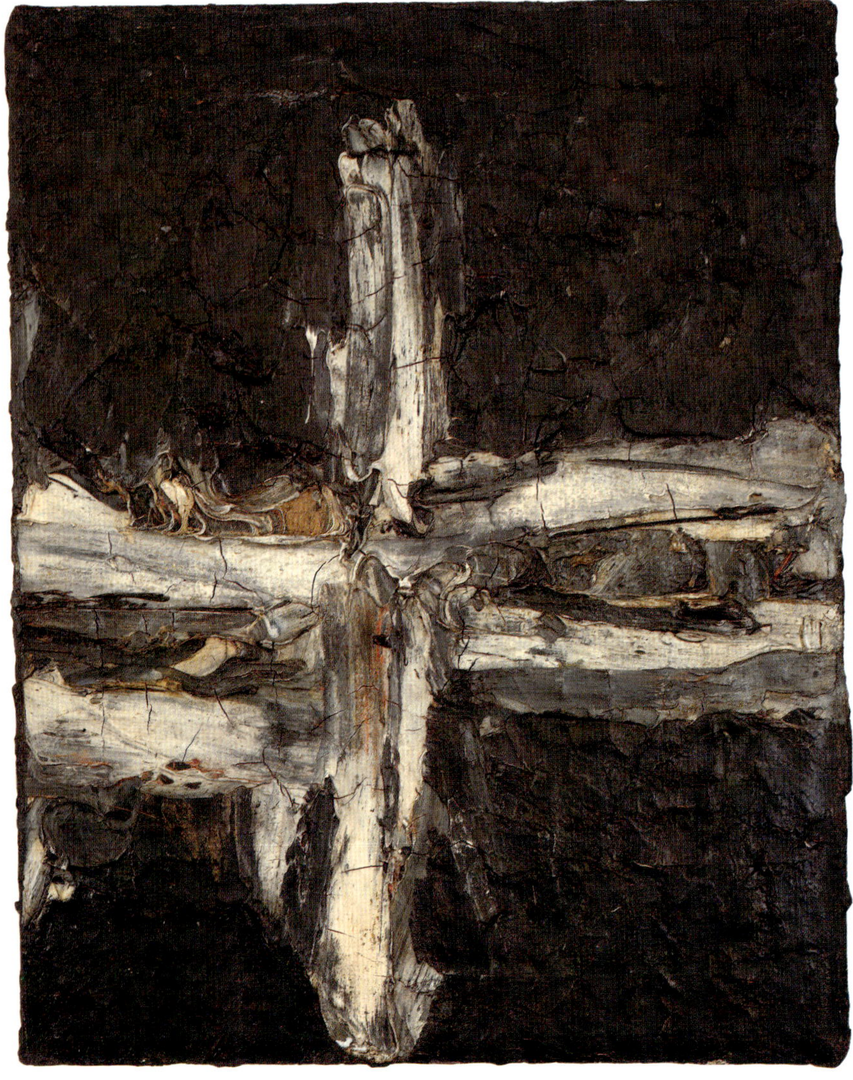

3

2. **Fragment of a Dream of God's,** 1950.
Oil on masonite, 20×30 in. (50.8×76.2 cm).
Collection of the artist.

3. **Untitled,** 1950–52.
Oil on canvas, 20 1/4×16 1/4 in. (51.4×41.2 cm).
Robert Miller Gallery, New York.

4. **Untitled,** 1950–52.
Oil on canvas, 64 1/2×54 3/4 in. (163.8×139 cm).
Robert Miller Gallery, New York.

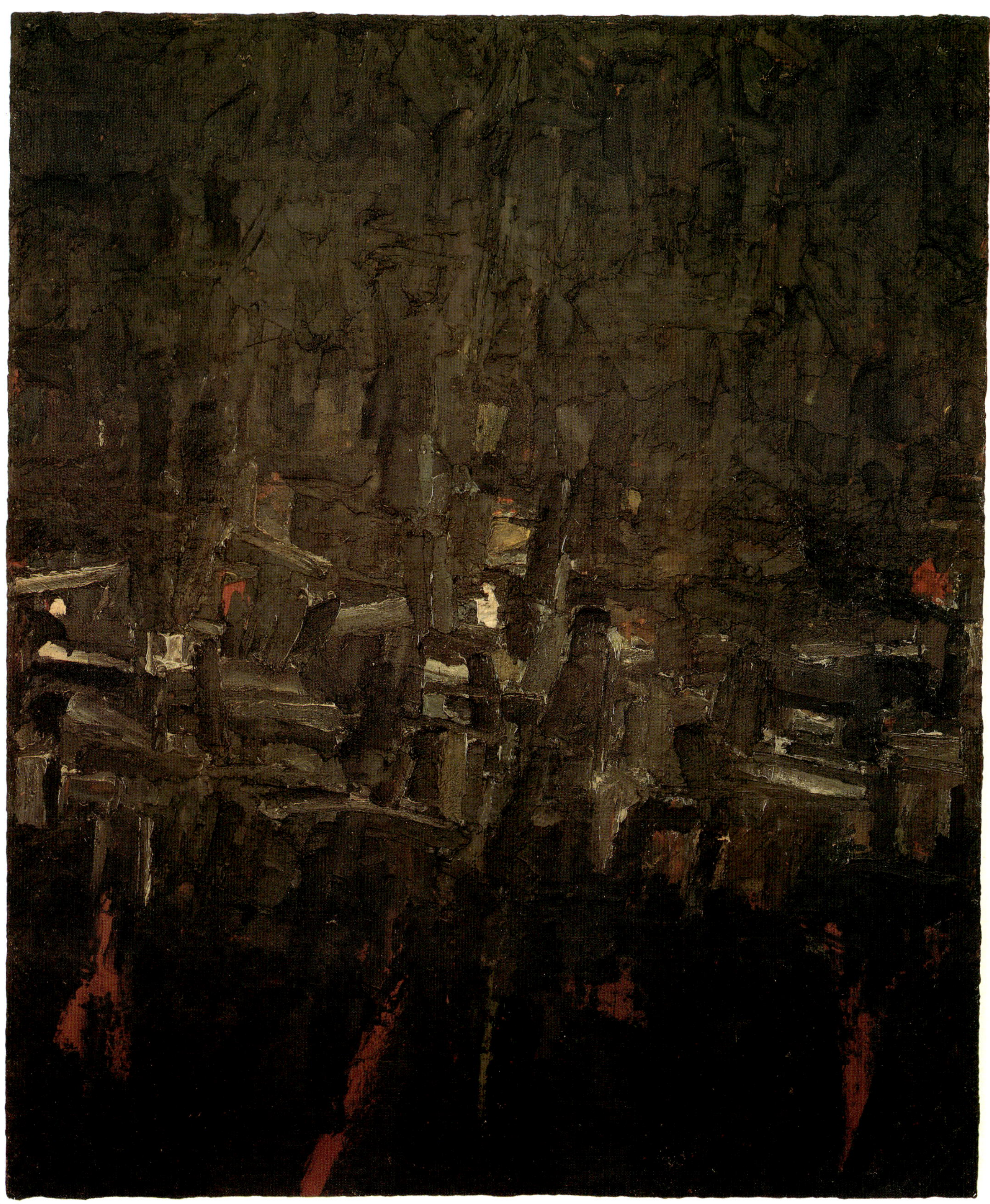

5. **Untitled,** 1950–52.
Oil on canvas, 43 1/2×34 1/4 in. (110.5×87 cm).
Robert Miller Gallery, New York.

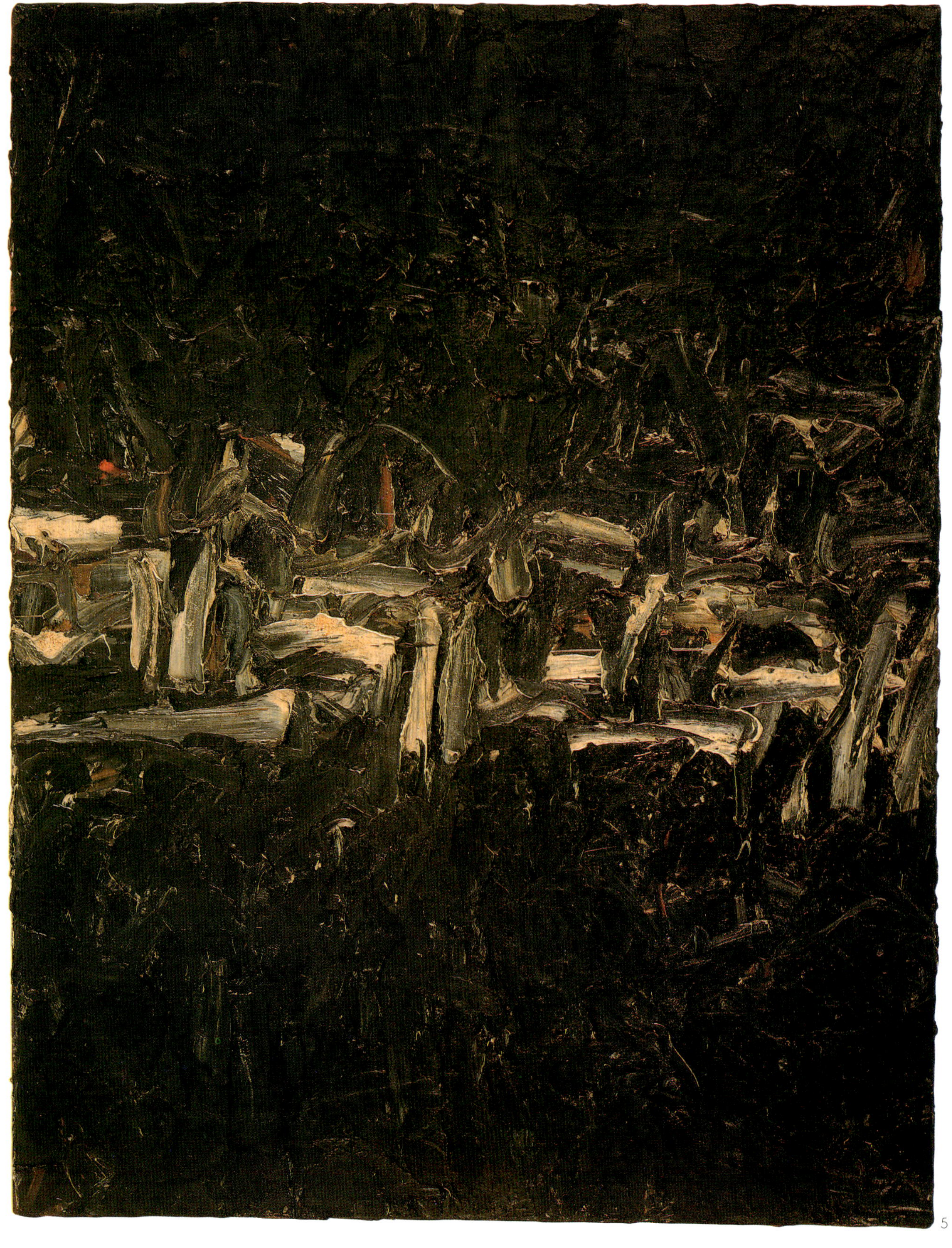

6. **Untitled,** 1950–52.
Oil on canvas, 72 1/4×46 3/4 in. (183.5×118.7 cm).
Robert Miller Gallery, New York.

7. **Untitled,** 1953.
Oil on canvas, 72×46 1/2 in. (183×118 cm).
Collection of the artist.

6

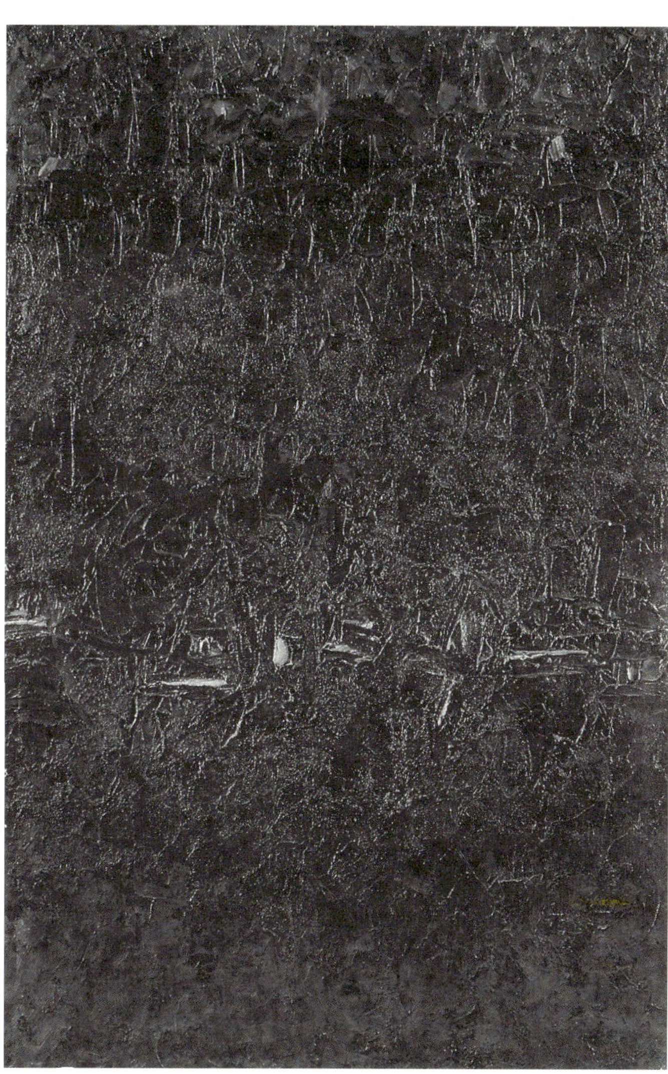
7

8. **Untitled No. 60,** 1954.
Oil on canvas, 96×72 in. (243.8×183 cm).
Collection of Mara Held, New York.

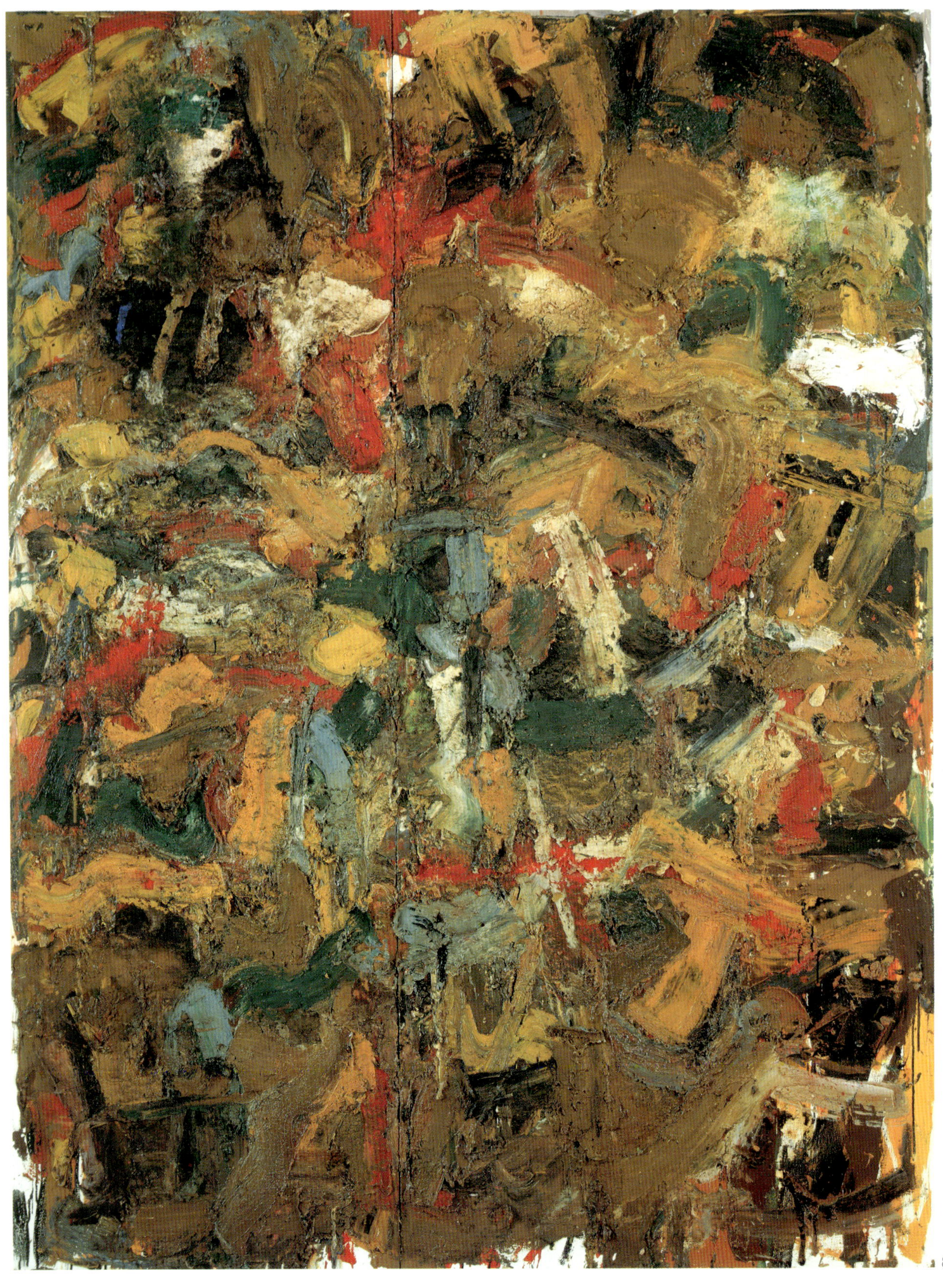

9. **Untitled,** 1955.
Oil on canvas, 72×96 in. (183×243.8 cm).
Robert Miller Gallery, New York.

10. **Untitled No. 57,** 1956.
Oil on canvas, 72×108 in. (183×274.3 cm).
American Medical Association Art Collection, Washington.

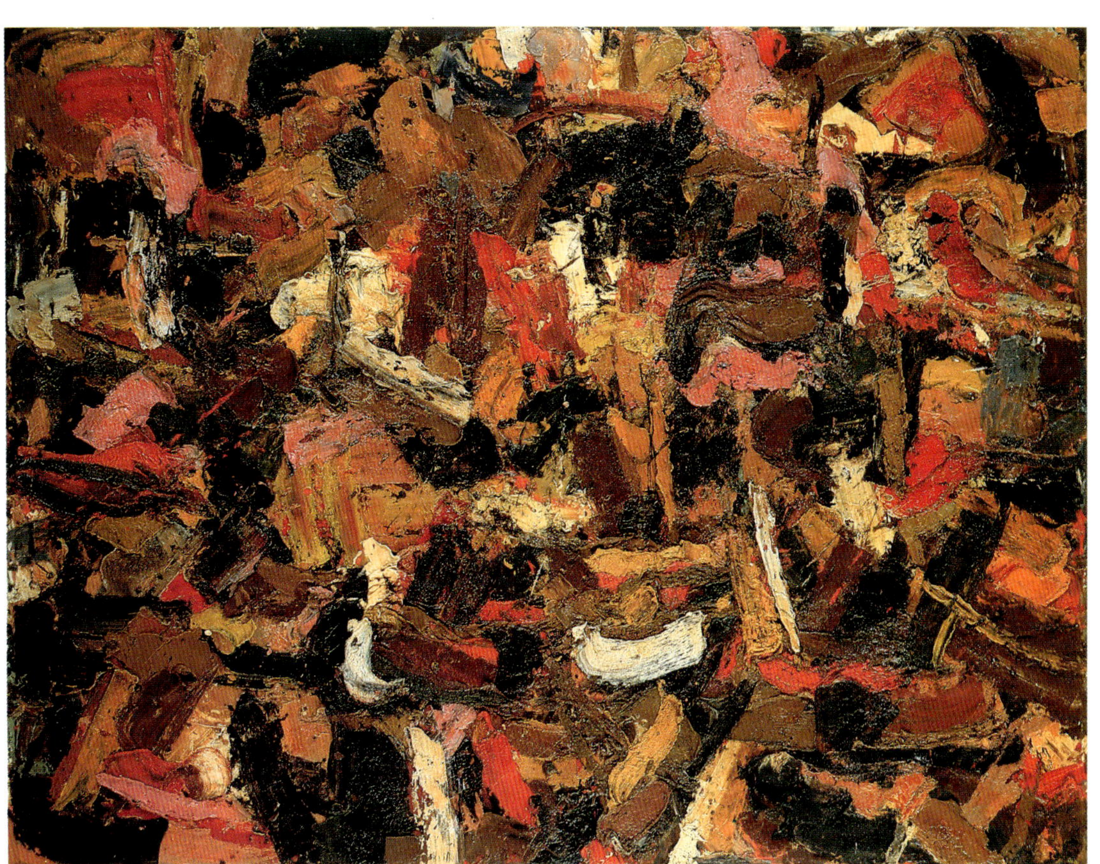

9

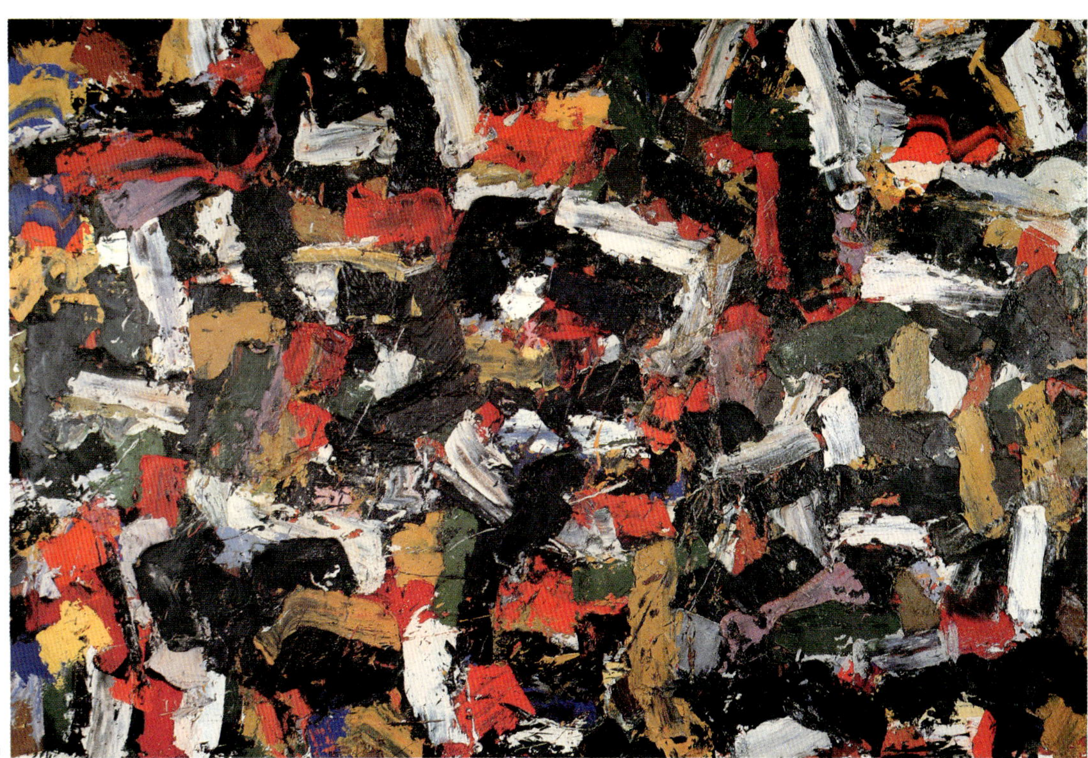

10

11. **Untitled No. 54,** 1956.
Oil on canvas, 108×64 in. (274.3×162.5 cm).
National Gallery of Victoria, Melbourne, Australia.

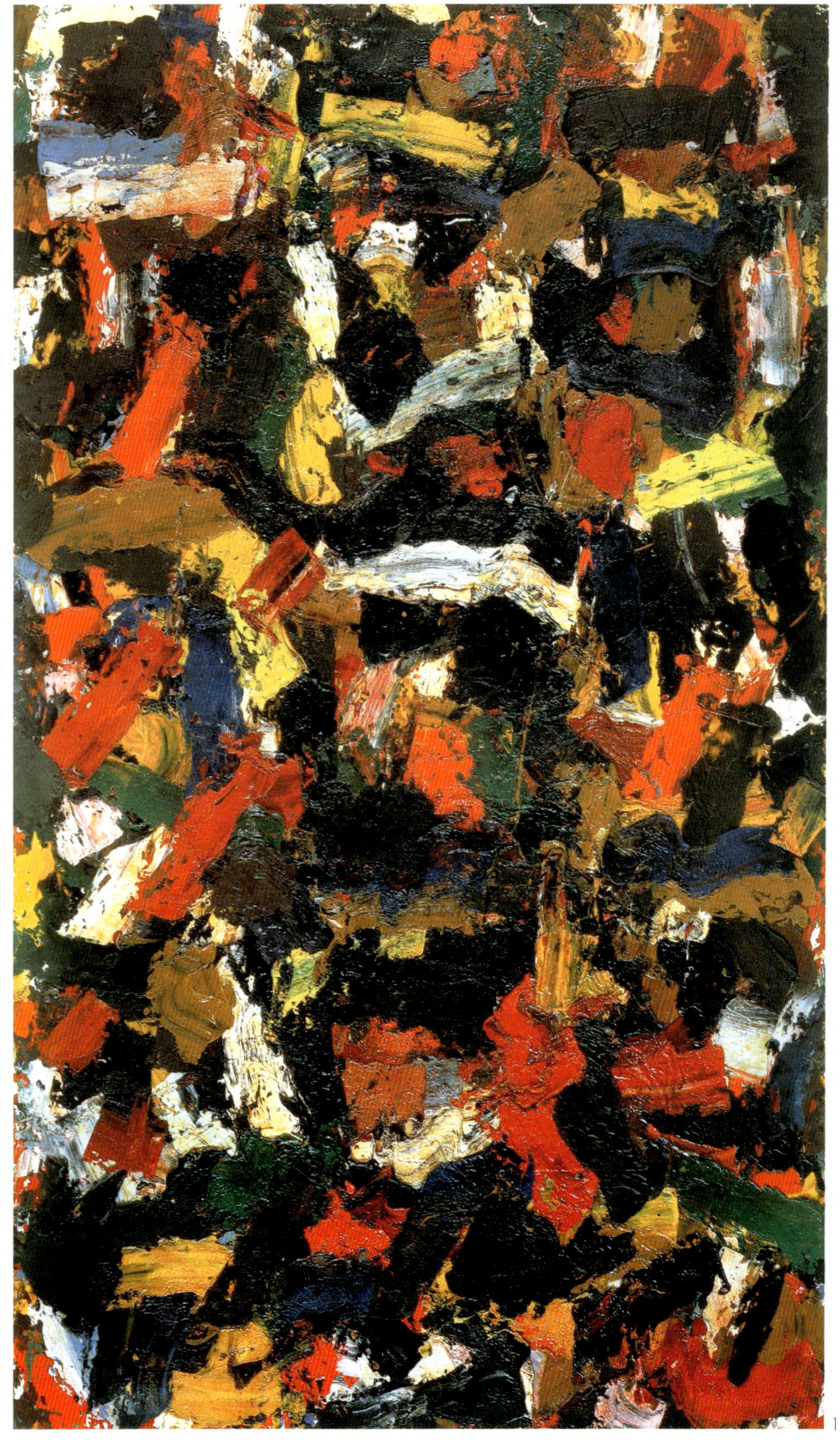

11

12. **Untitled,** 1958.
Oil on canvas, 72×108 in. (183×274.3 cm).
Robert Miller Gallery, New York.

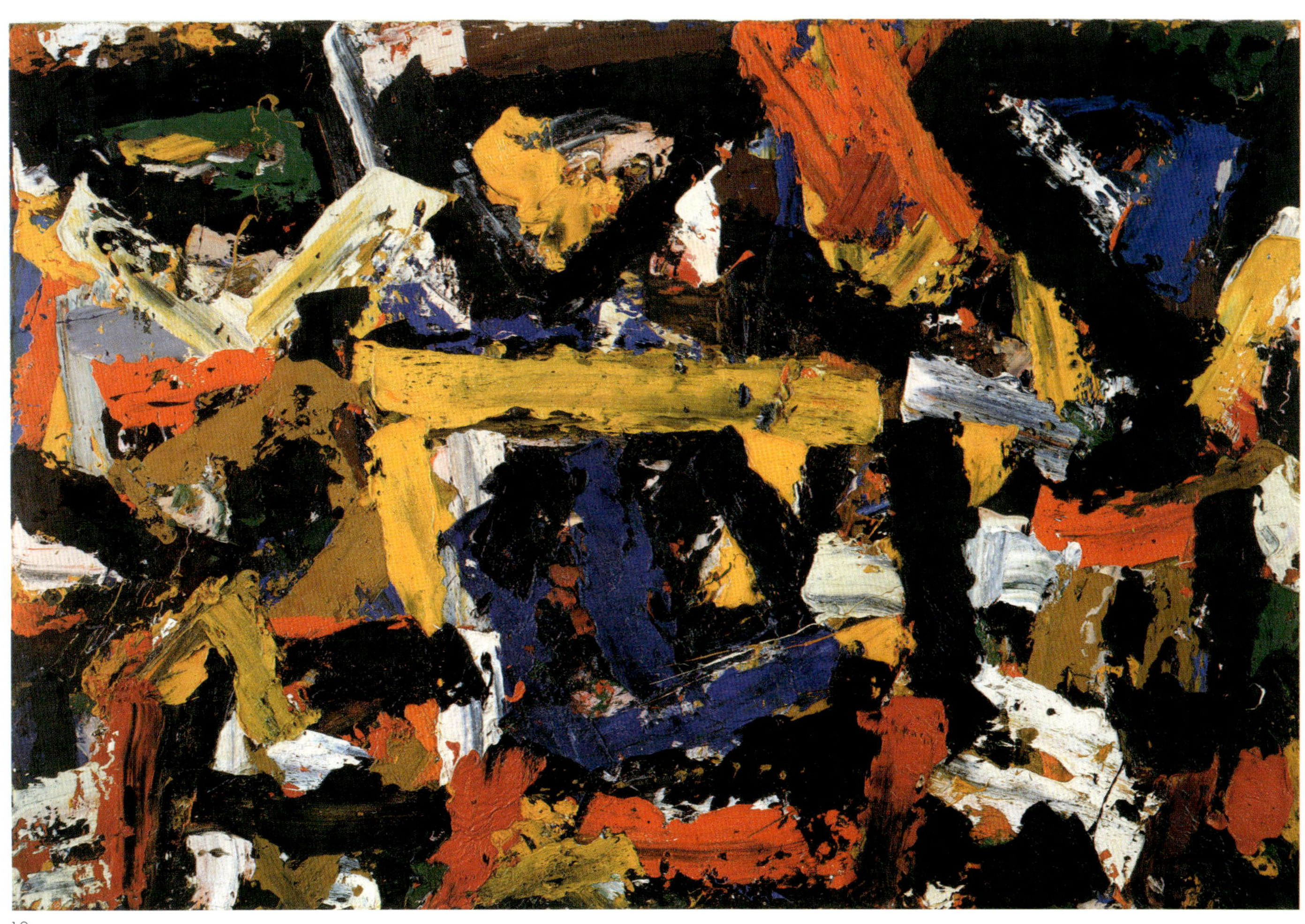

12

13. **Taxicab IV,** 1959.
Acrylic on paper mounted on canvas, 107×268 in. (271.8×680.7 cm).
Robert Miller Gallery, New York.

14. **Untitled No. 46,** 1959.
Oil on canvas, 72×54 in. (183×137 cm).
Albright-Knox Art Gallery, Buffalo, New York
(Gift of Seymour H. Knox).

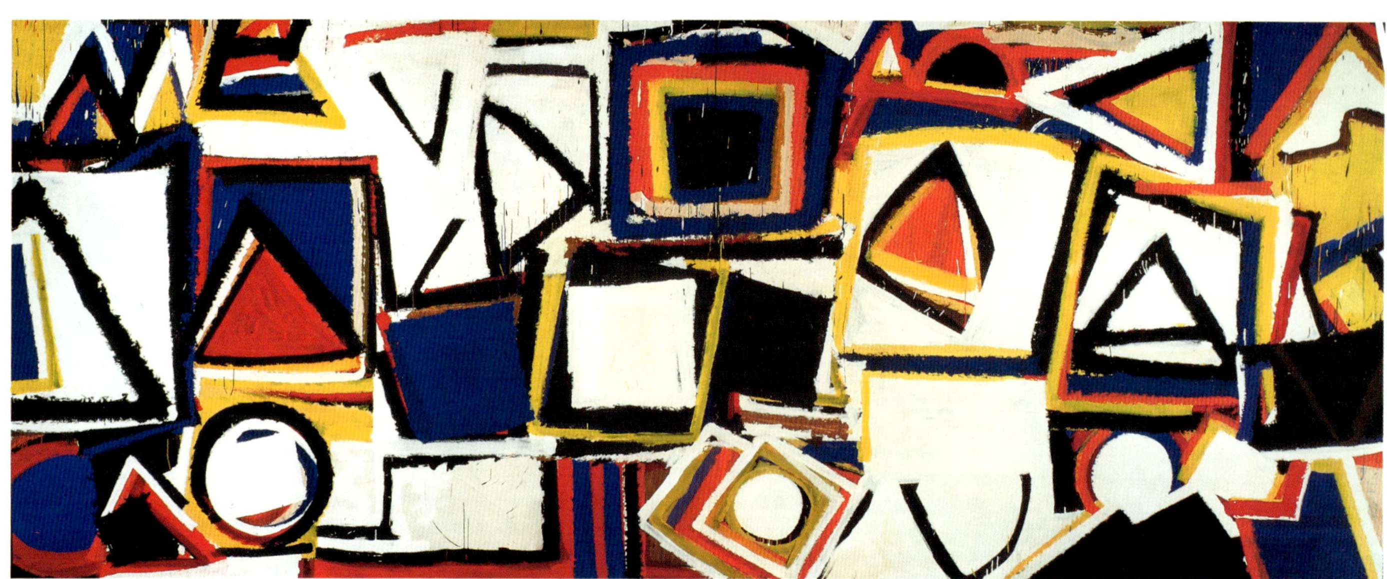

13

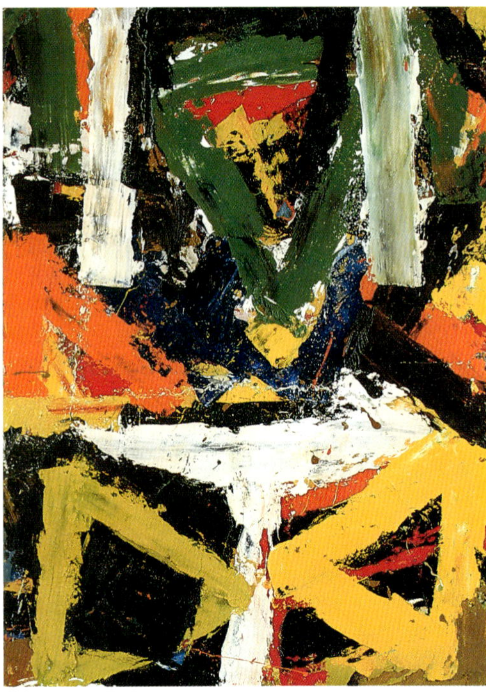

14

15. **Untitled,** 1960.
Acrylic on linen, 114½×164¼ in. (291.3×417.5 cm).
Robert Miller Gallery, New York.

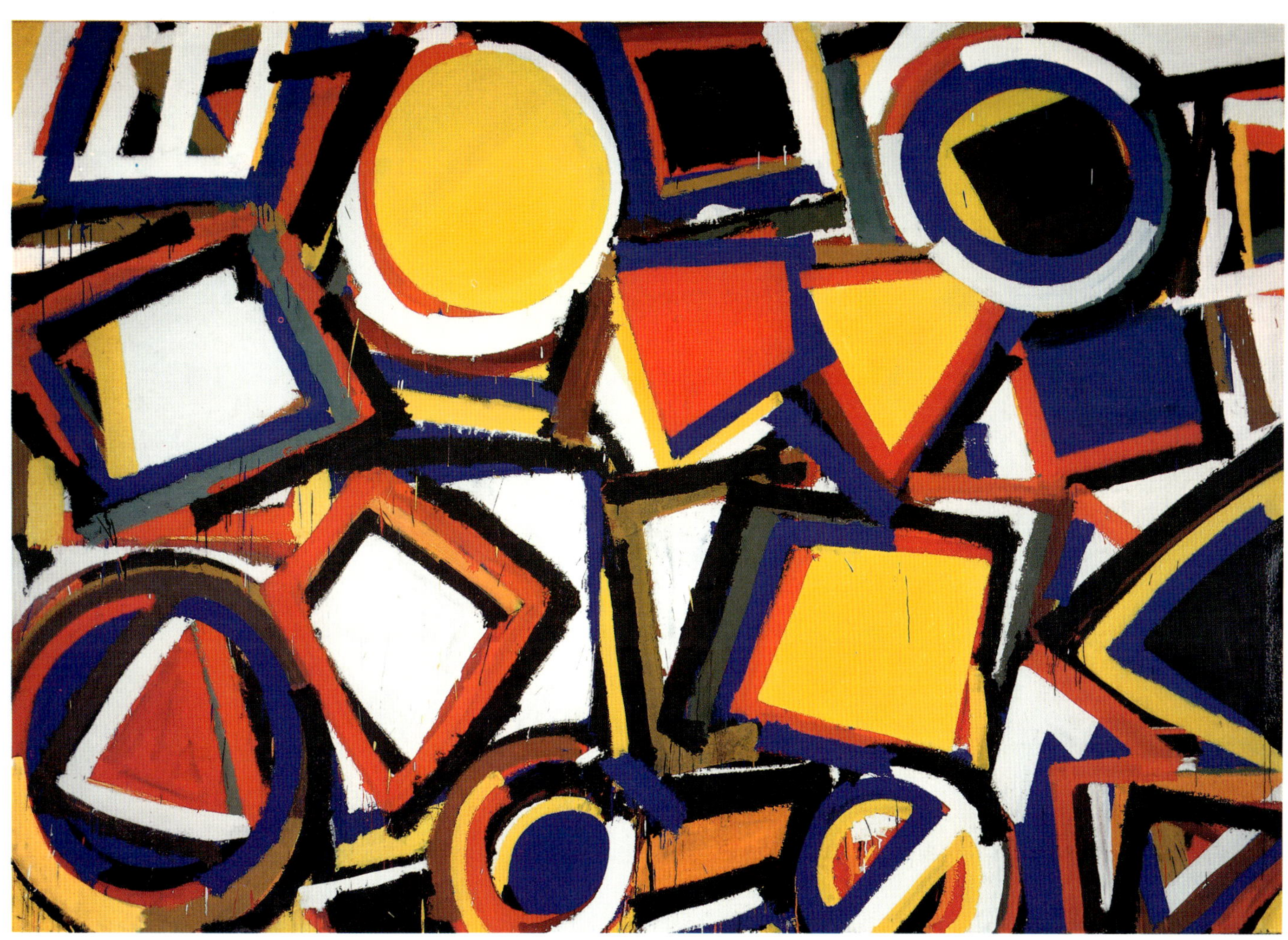

15

16. **House of Cards,** 1960.
Acrylic on canvas, 114¼×253¼ in. (290.5×643.5 cm).
San Francisco Museum of Modern Art (Gift of Mrs. George Poindexter).

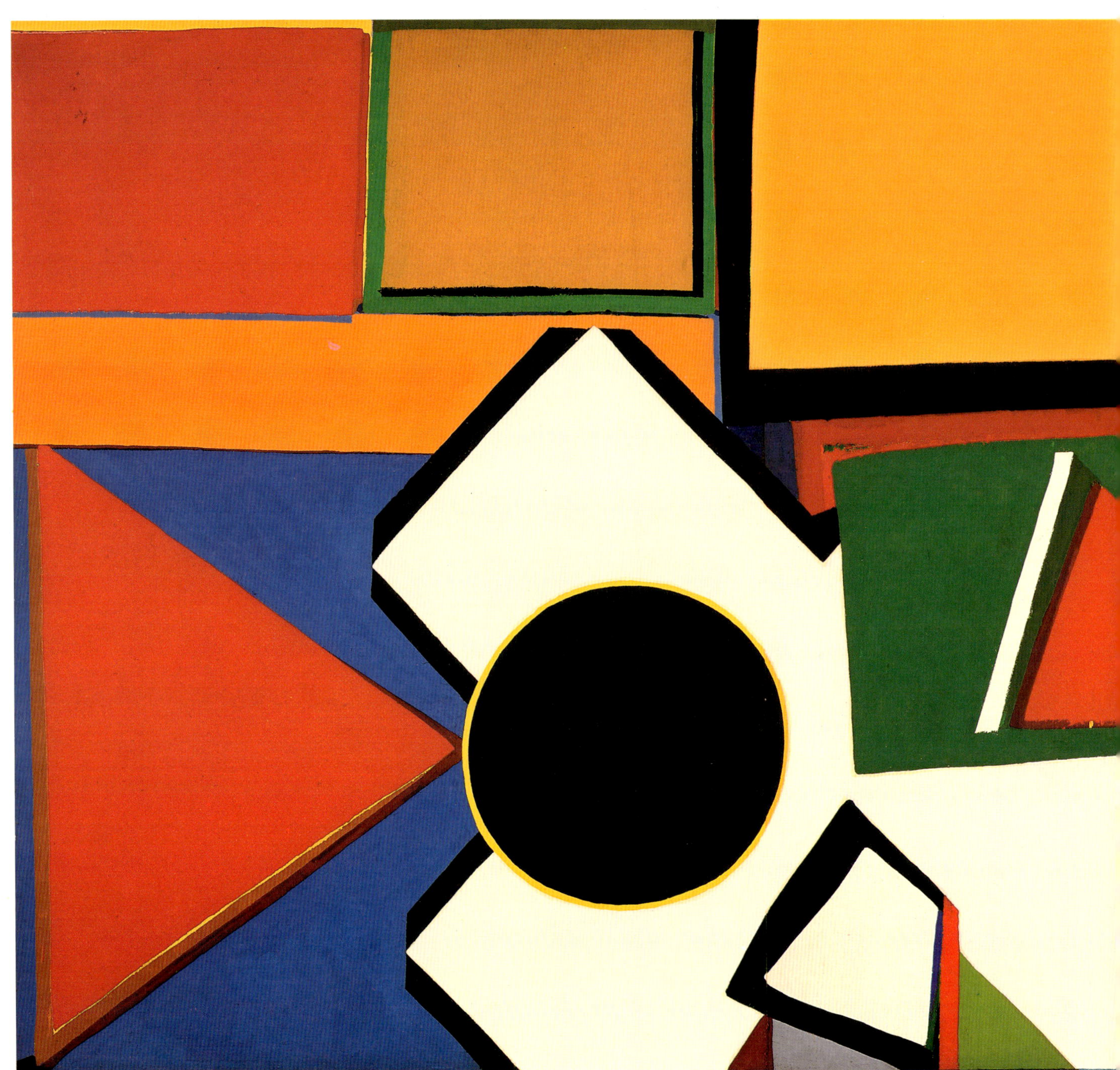

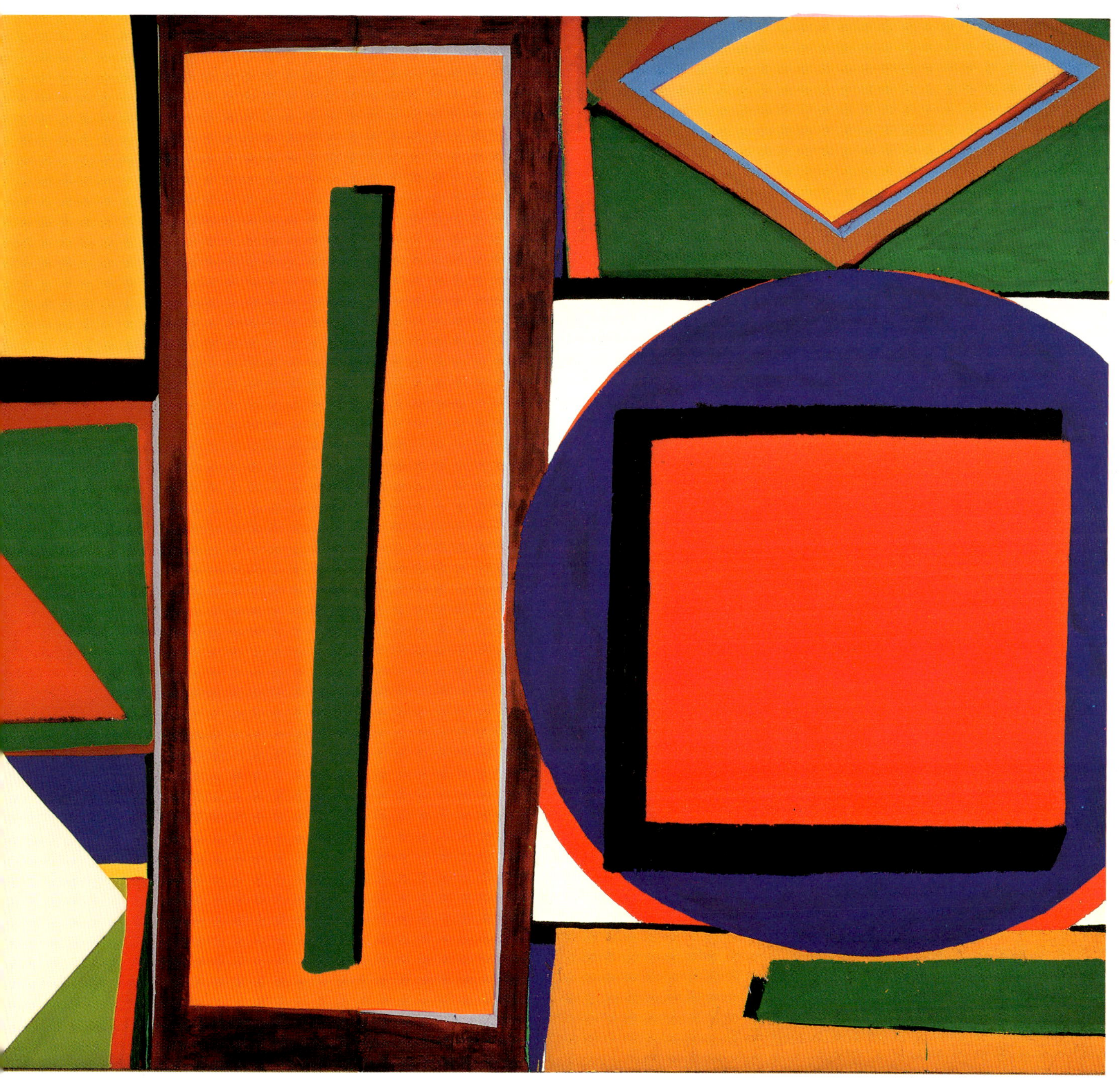

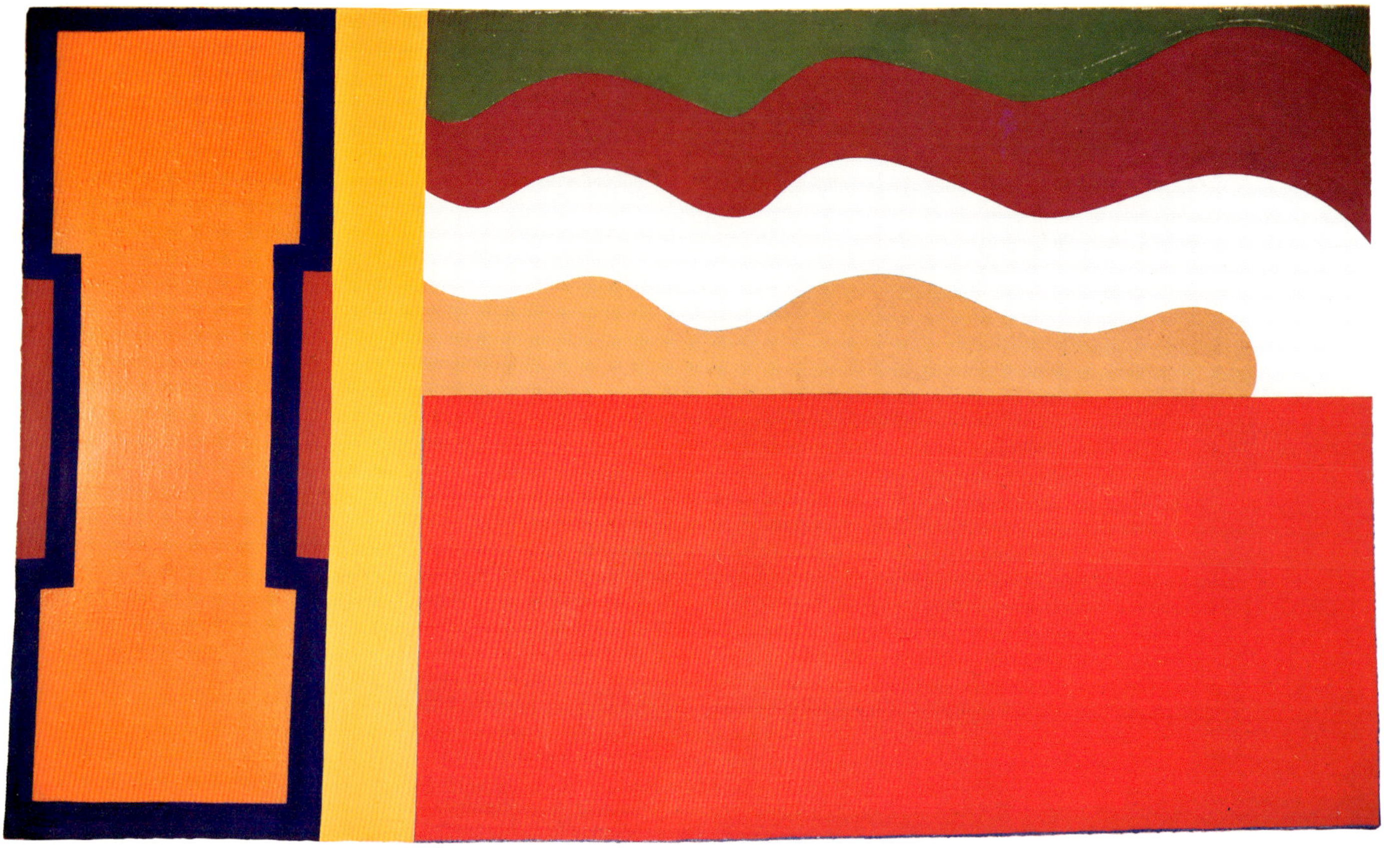

17

18

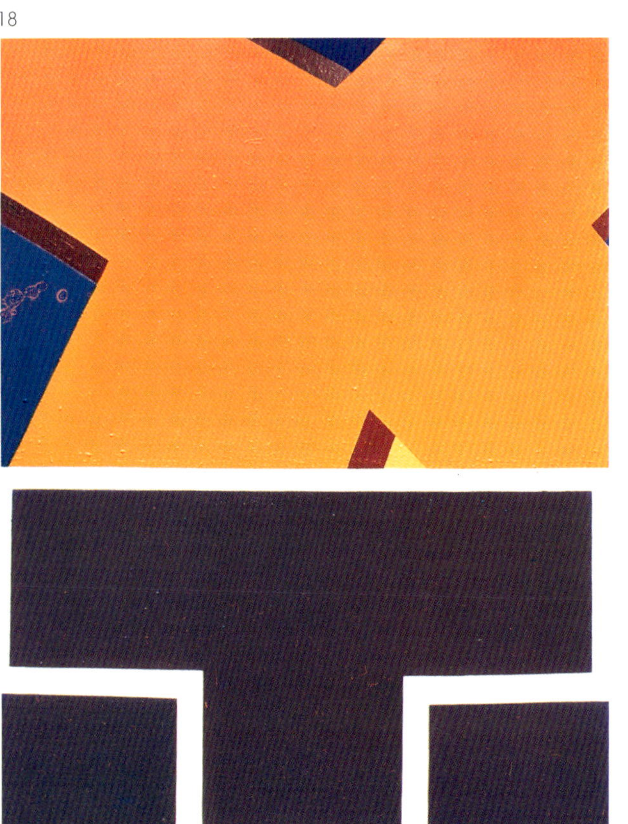

19

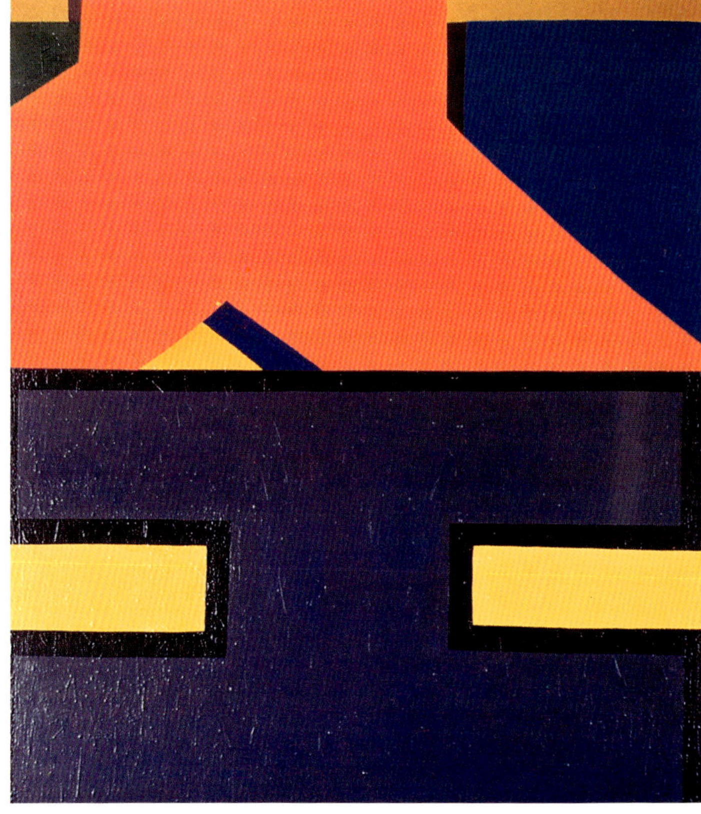

17. **I-Beam,** 1961–62.
Acrylic on canvas, 114×192 in. (289.5×487.5 cm).
Collection of Mara Held, New York.

18. **Ivan the Terrible,** 1961.
Acrylic on canvas, 144×114 in. (365.8×289.5 cm).
André Emmerich Gallery, New York.

19. **Y and I,** 1961.
Acrylic on canvas, 126×108 5/8 in. (320×276 cm).
Private collection.

20. **Maltese Cross,** 1964.
Acrylic on canvas, 114×114 in. (289.5×289.5 cm).
Collection of Mrs. Morton J. Hornick.

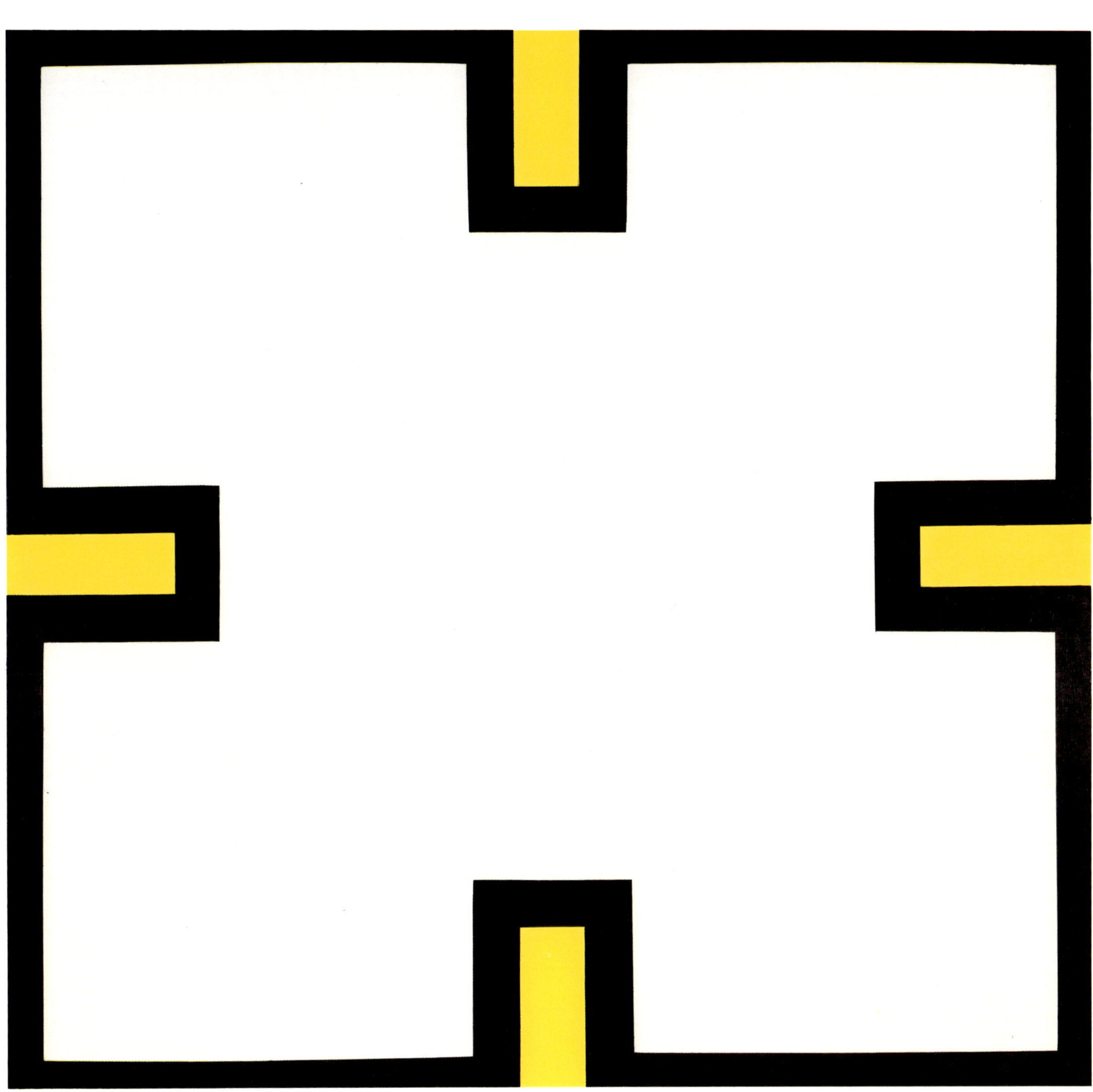

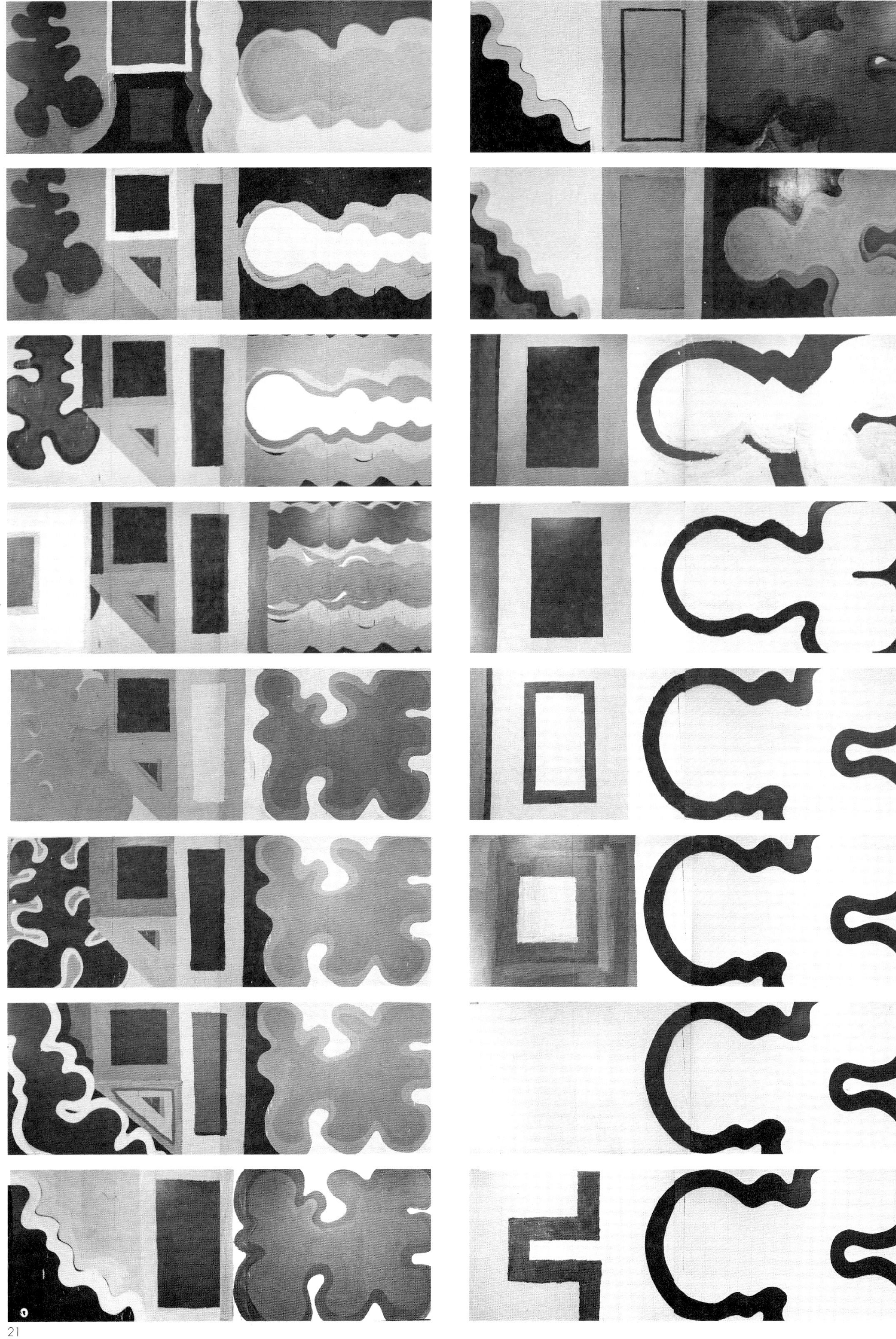

21. Stages of **Genesis,** 1963.
Photographed in the artist's studio, 1963.

22. **Genesis,** 1963.
Acrylic on canvas, 114×336 in. (289.5×853.5 cm).
Emanuel Hoffman-Foundation Kunstmuseum, Basel.

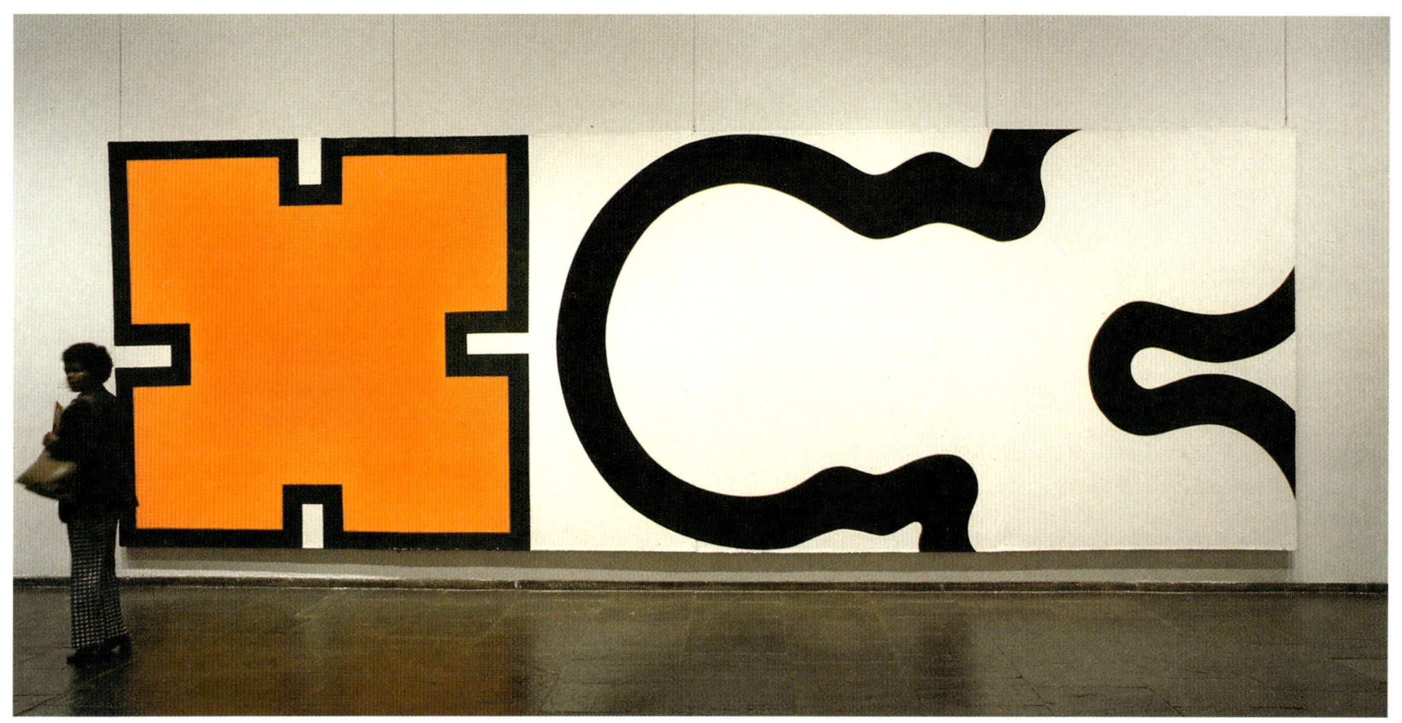

22

23. **The Big D,** 1964.
Acrylic on canvas, 144×114 in. (365.8×289.5 cm).
Collection of Mara Held, New York.

24. **The Big A,** 1962.
Acrylic on canvas, 120×168 in. (304.8×426.7 cm).
Staatlich Museen Preussischer Kulturbesitz, Nationalgalerie,
Berlin (Purchase Verein der Freunde der Nationalgalerie, 1980).

25. **The Big N,** 1965.
Acrylic on canvas, 108 3/8×108 in. (275.5×274.3 cm).
Collection, The Museum of Modern Art, New York (Mrs. Armand P. Bartos Fund).

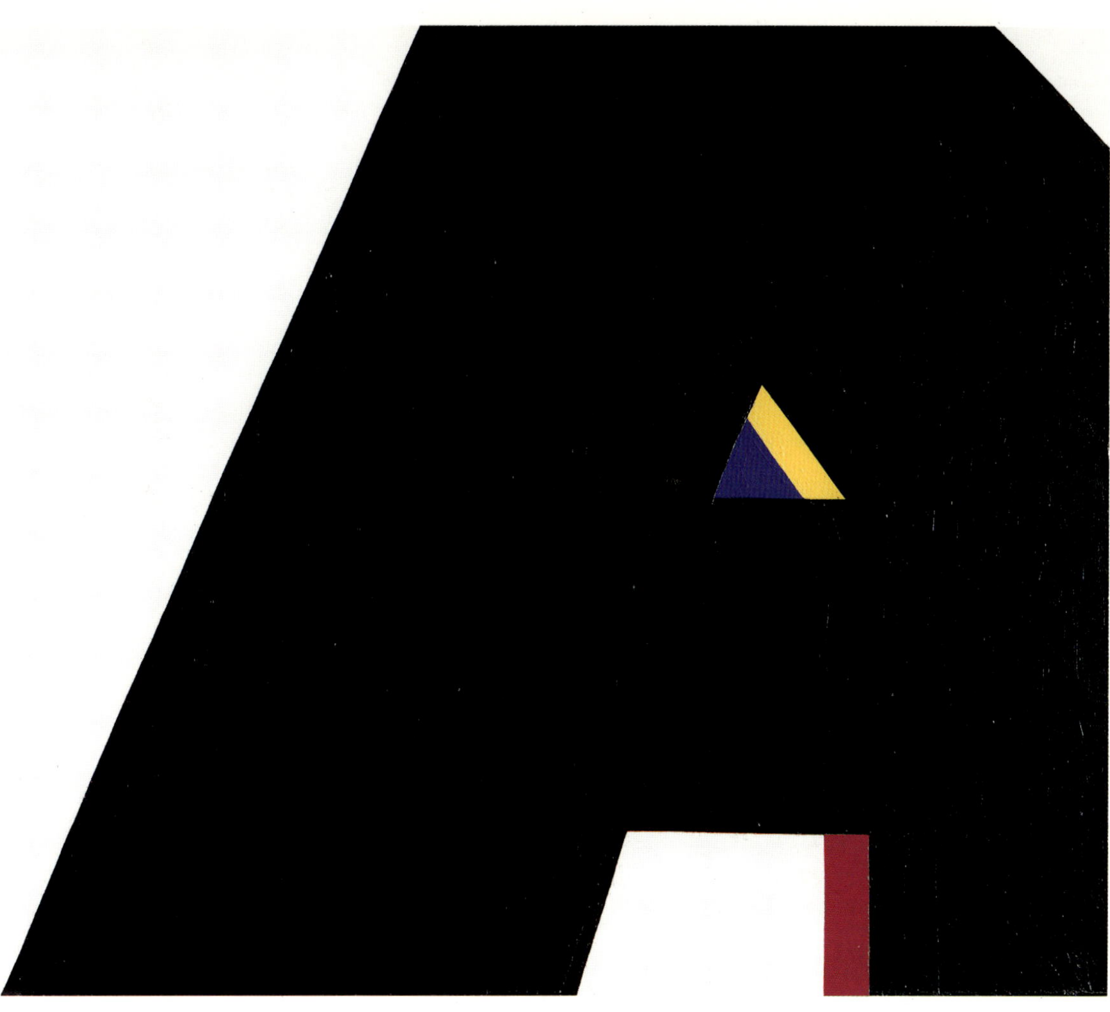

24

25

26. **The Yellow X,** 1965.
Acrylic on canvas, 144×180 in.
(365.8×457.2 cm).
Private collection.

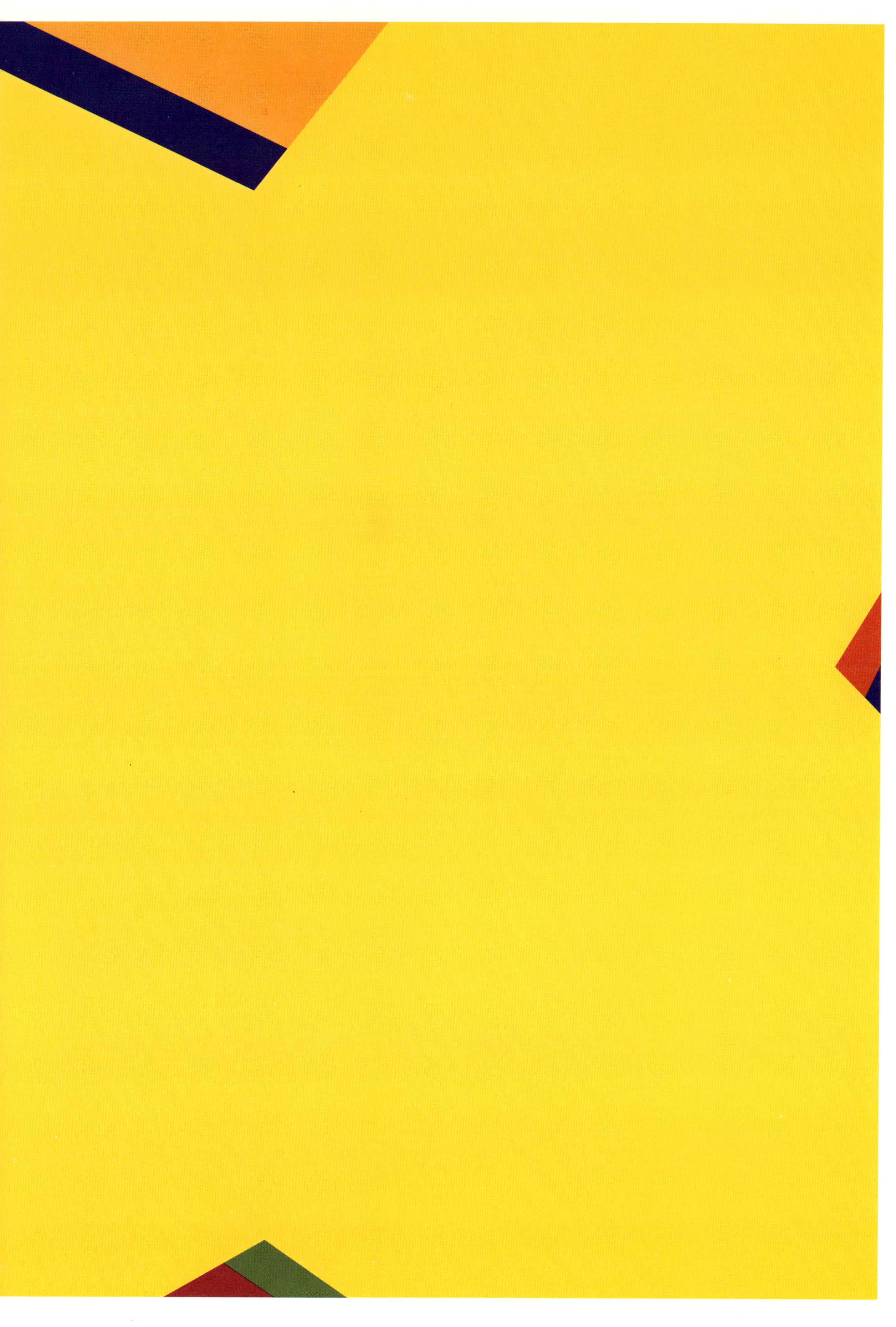

27. **The Dowager Empress,** 1965.
Acrylic on canvas,
96×72 in. (243.8×183 cm).
Whitney Museum of American Art,
New York (Gift of the Friends of the
Whitney Museum of American Art).

28. **Greek Garden,** 1966.
Acrylic on canvas,
114×672 in. (3.65×17 m).
The Metropolitan Musem of Art, New York.

29. **Upside Down Triangle,** 1966.
Acrylic on canvas,
114×168 in. (289.5×426.7 cm).
Collection of the artist.

30. **Bastion,** 1967.
Acrylic on canvas,
114×114 in. (289.5×289.5 cm).
Collection of the artist.

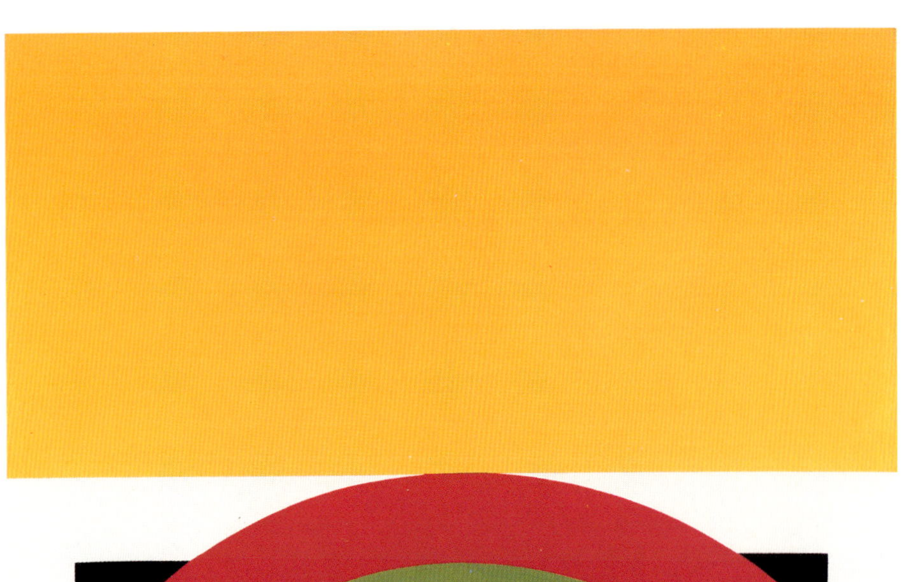

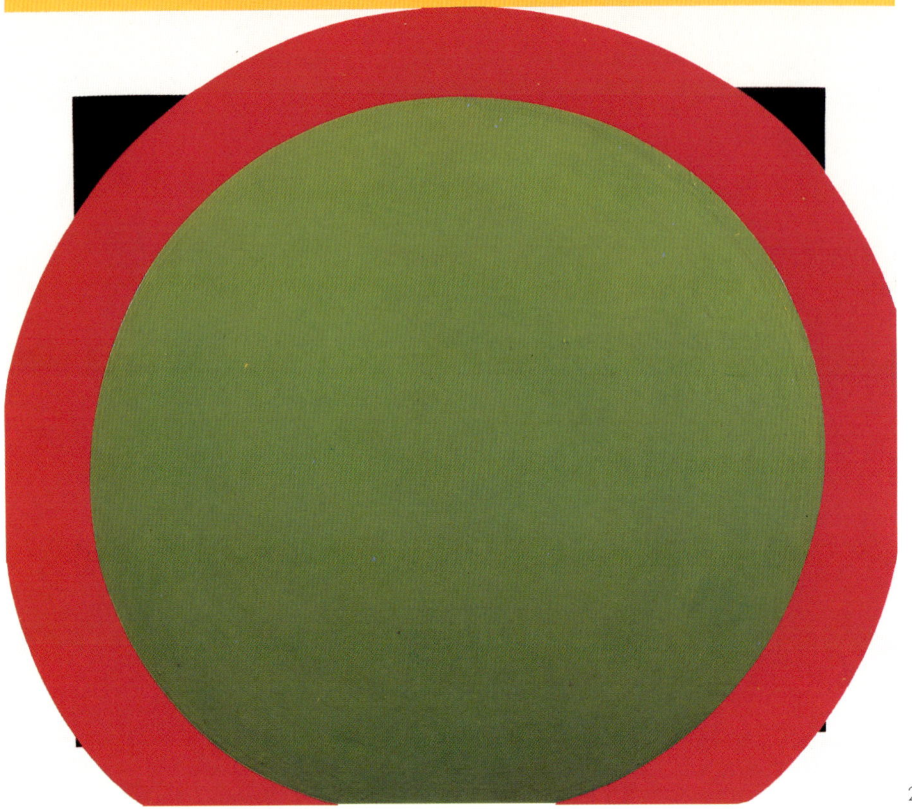

27

28

29

30

31 and 32. **I and We** (murals), 1967.
Acrylic on canvas, each 108×252 in. (274.3×640 cm).
Tower East, Cleveland (Collection Frank H. Porter).

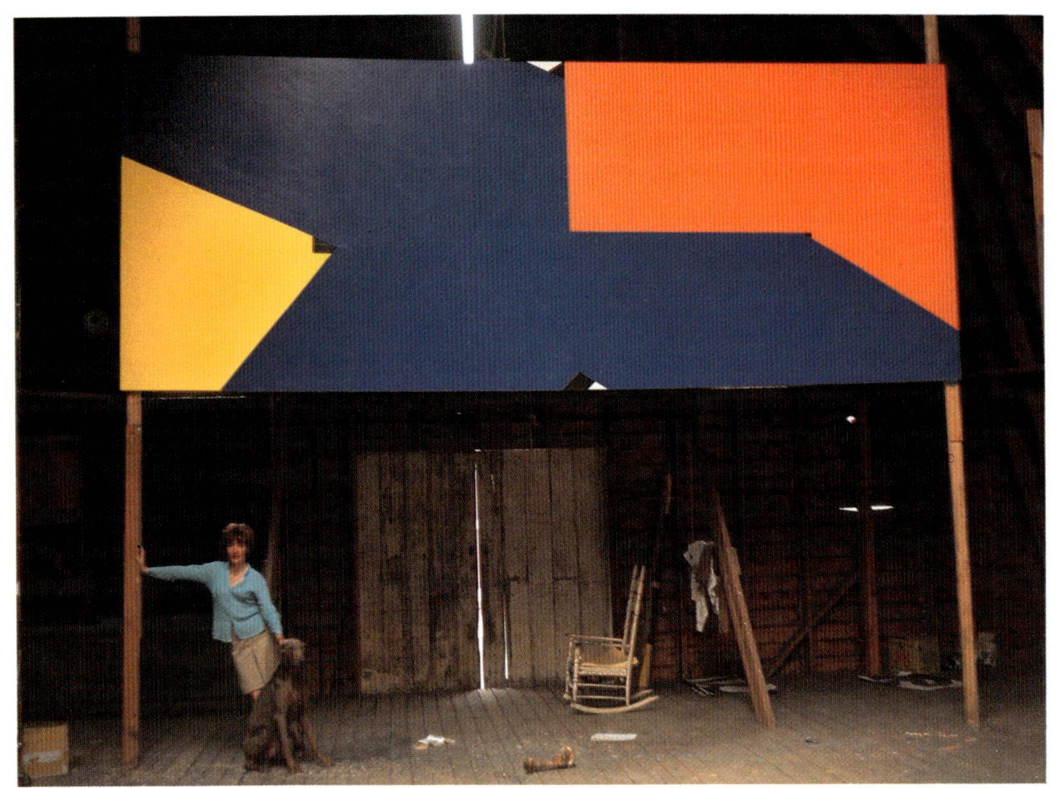

31

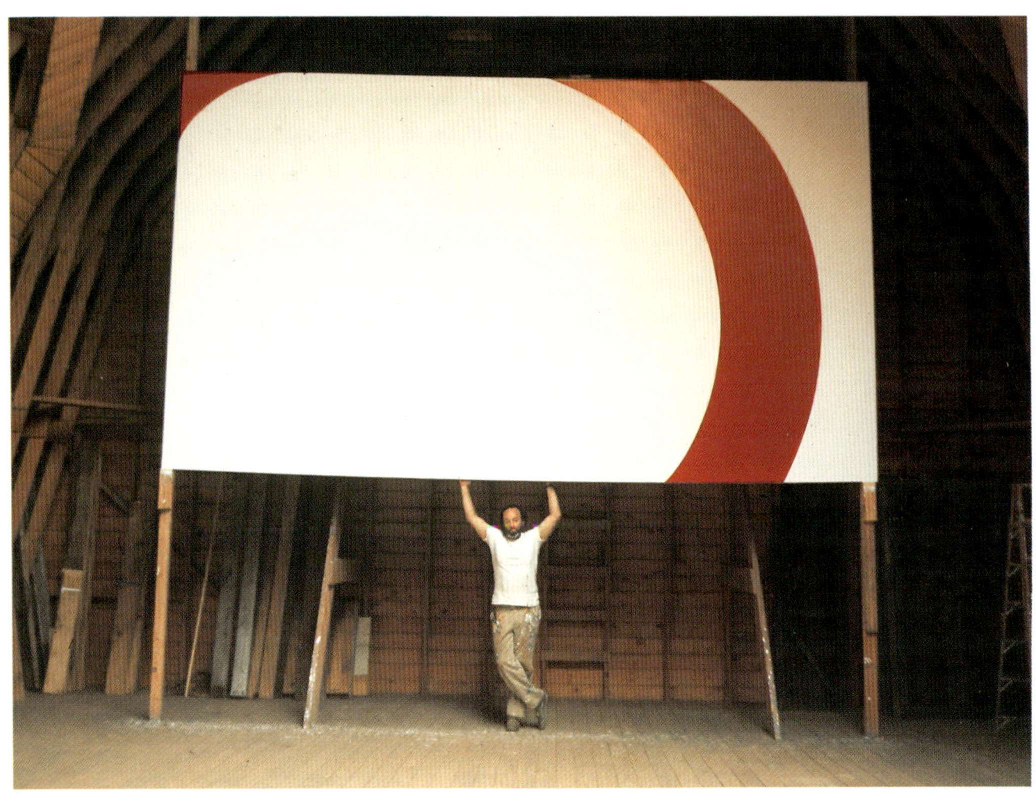

32

33. **Mao,** 1967.
Acrylic on canvas, 114×114 in. (289.5×289.5 cm).
André Emmerich Gallery, New York.

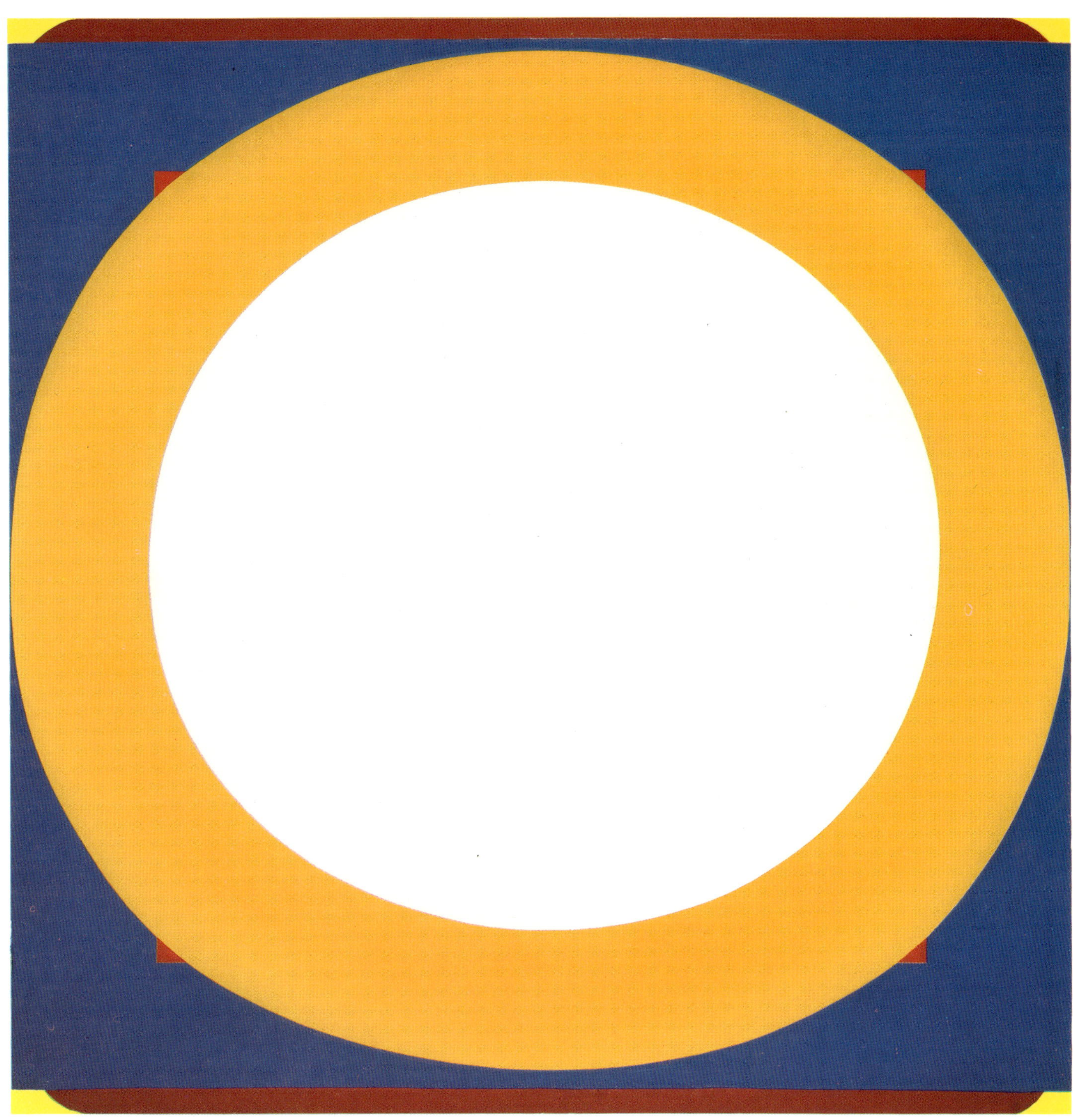

33

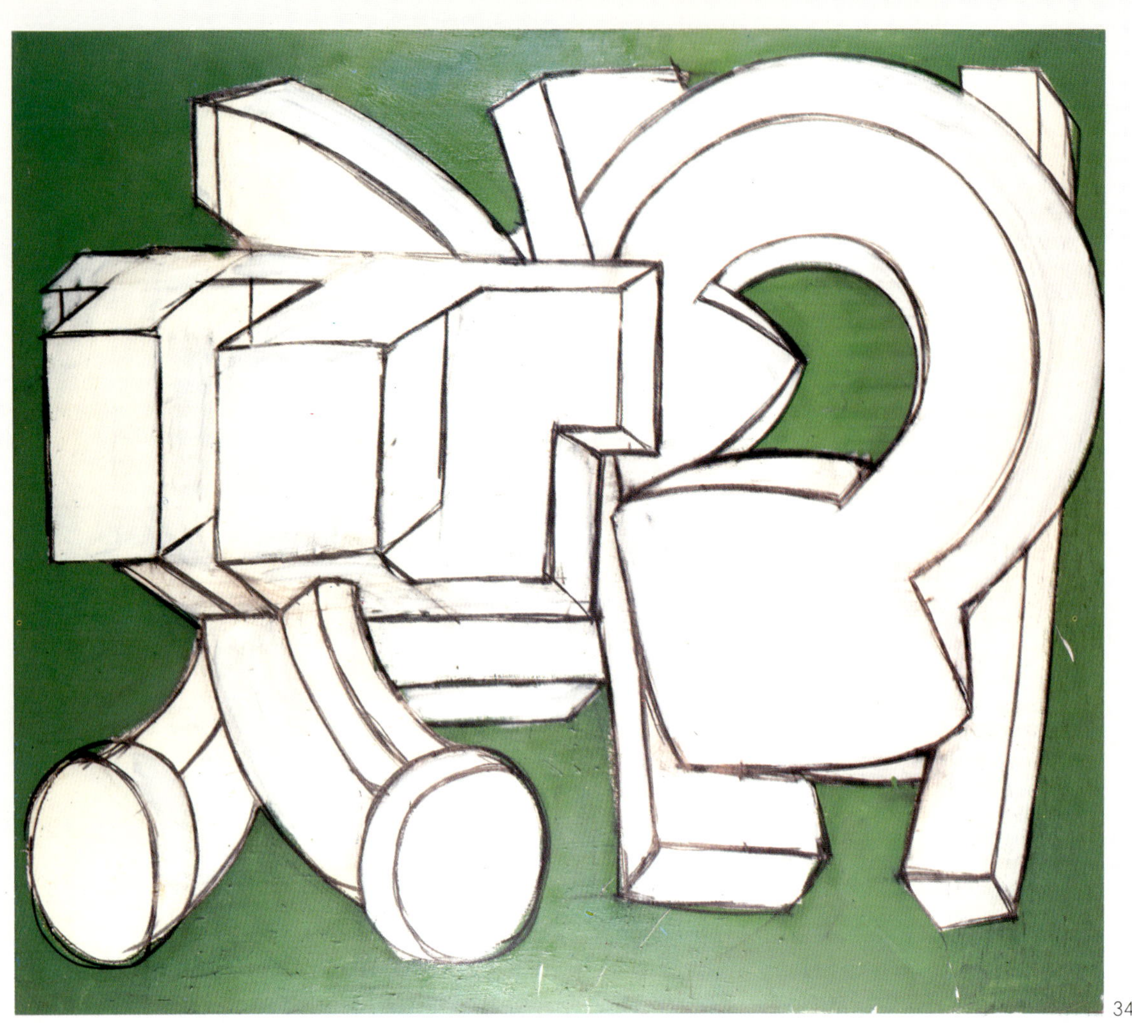

34

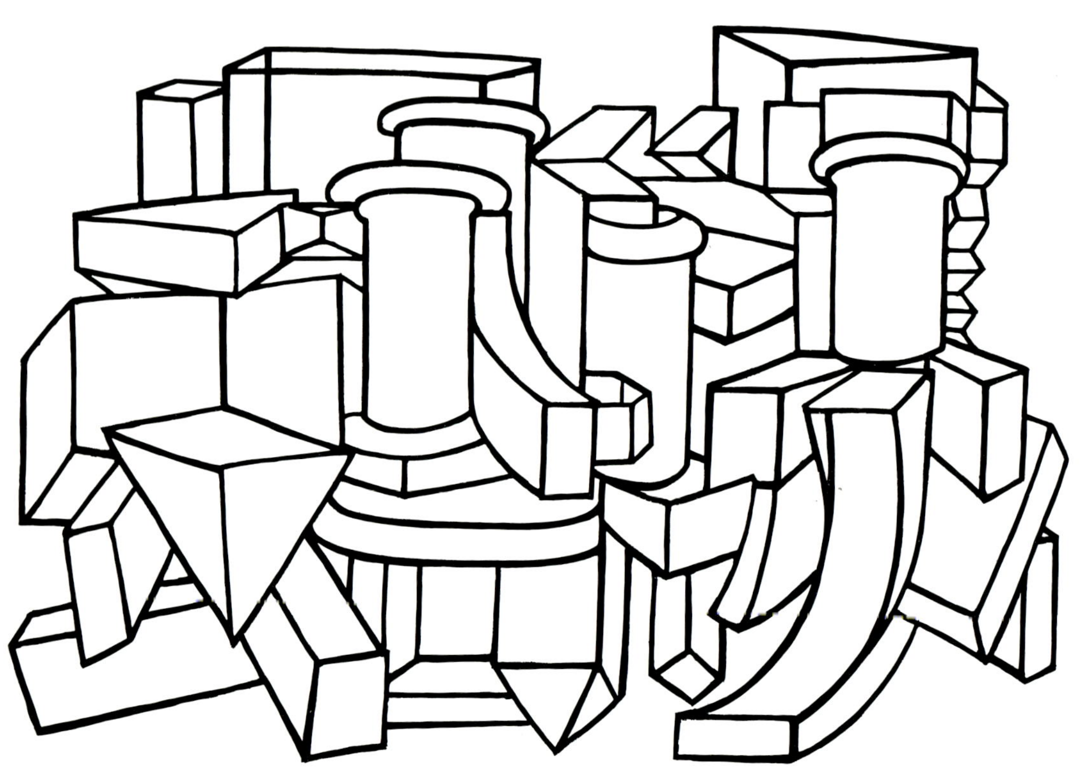

34. **Untitled (Black, White, and Green),** 1967.
Charcoal and acrylic on canvas, 87×100 in. (221×254 cm).
Collection of the artist.

35. **Four Columns,** 1967.
Acrylic on canvas, 114×144 in. (289.5×365.8 cm).
Collection of the artist.

36. **B/W VI,** 1967.
Acrylic on canvas, 114×114 in. (289.5×289.5 cm).
Collection of the artist.

37. **B/W VIII,** 1967.
Acrylic on canvas, 114×114 in. (289.5×289.5 cm).
Collection of Mrs. Watson Blair, New York.

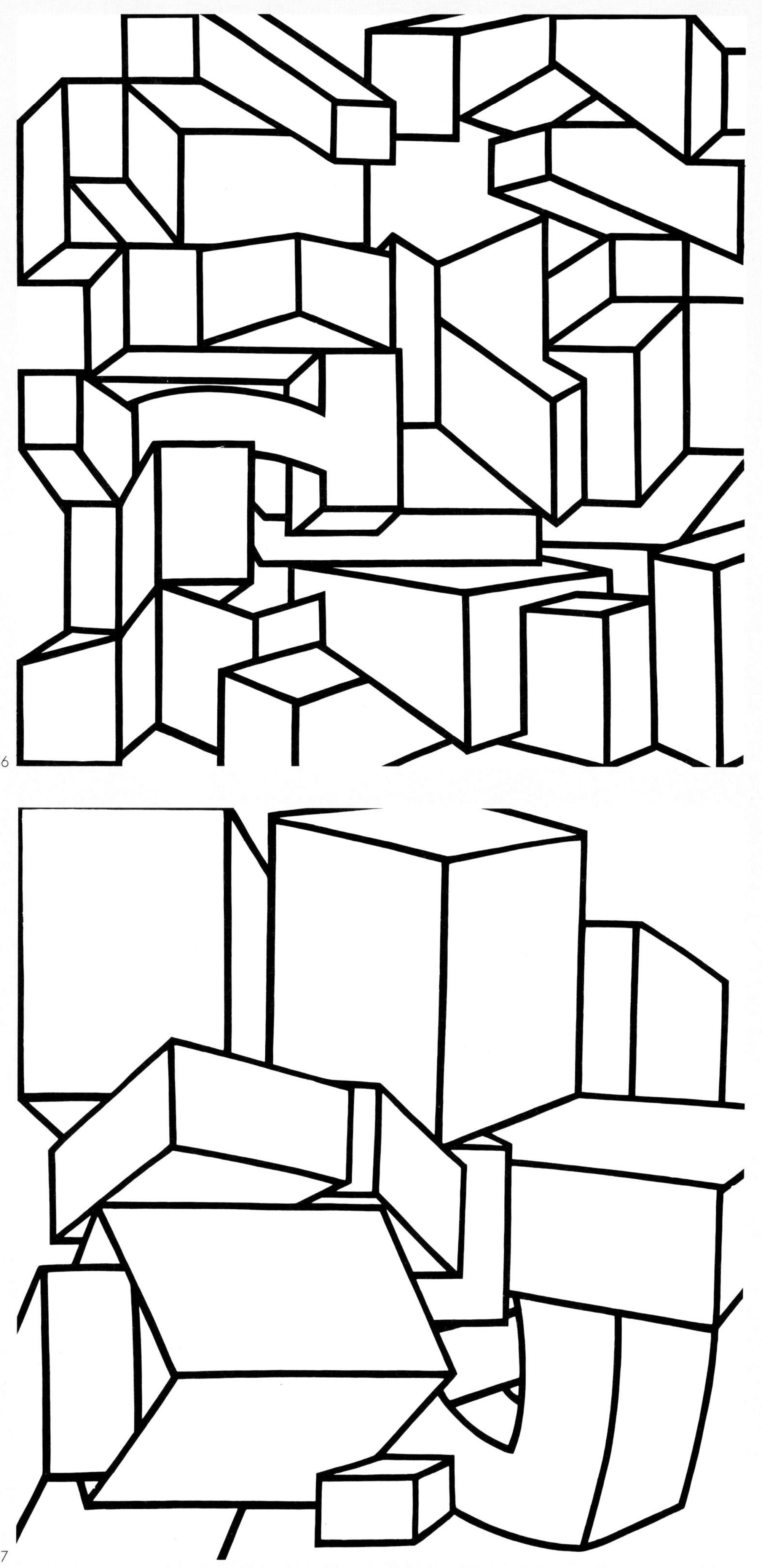

36

37

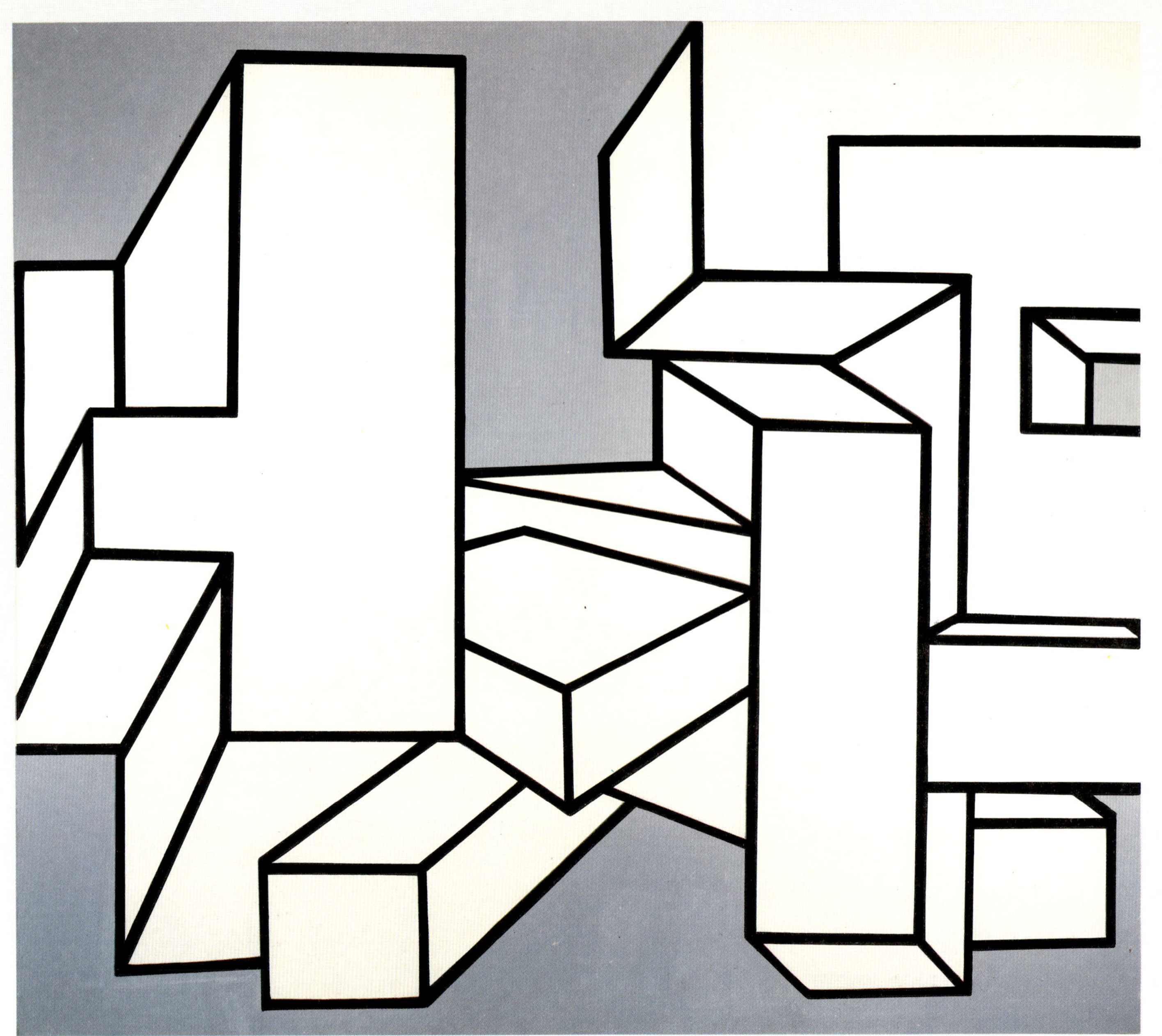

38

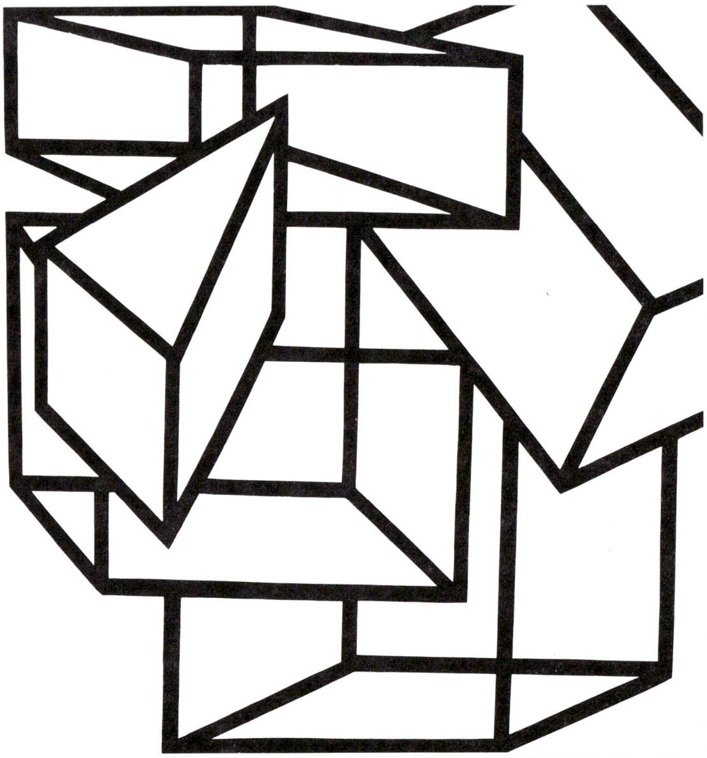

39

38. **Gateway,** 1967.
Acrylic on canvas, 114×144 in. (289.5×365.8 cm).
Collection of the artist.

39. **Phoenicia I,** 1969.
Acrylic on canvas, 48 3/8×48 3/8 in. (123.8×123.8 cm).
Private collection.

40. **Phoenicia V,** 1969.
Acrylic on canvas, 96×132 in. (243.8×335.2 cm).
Whereabouts unknown.

41. **Phoenicia IX,** 1969.
Acrylic on canvas, 114×144 in. (289.5×365.8 cm).
Israel Museum, Jerusalem.

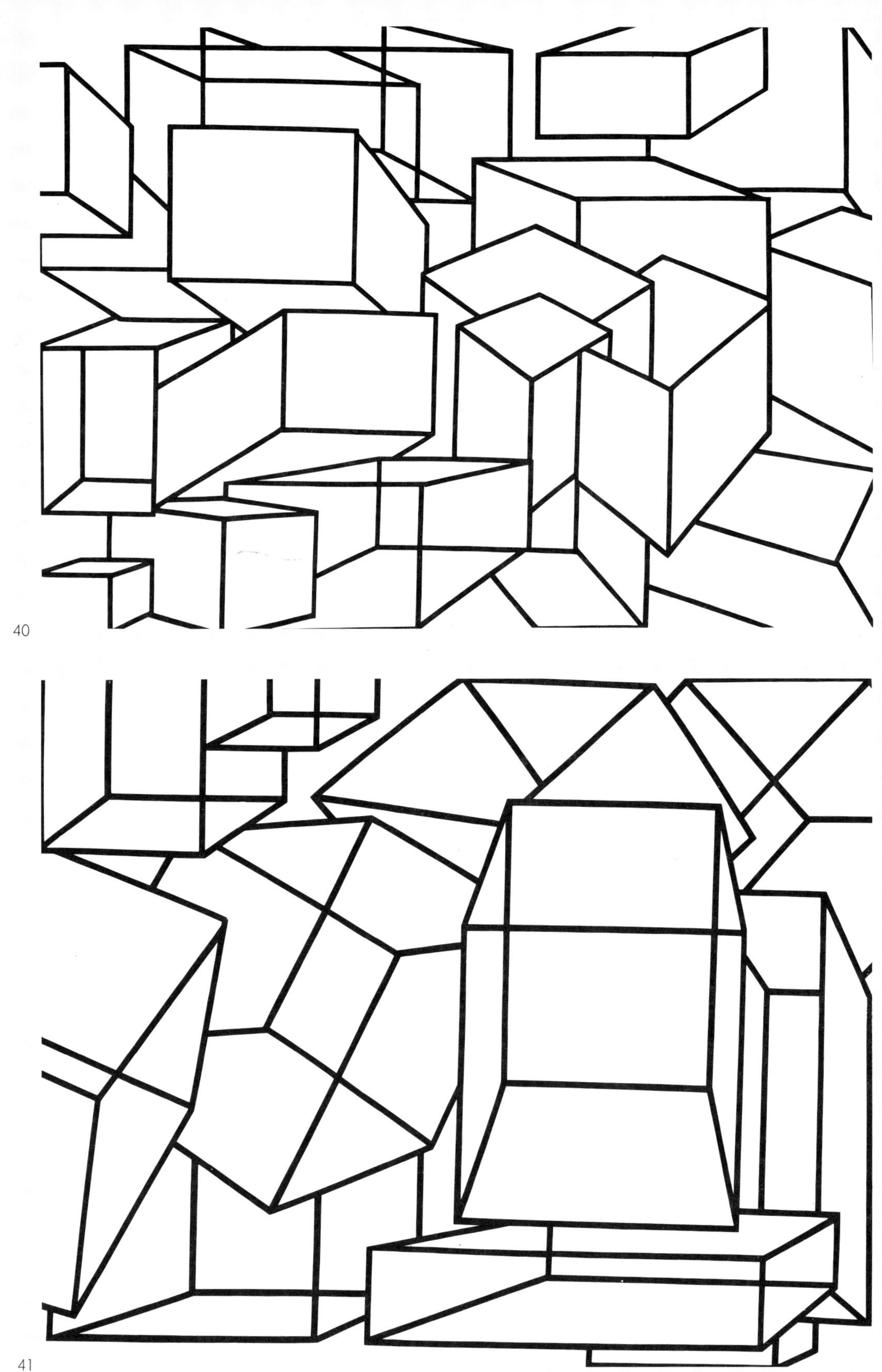

40

41

42. **Rothko's Canvas** (mural), 1969–70.
Acrylic on canvas, 120×1080 in. (3.08×27.43 m).
State of New York, Governor Nelson A. Rockefeller
Empire State Plaza, Albany.

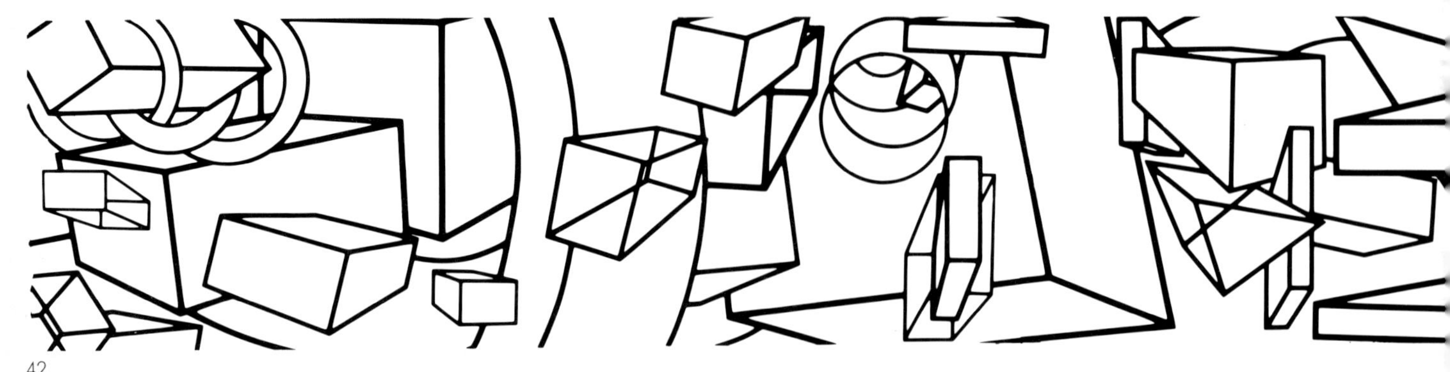

42

43. **Promised Land,** 1969–70.
Acrylic on canvas, 114×240 in. (289.5×609.5 cm).
Private collection.

44. **Eusopus I,** 1969.
Acrylic on canvas, 114×144 in. (289.5×365.8 cm).
Collection of the artist.

43

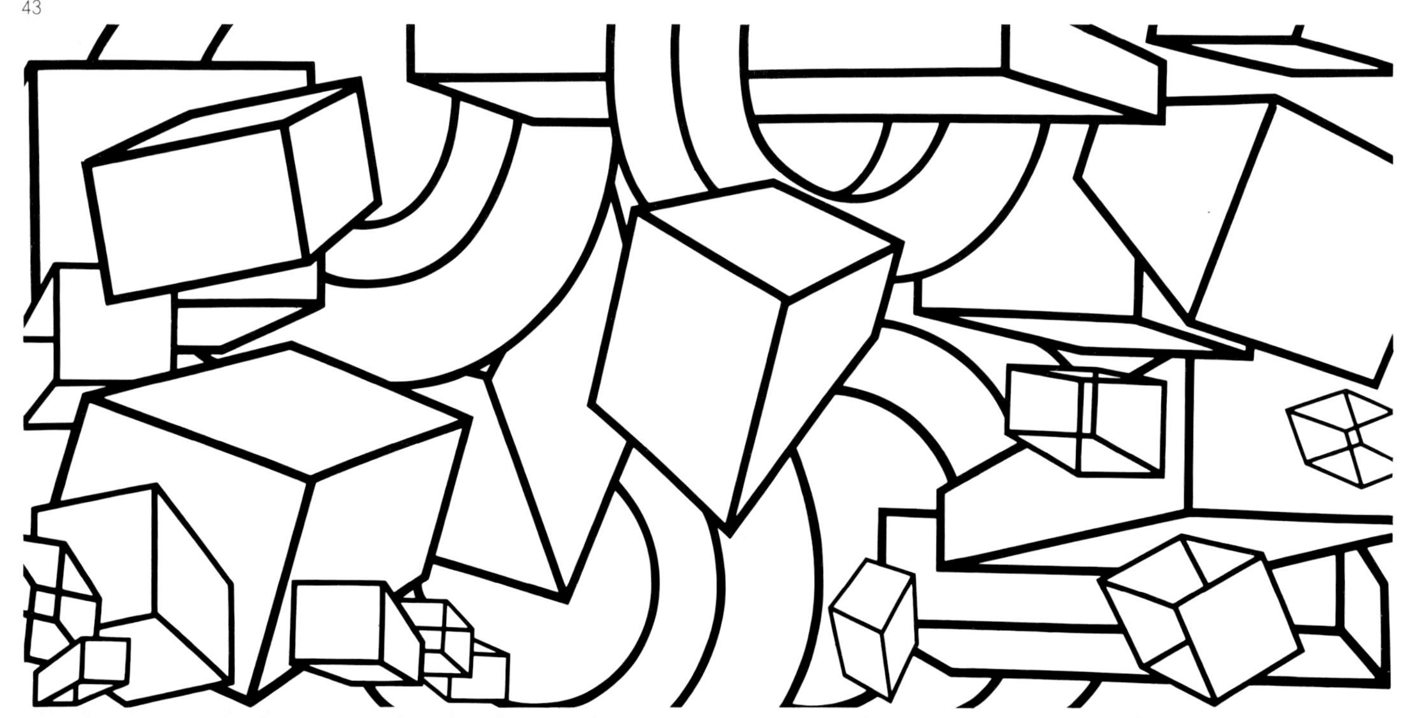

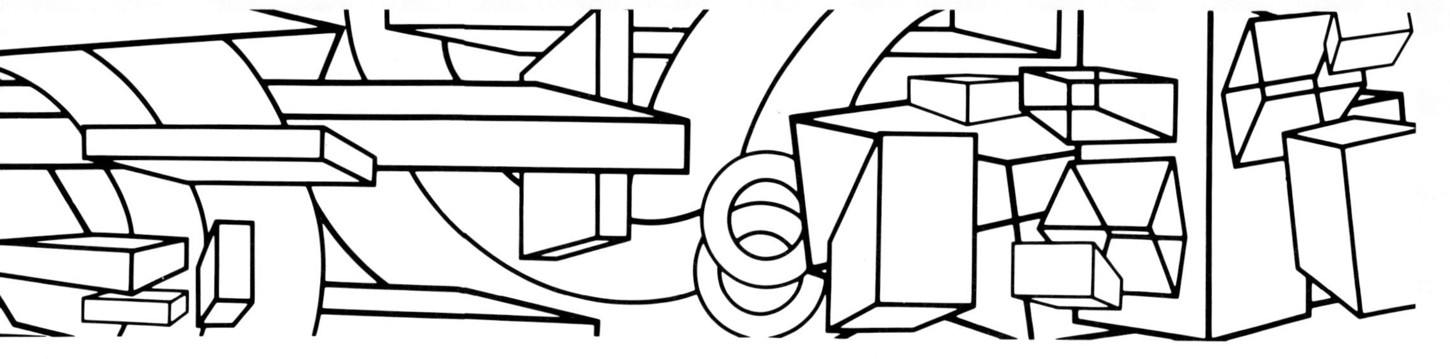

44

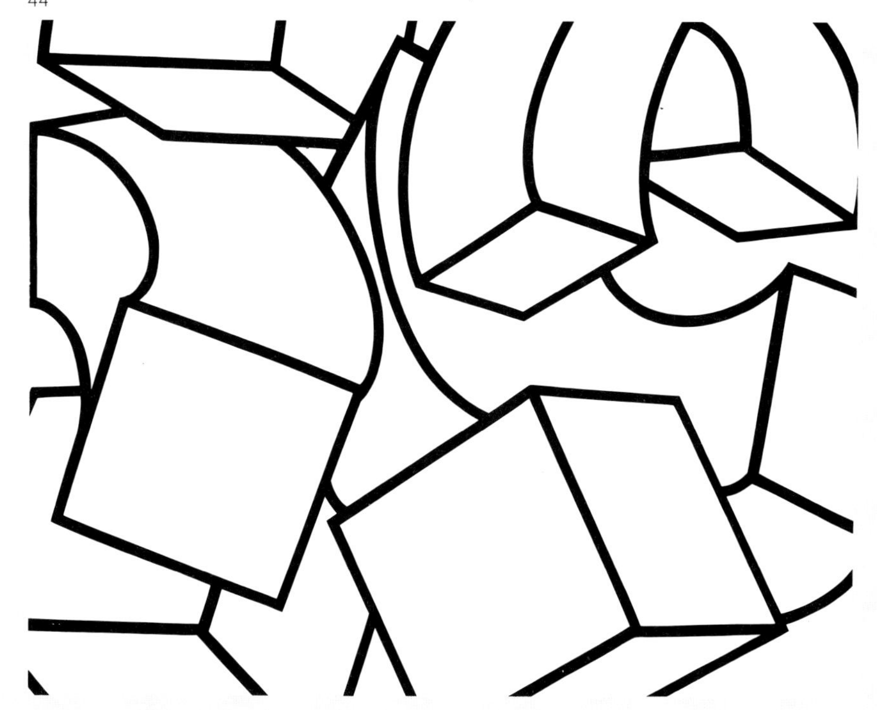

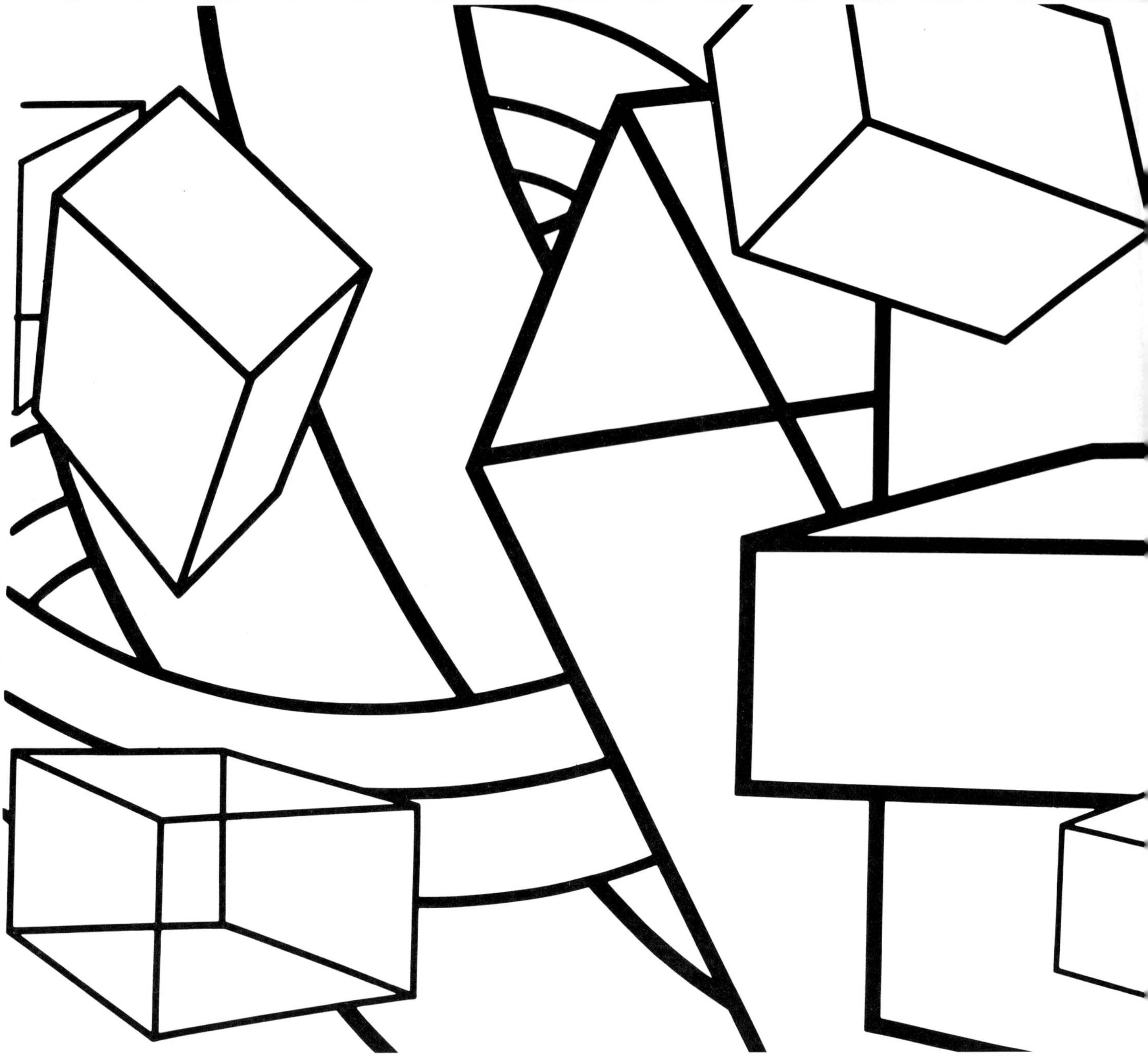

45

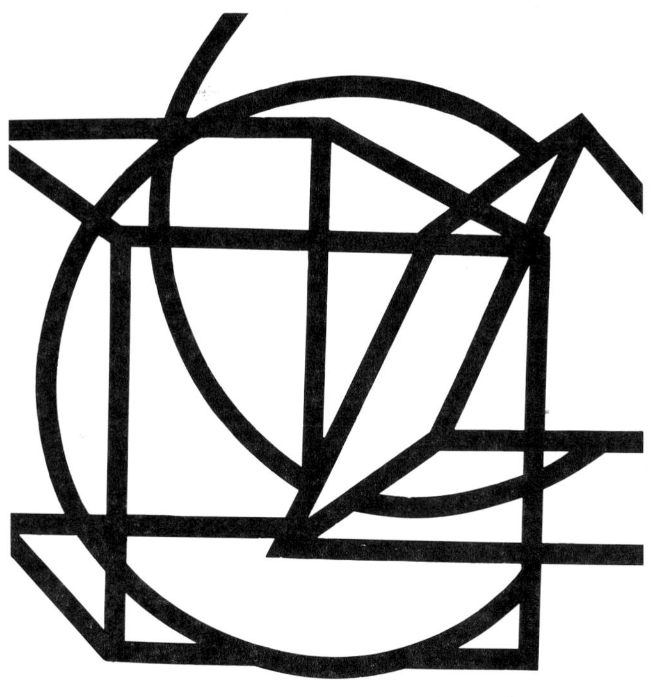

46

45. **Noah's Focus I,** 1970.
Acrylic on canvas, 138×300 in. (350.5×762 cm).
Collection of the artist.

46. **MO-T-6,** 1971.
Acrylic on canvas, 24×24 in. (61×61 cm).
Private collection, Farmington Hills, Michigan.

47. **MO-T-7,** 1971.
Acrylic on canvas, 30×41 in. (76.2×104.2 cm).
Collection of Jack Waser, Weiningen, Switzerland.

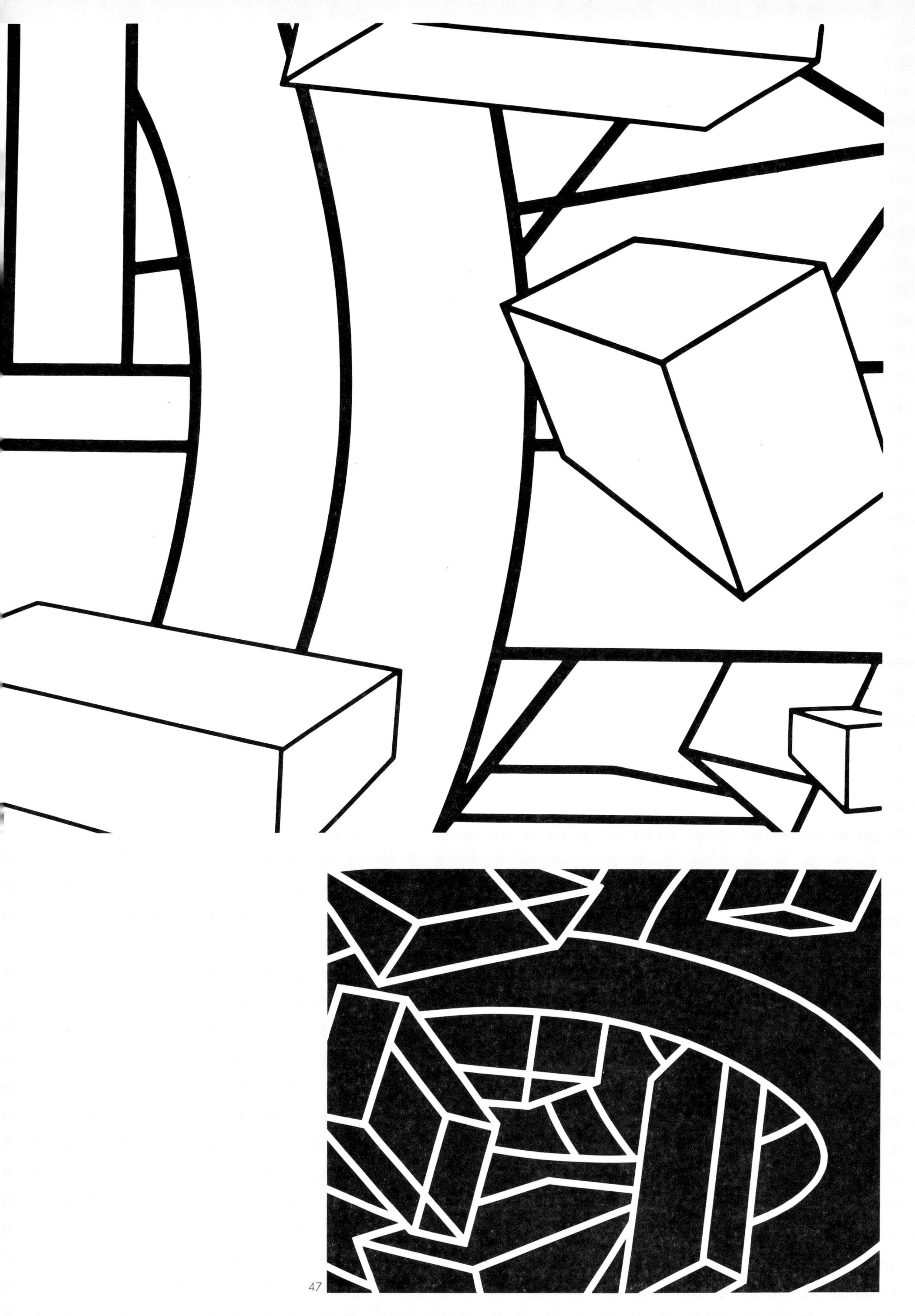

48. **Black Nile II,** 1971.
Acrylic on canvas, 90×90 in. (228.5×228.5 cm).
Private collection.

49. **Skywatch I,** 1971.
Acrylic on canvas, diameter 60 in. (152.4 cm).
Akron Art Museum, Ohio.

50. **Skywatch II,** 1972.
Acrylic on canvas, diameter 72 in. (183 cm).
Australian National Gallery, Canberra.

51. **Southeast,** 1972.
Acrylic on canvas, 138×168 in. (350.5×426.7 cm).
Collection of the artist.

48

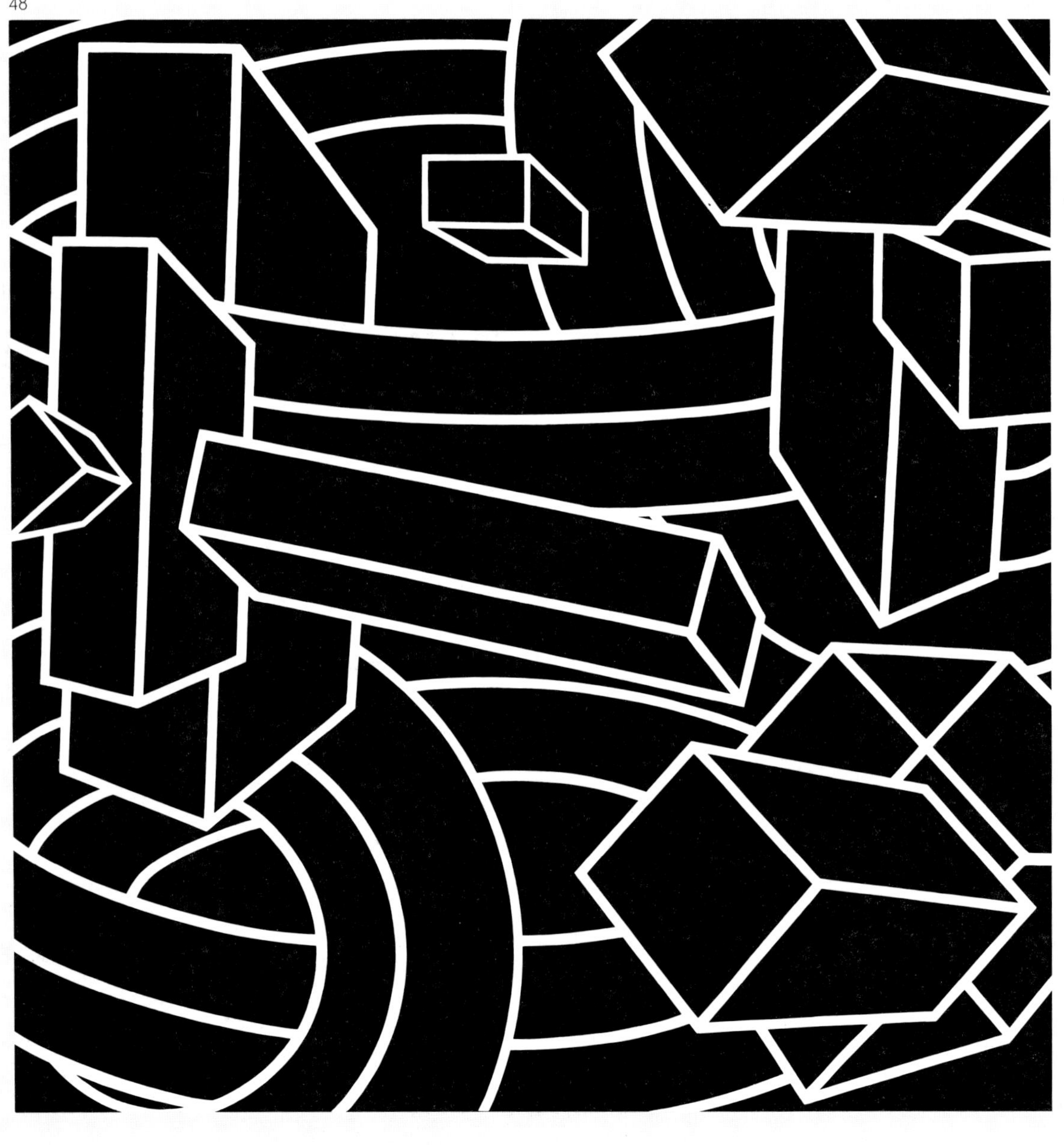

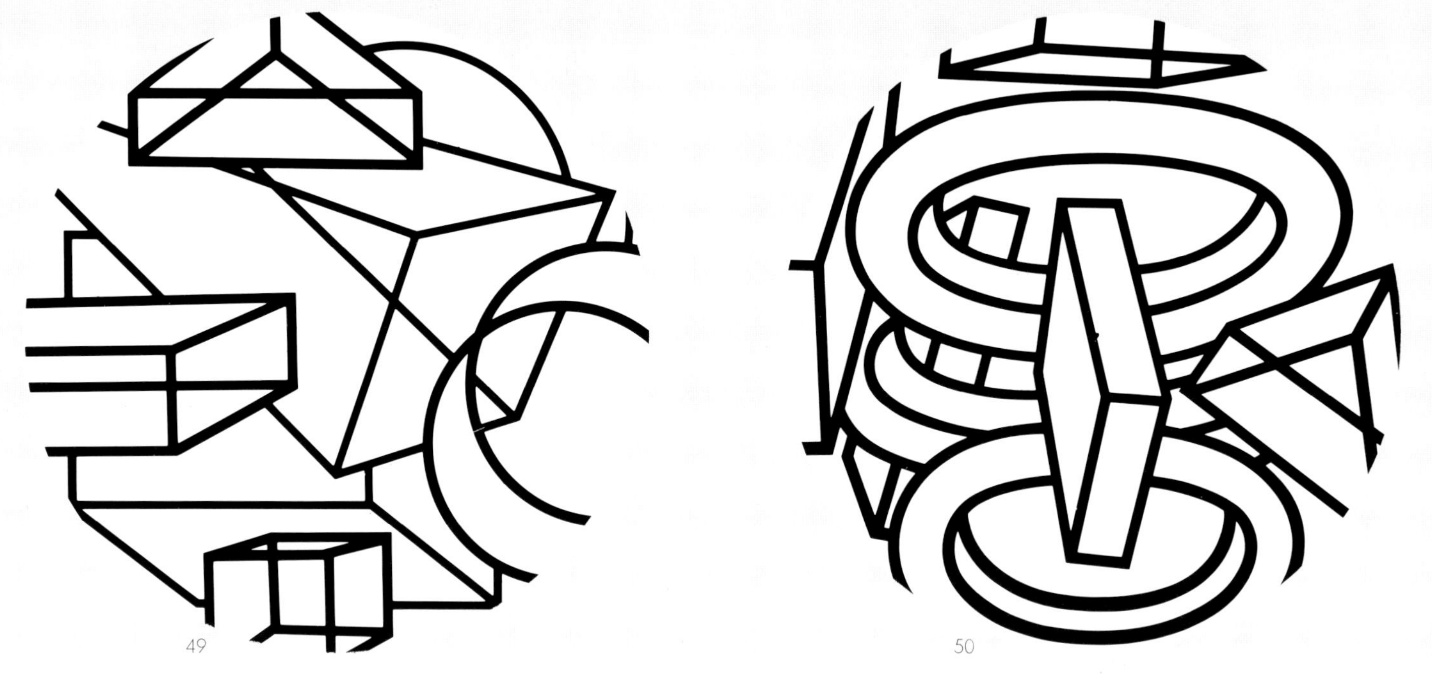

49

50

51

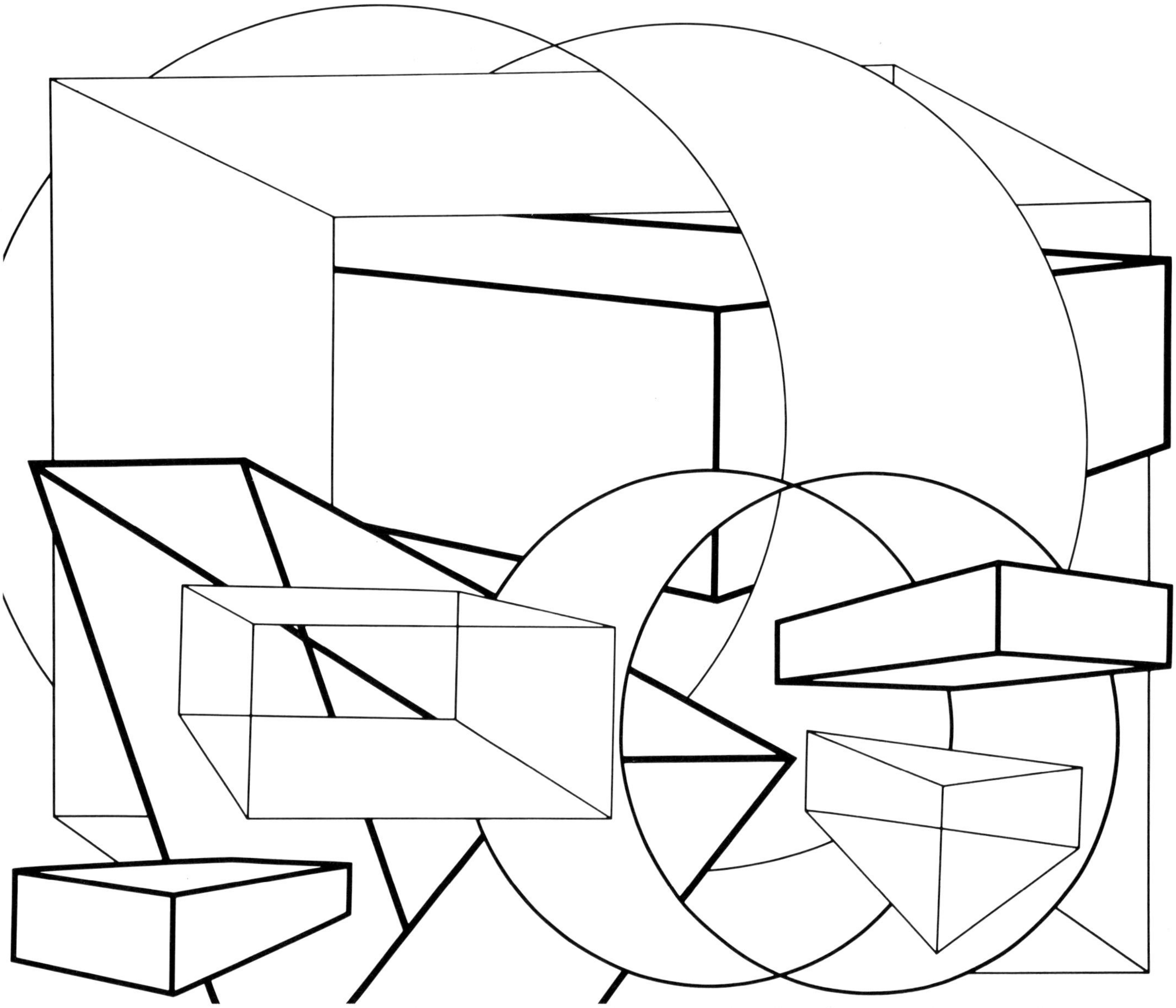

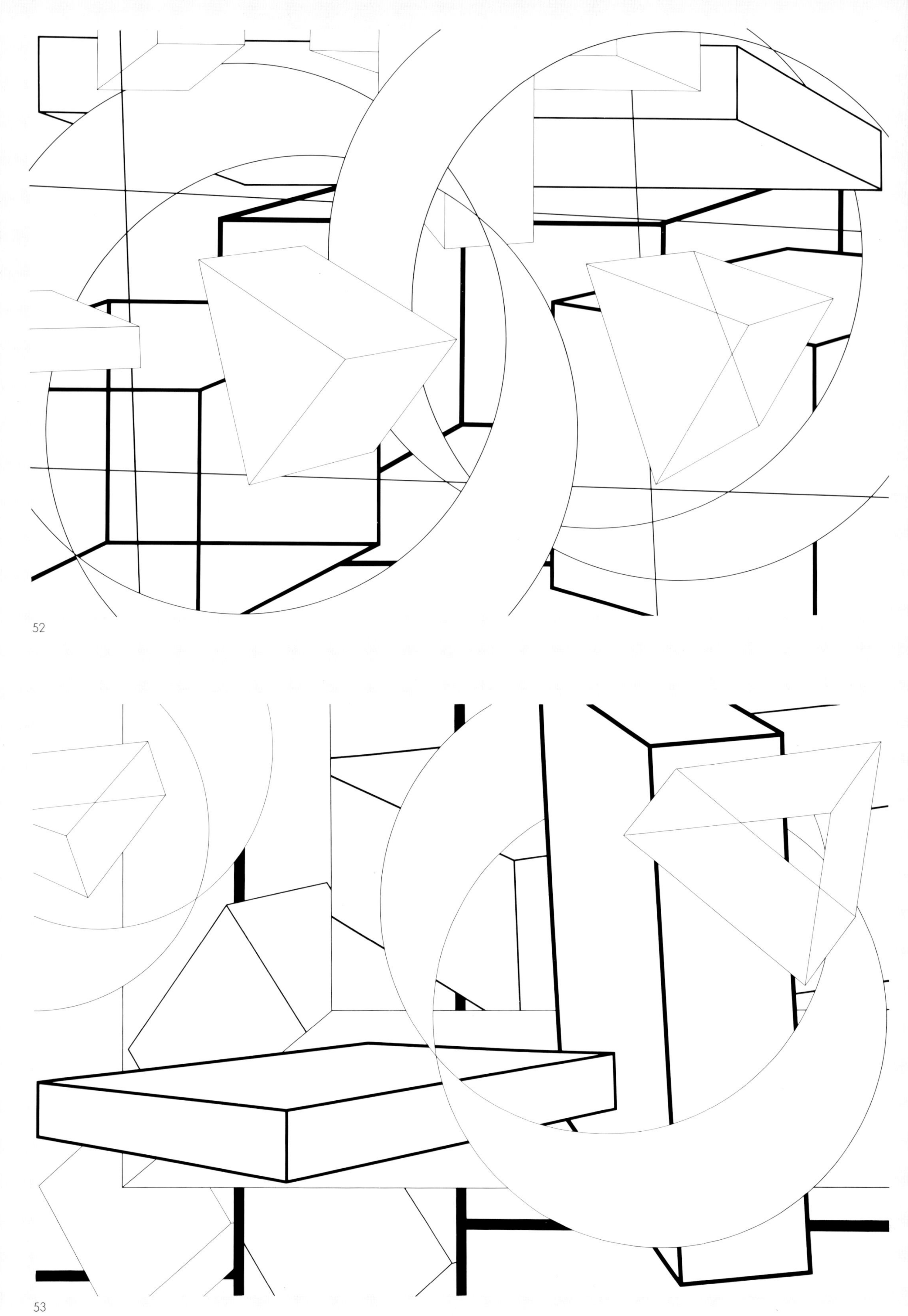

52

53

52. **South-Southwest,** 1973.
Synthetic polymer on canvas, 96×144 in. (243.8×365.8 cm).
Whitney Museum of American Art, New York (Purchase).

53. **Southwest,** 1973.
Acrylic on canvas, 114×168 in. (289.5×426.7 cm).
Collection of the artist.

54. **East-Southwest,** 1973.
Acrylic on canvas, 84×96 in. (213.4×243.8 cm).
Collection of Hannelore B. Schulhof, New York.

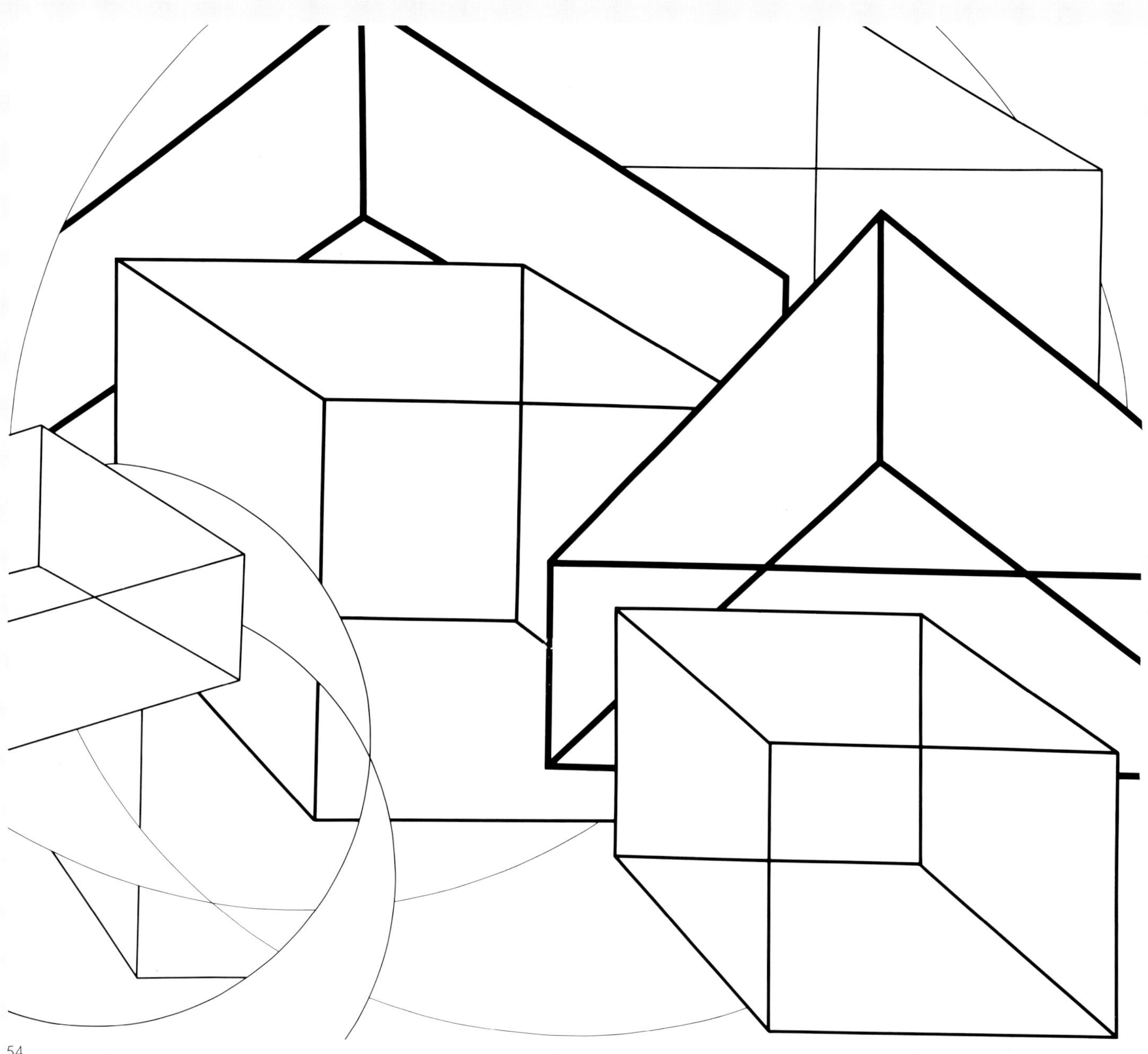

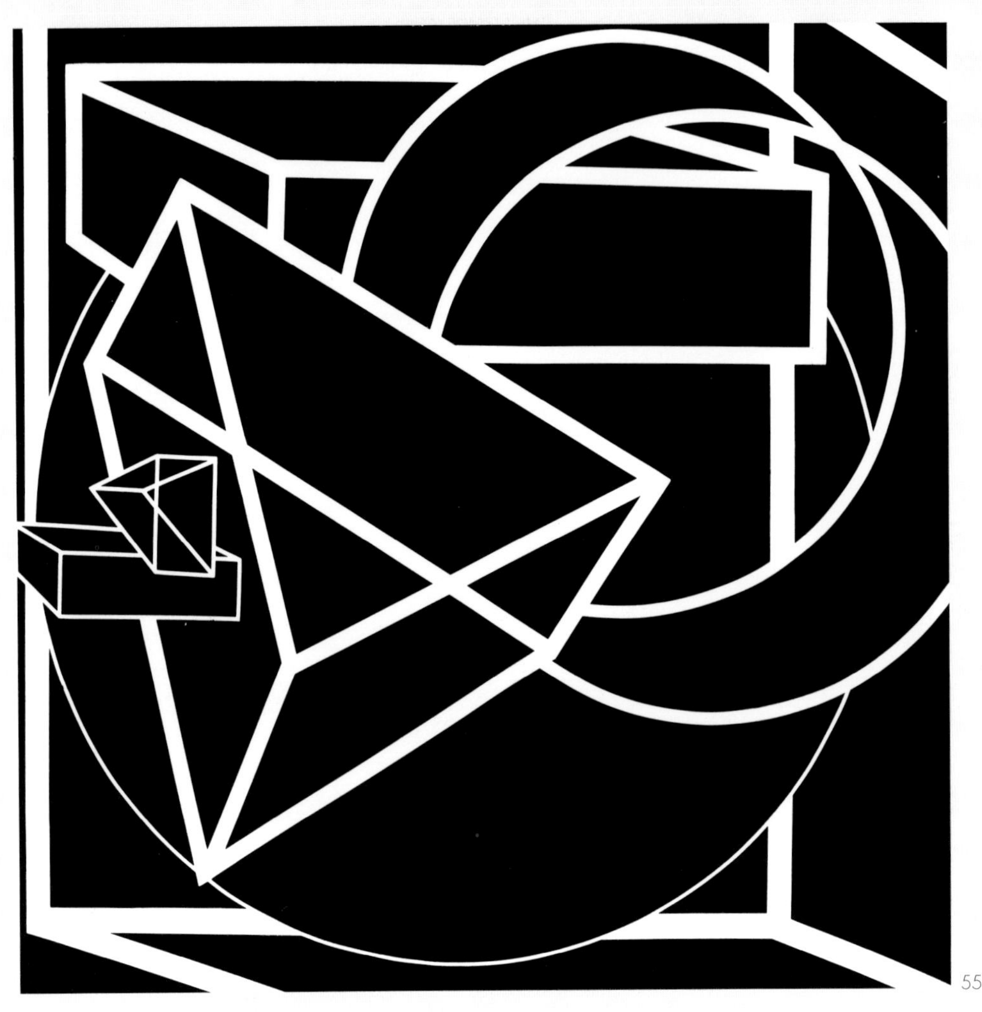

55

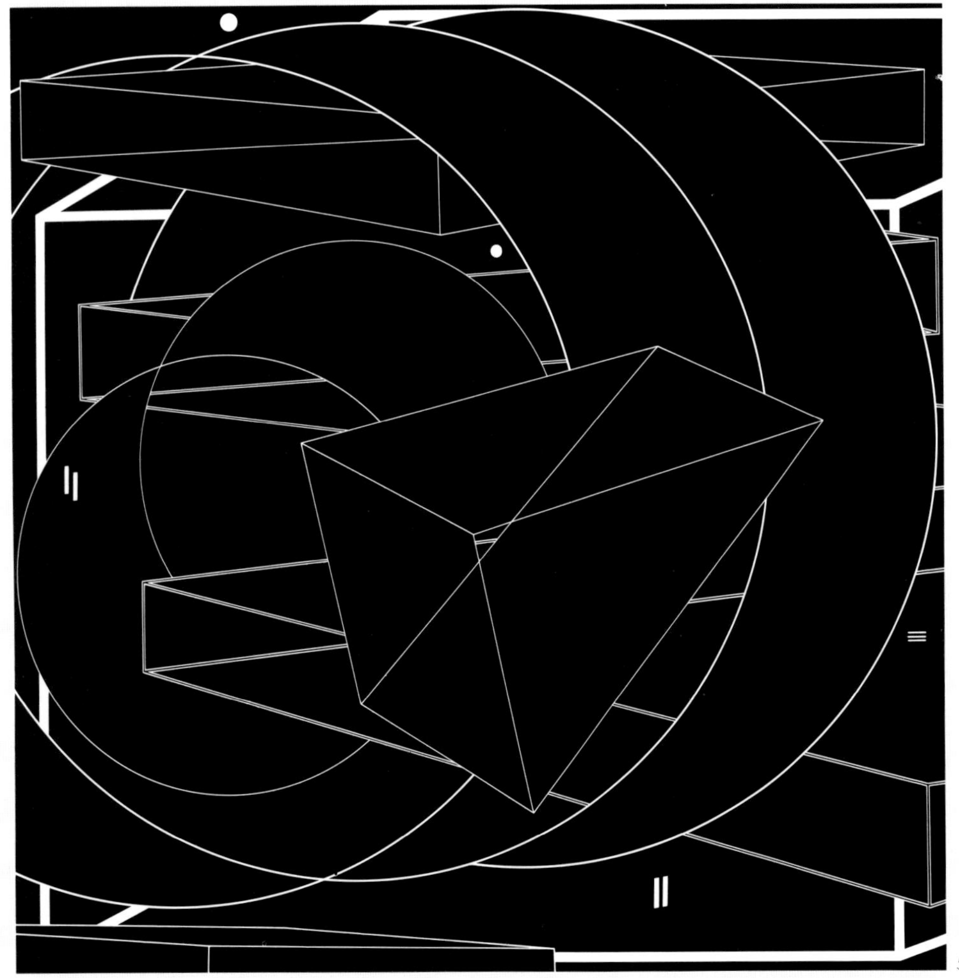

56

55. **Flemish II,** 1972.
Acrylic on canvas,
60×60 in. (152.4×152.4 cm).
Private collection.

56. **Flemish XII,** 1975.
Acrylic on canvas,
60×60 in. (152.4×152.4 cm).
Collection of John and Cynthia Cross,
Ann Arbor, Michigan.

57. **Solar Wind I,** 1973.
Acrylic on canvas,
114×114 in. (289.5×289.5 cm).
Galerie Renée Ziegler, Zurich.

58. **Jupiter I,** 1973.
Acrylic on canvas,
72×96 in. (183×243.8 cm).
Collection of Spencer and Myrna
Partrich, Bloomfield Hills, Michigan.

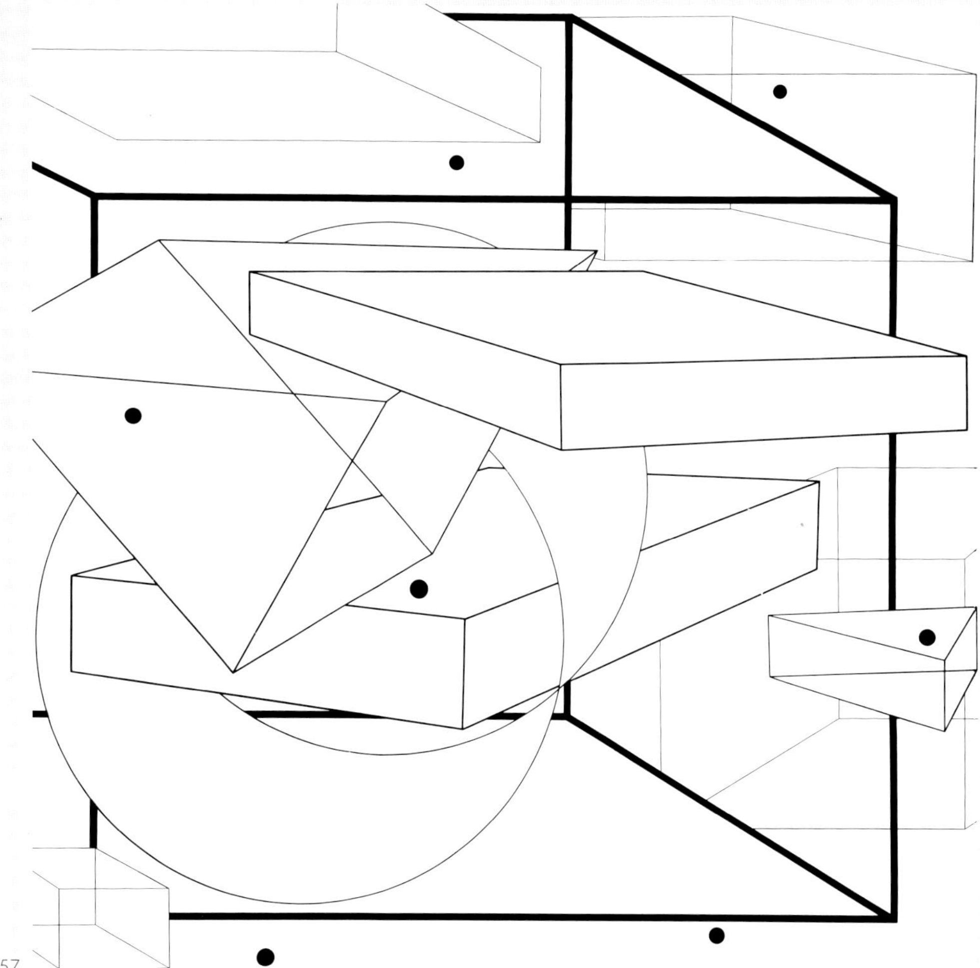

57

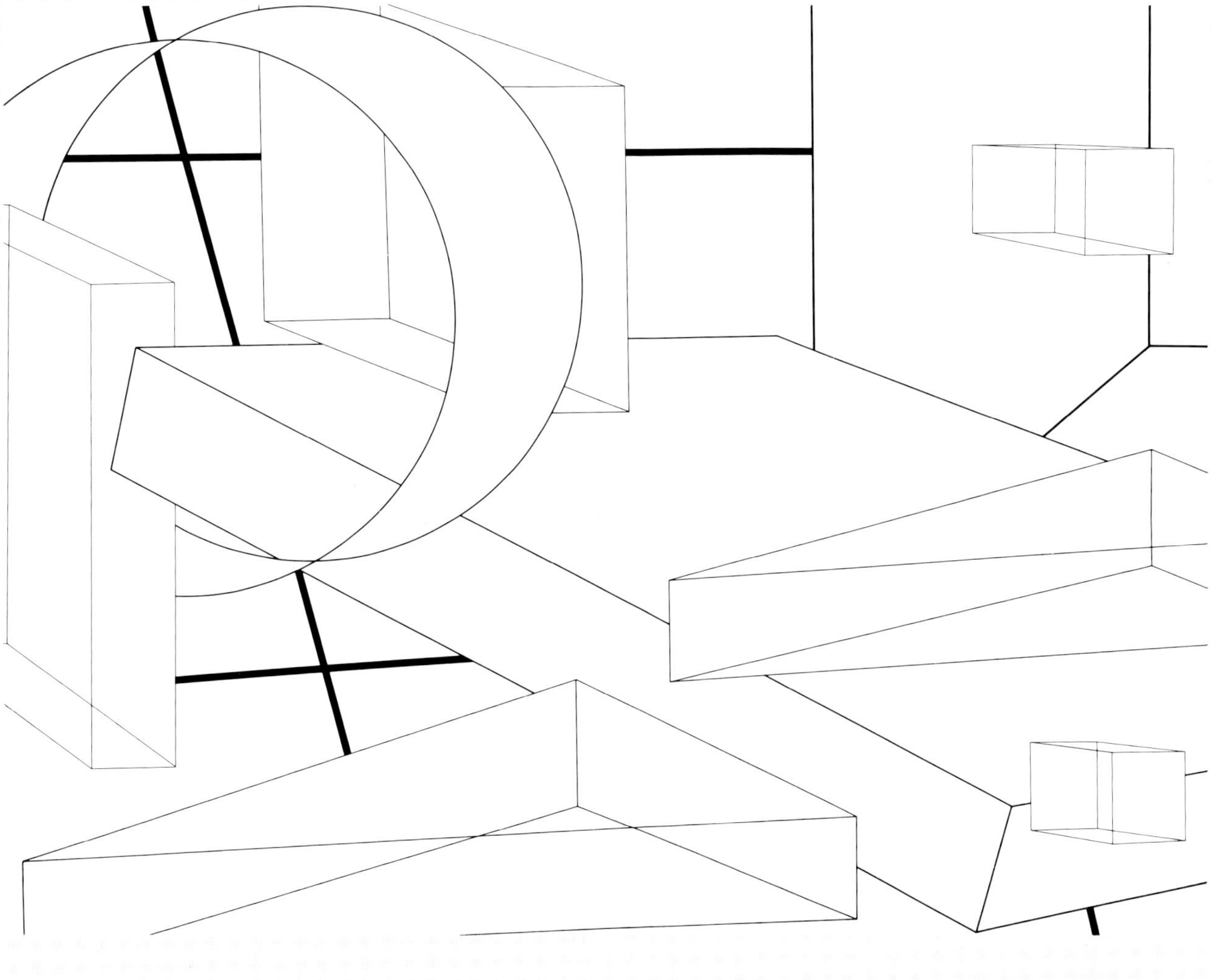

58

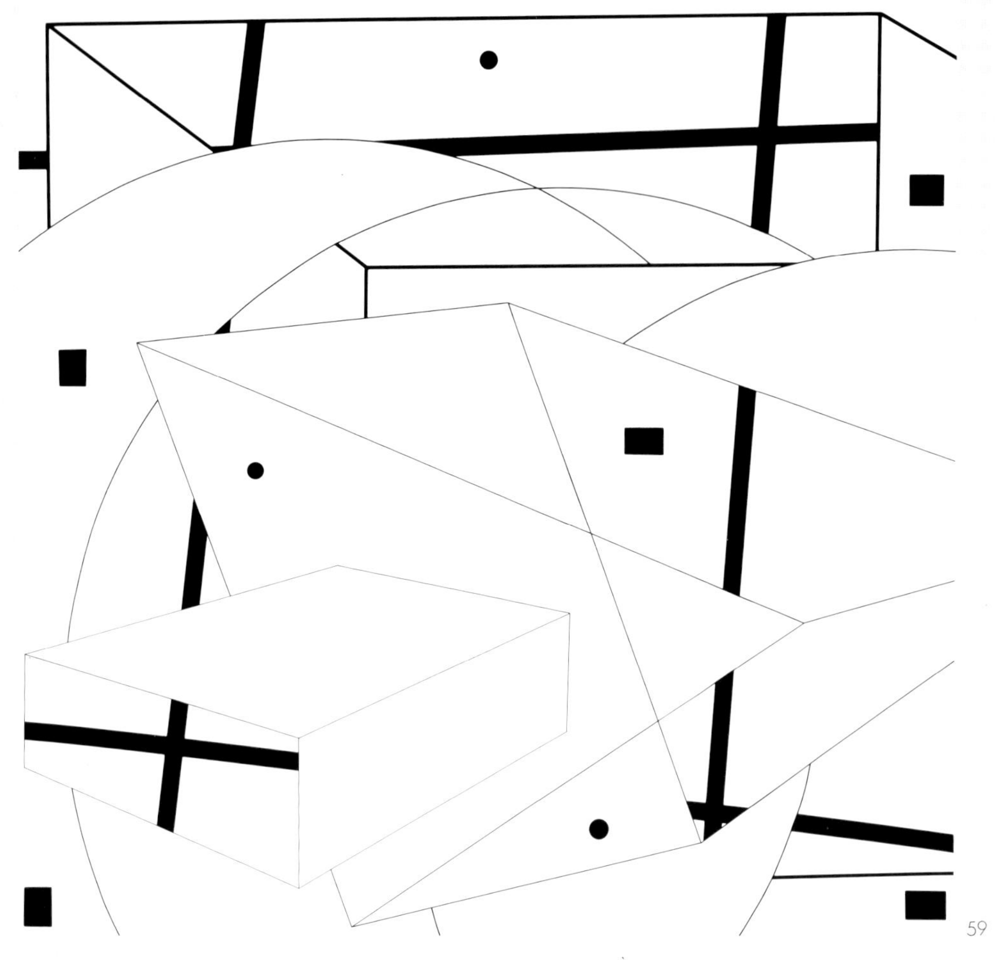
59

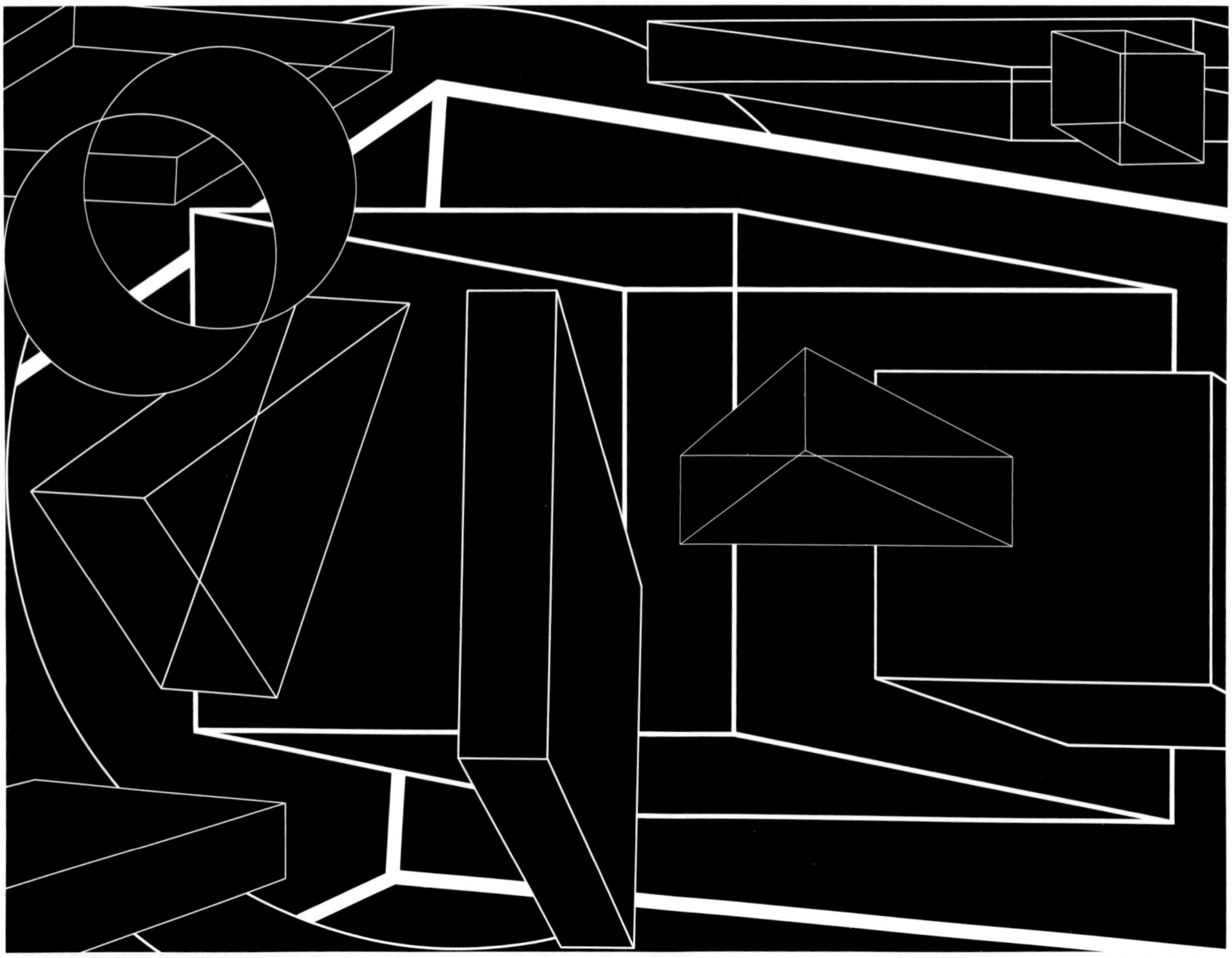

60

59. **Solar Wind III,** 1974.
Acrylic on canvas, 84×84 in. (213.4×213.4 cm).
The Brooklyn Museum, New York.

60. **Black Nile VI,** 1974.
Acrylic on canvas, 72×96 in. (183×243.8 cm).
Private collection.

61. **Mercury Zone II,** 1975.
Acrylic on canvas, 72×60 in. (183×152.4 cm).
Collection of Mr. Walter Netsch, Jr., Chicago.

62. **Stereo III,** 1975.
Acrylic on canvas, 72×60 in. (183×152.4 cm).
Private collection, Birmingham, Michigan.

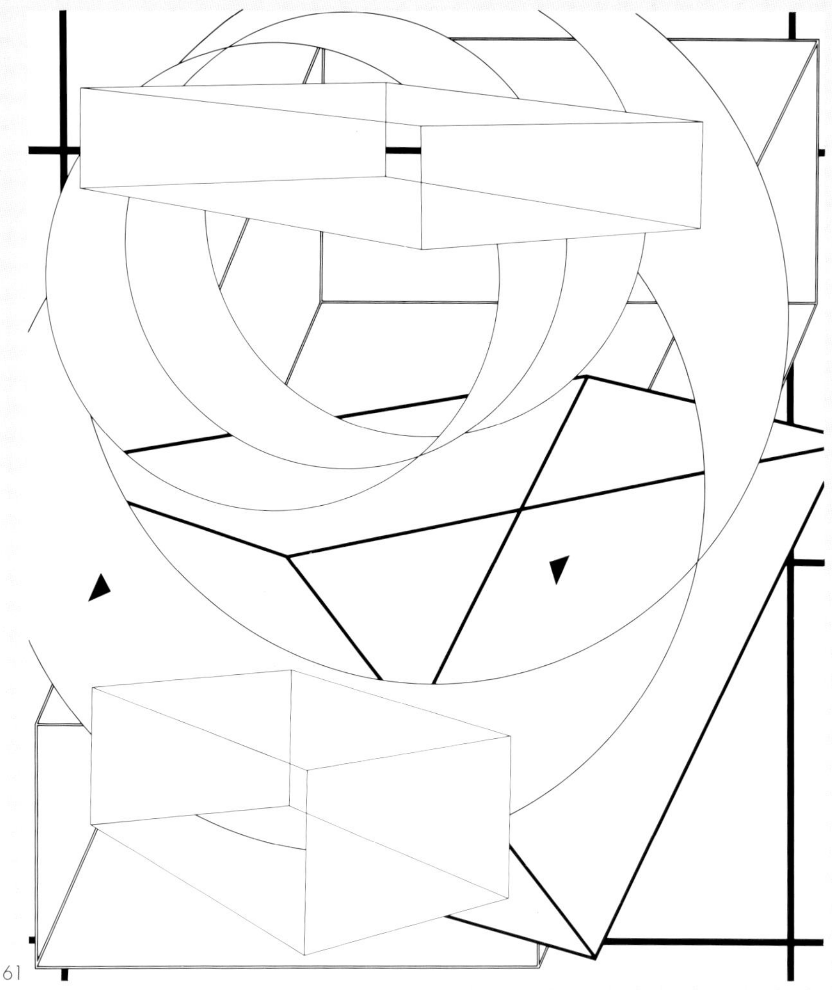

61

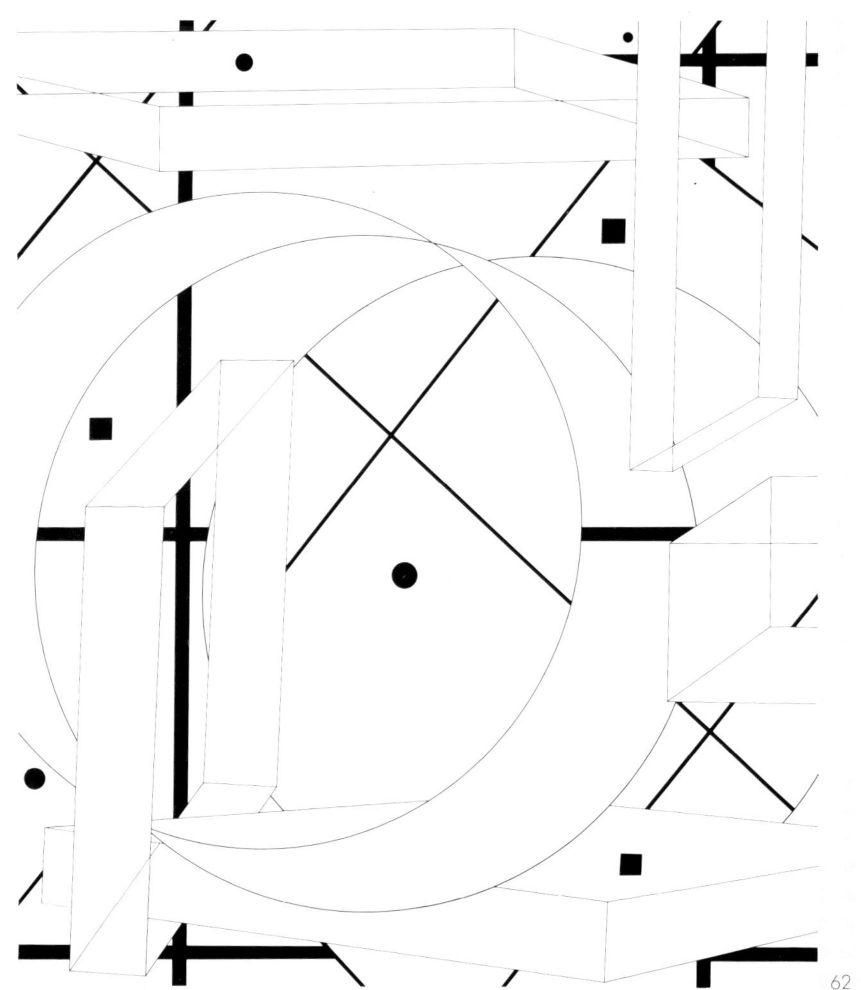

62

63. **Mercury Zone III,** 1975.
Acrylic on canvas, 96×143 in. (243.8×363.2 cm).
The Metropolitan Museum of Art, New York
(George A. Hearn Fund, 1976).

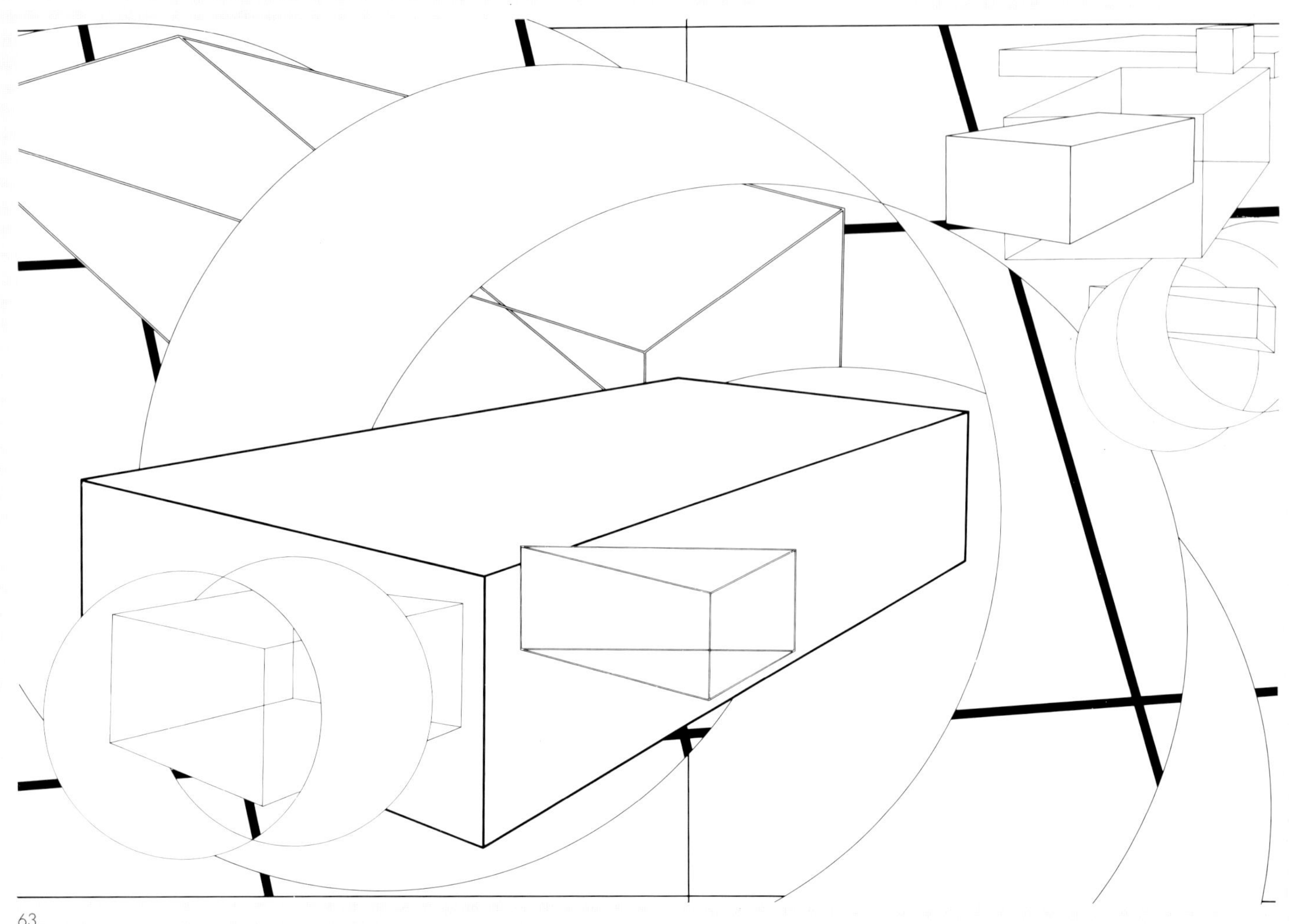

63

64. **Mercury Zone VIII,** 1976.
Acrylic on canvas, 108×108 in. (274.3×274.3 cm).
Private collection.

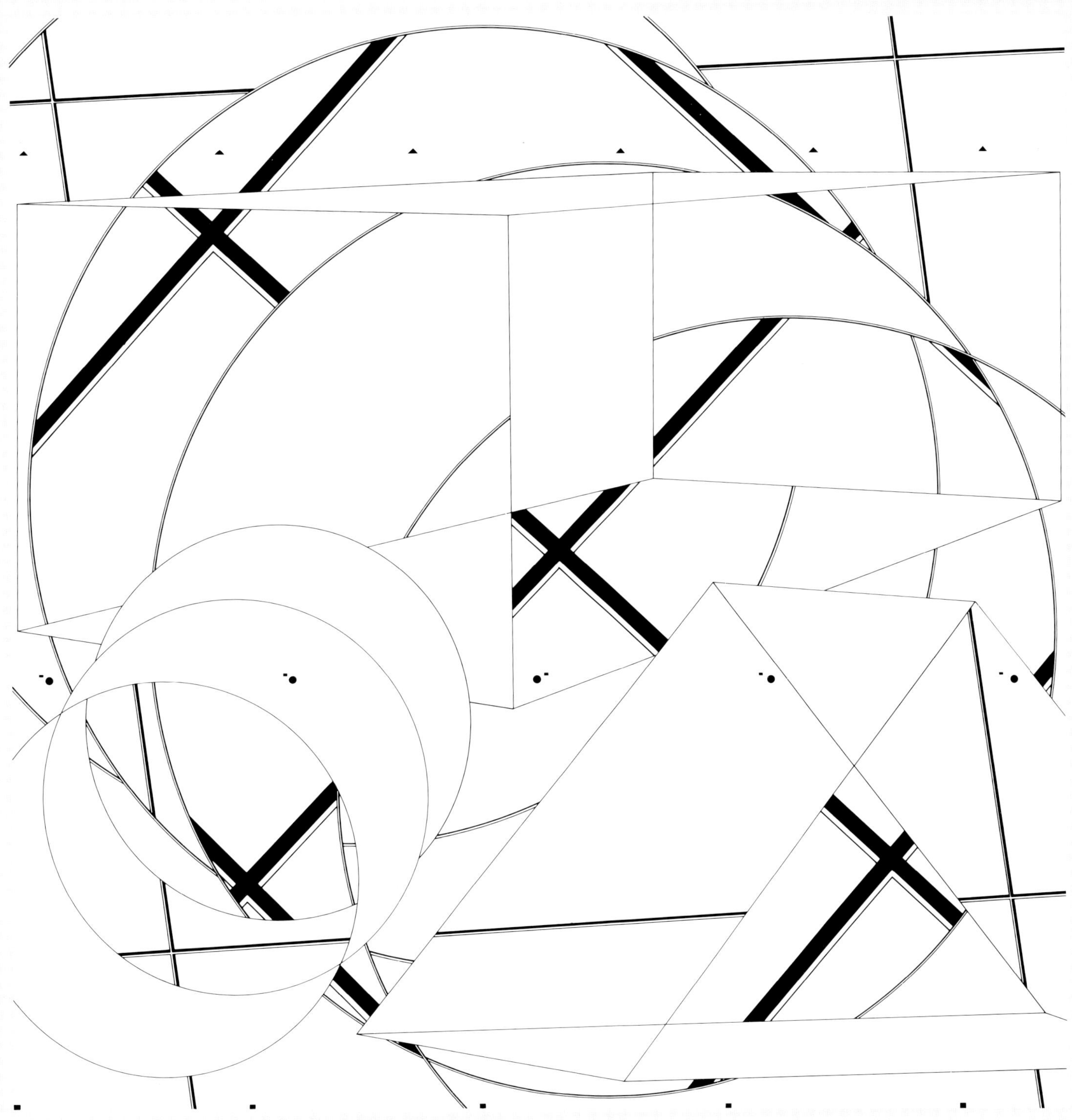

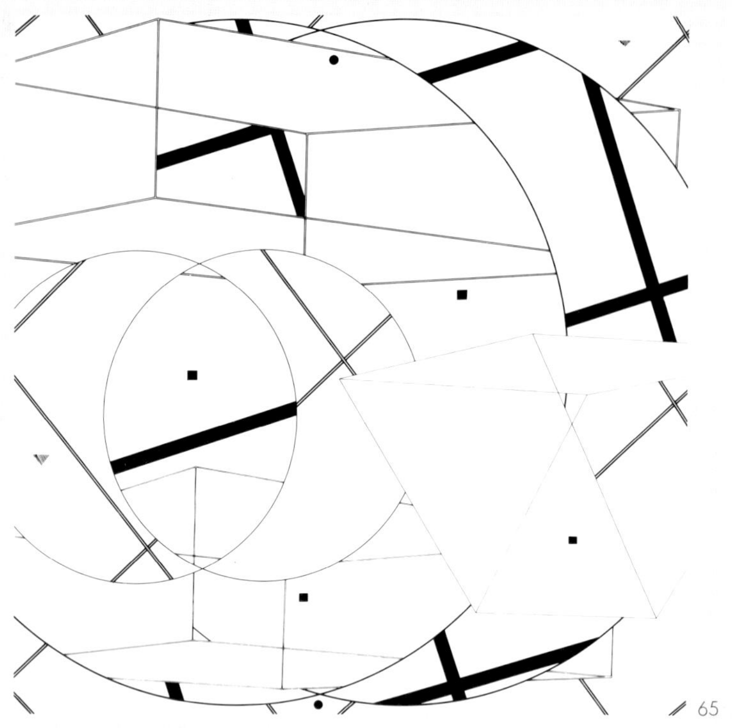

65

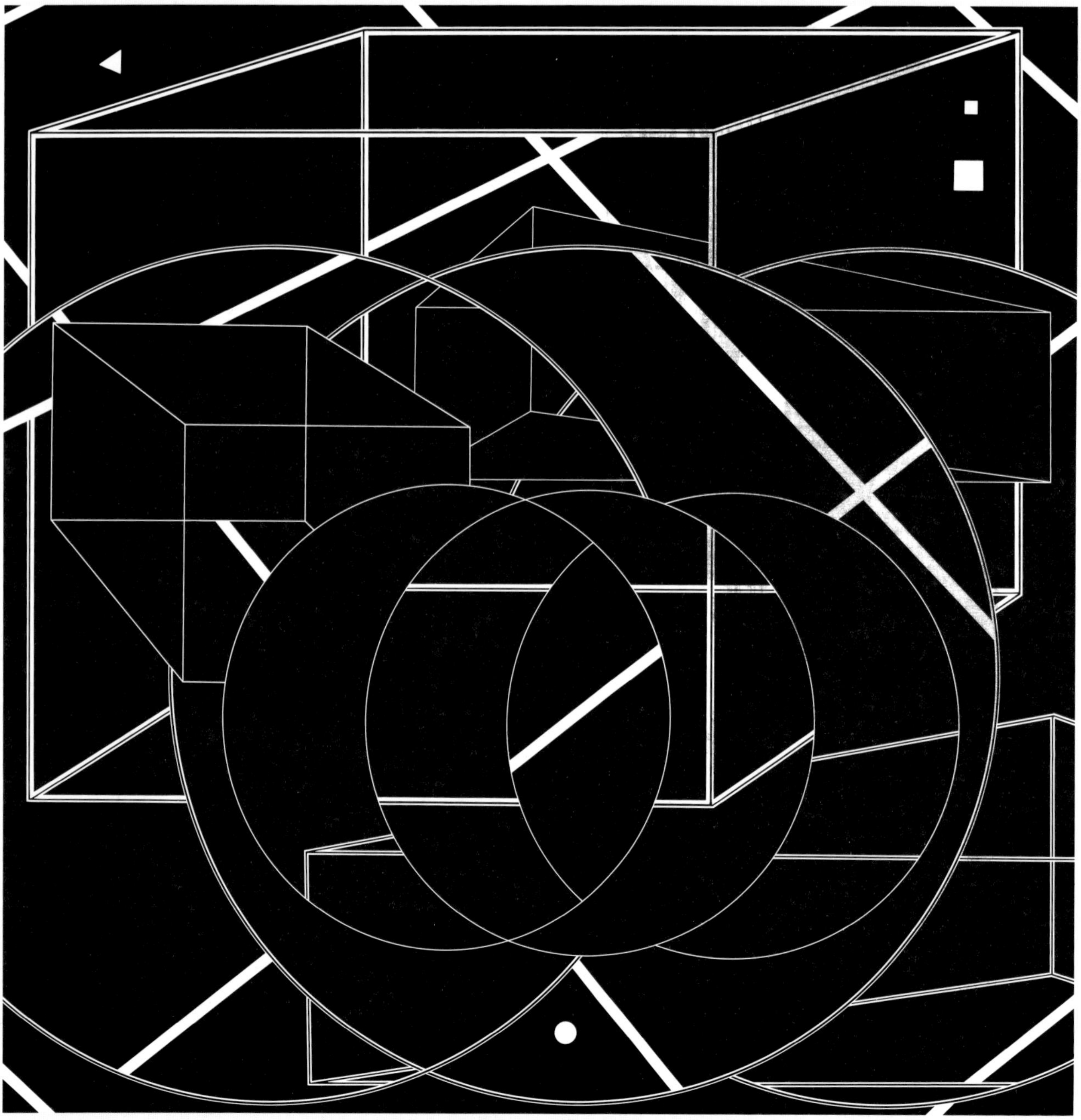

66

65. **Mercury Zone VI,** 1976.
Acrylic on canvas, 60×60 in. (152.4×152.4 cm).
Private collection.

66. **Volta I,** 1976.
Acrylic on canvas, 84×84 in. (213.4×213.4 cm).
Collection of Mr. and Mrs. Neil Rosenstein,
Beverly Hills, California.

67. **Volta IV,** 1977.
Acrylic on canvas, 48×48 in. (122×122 cm).
Collection of Mr. and Mrs. Donald Benyas,
Southfield, Michigan.

68. **Volta II,** 1976.
Acrylic on canvas, 84×84 in. (213.4×213.4 cm).
Private collection.

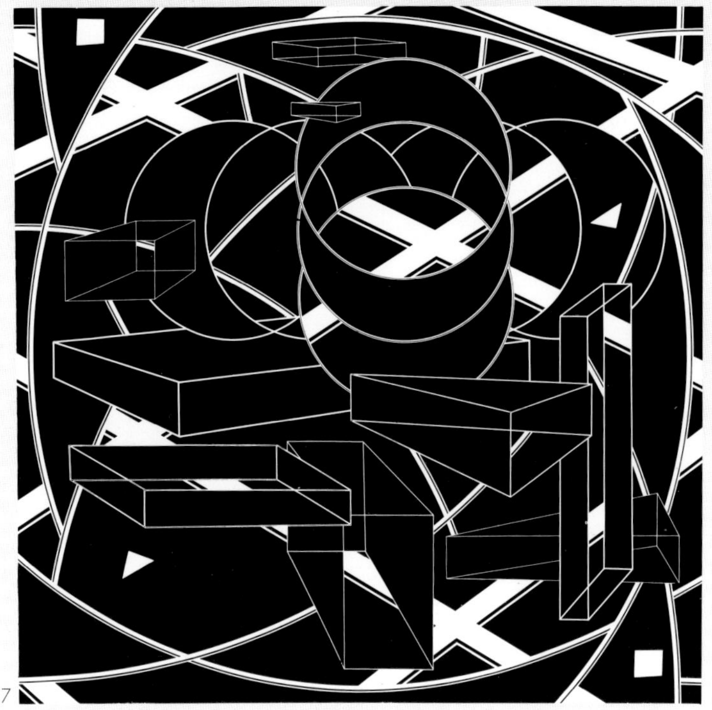

67

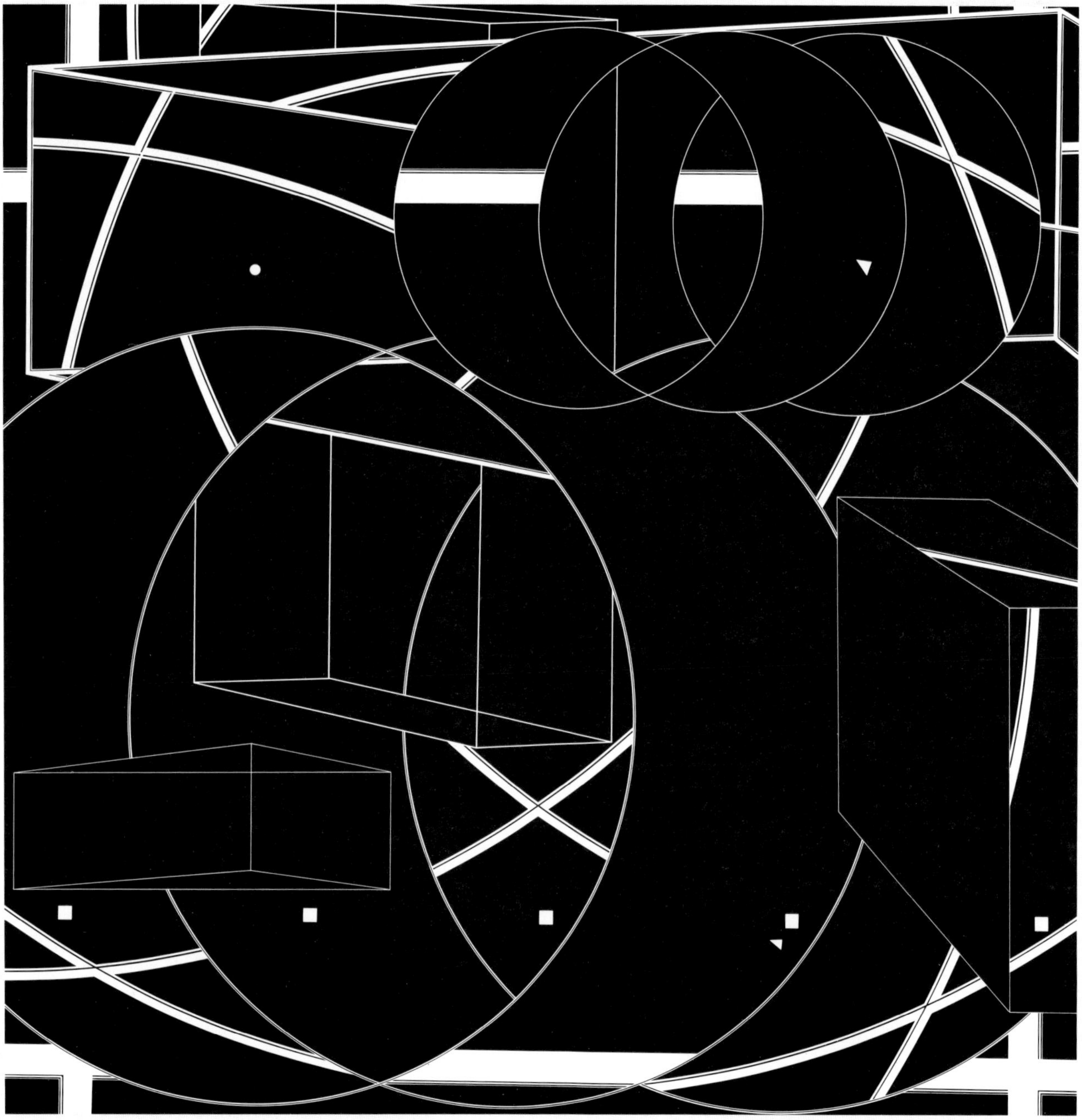

68

69. **Volta V,** 1977.
Acrylic on canvas, 96×144 in. (243.8×289.5 cm).
Hirshhorn Museum and Sculpture Garden, Smithsonian Institution, Washington, D.C.

70. **Volta VII,** 1978.
Acrylic on canvas, 60×60 in. (152.4×152.4 cm).
Collection of Forbes Cohen Properties, Southfield, Michigan.

71. **Volta VIII,** 1978.
Acrylic on canvas, 48×48 in. (122×122 cm).
Richard Brown Baker Collection, New York.

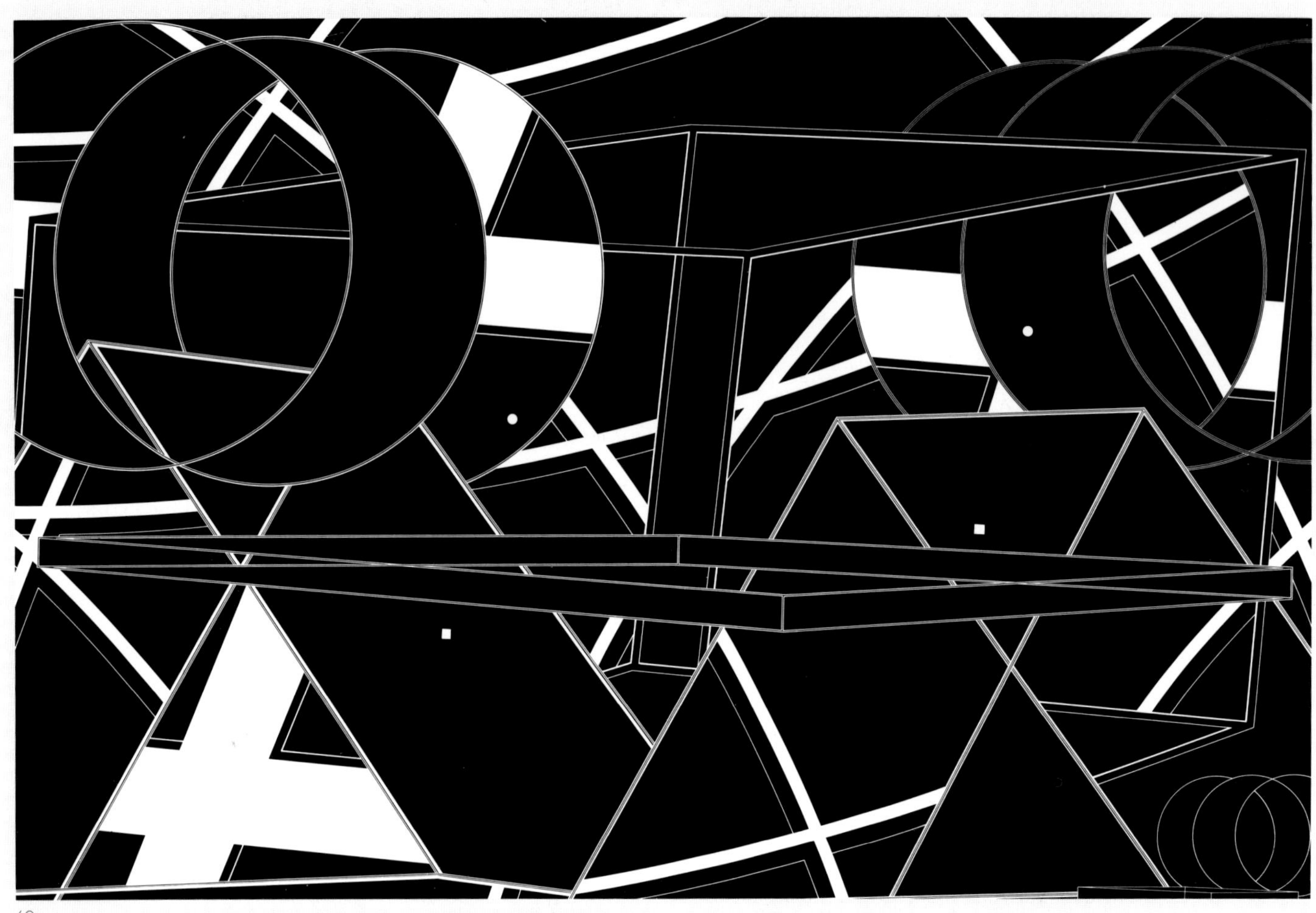

69

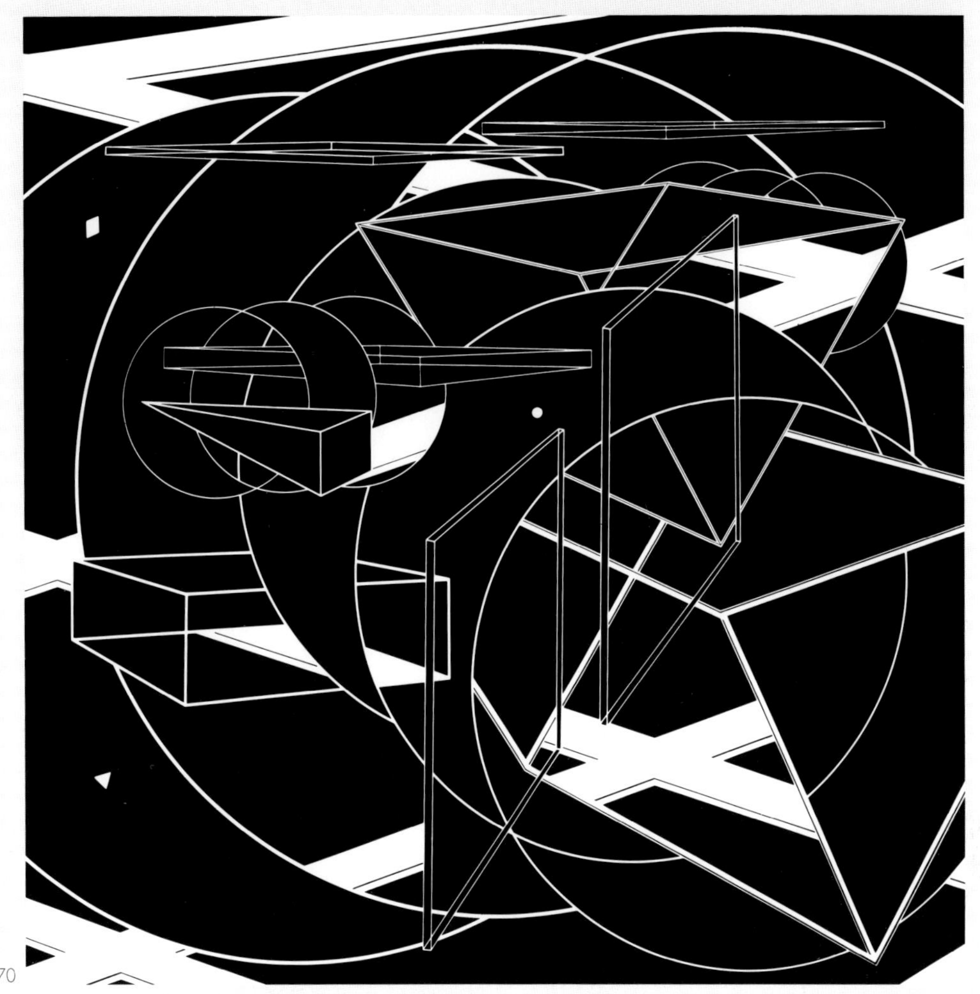

70

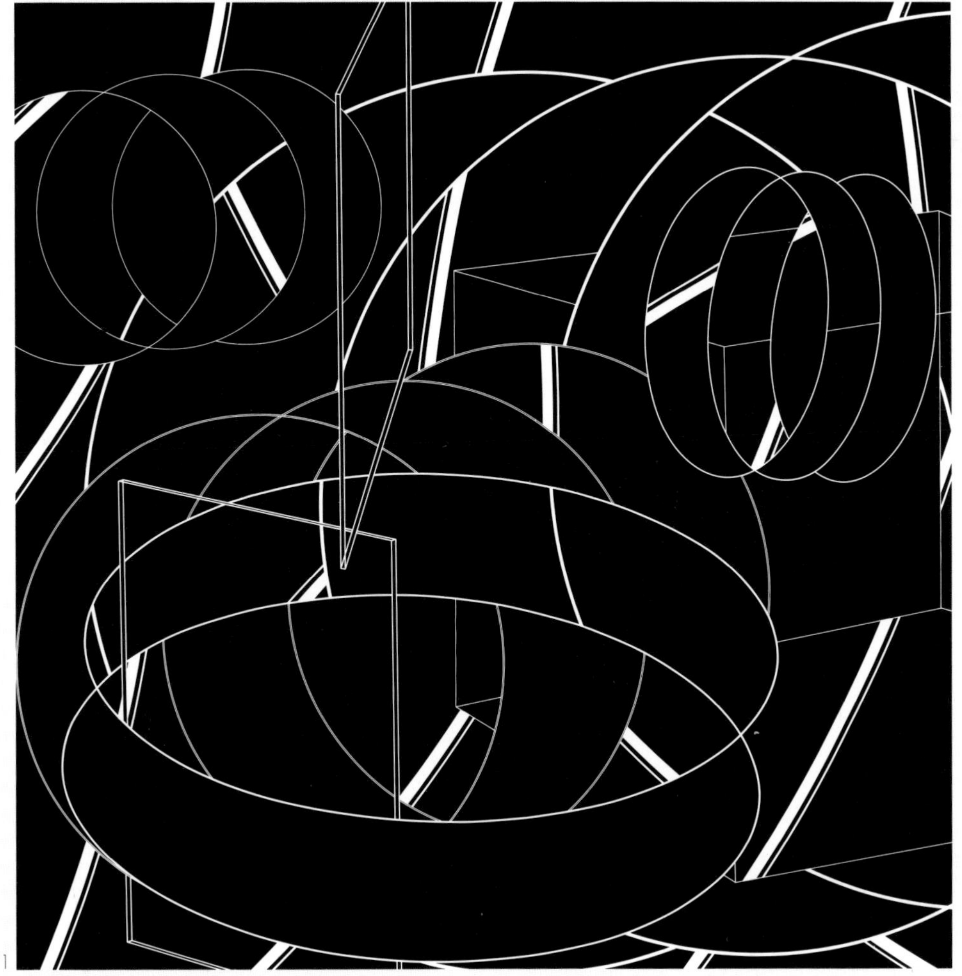

71

72 and 74. **Order/Disorder/Ascension/Descension** (murals), 1976.
Acrylic on canvas, each 156×1080 in. (3.96×27.5 m).
Mid-Atlantic Program Center of the Social Security Administration, Philadelphia (Commissioned by the Art-in-Architecture Program, United States General Services Administration).

73. **Inversion IV,** 1977.
Acrylic on canvas, 96×144 in. (243.8×365.8 cm).
Collection, The Museum of Modern Art, New York (Mr. and Mrs. David Kluger Fund and promised gift of the artist).

72

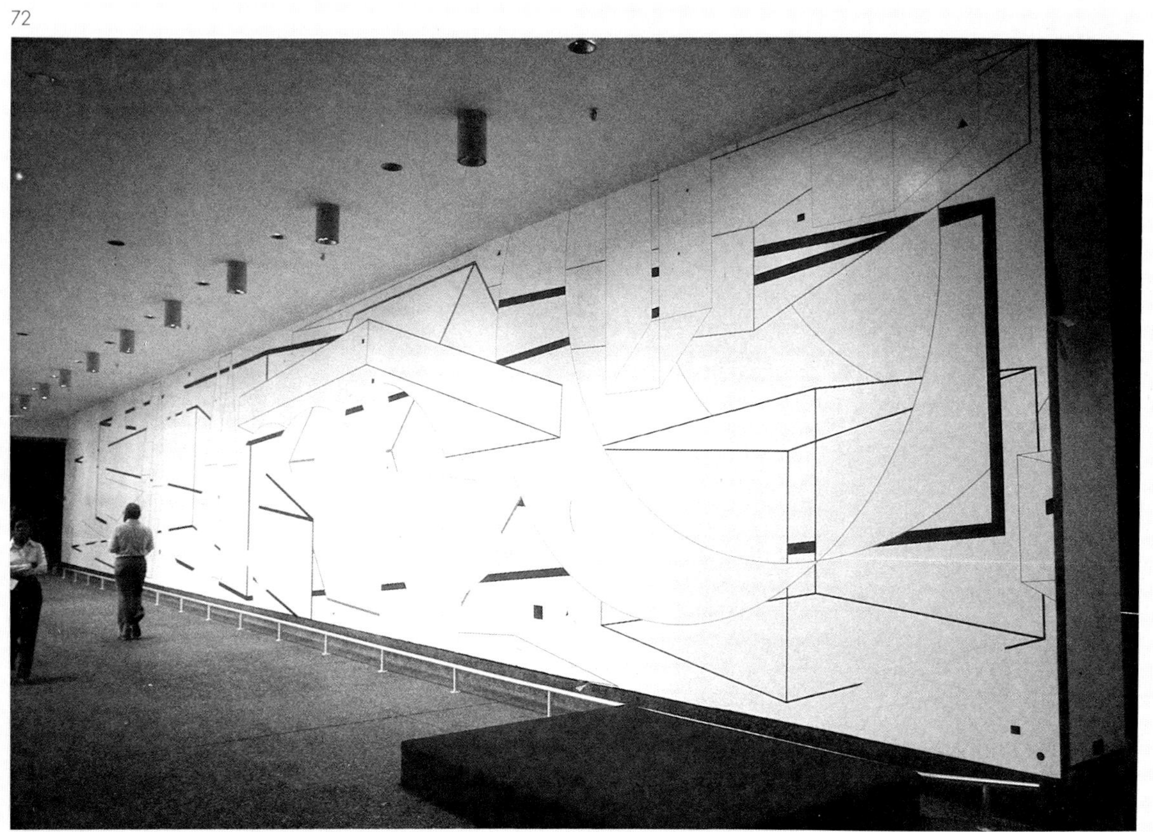

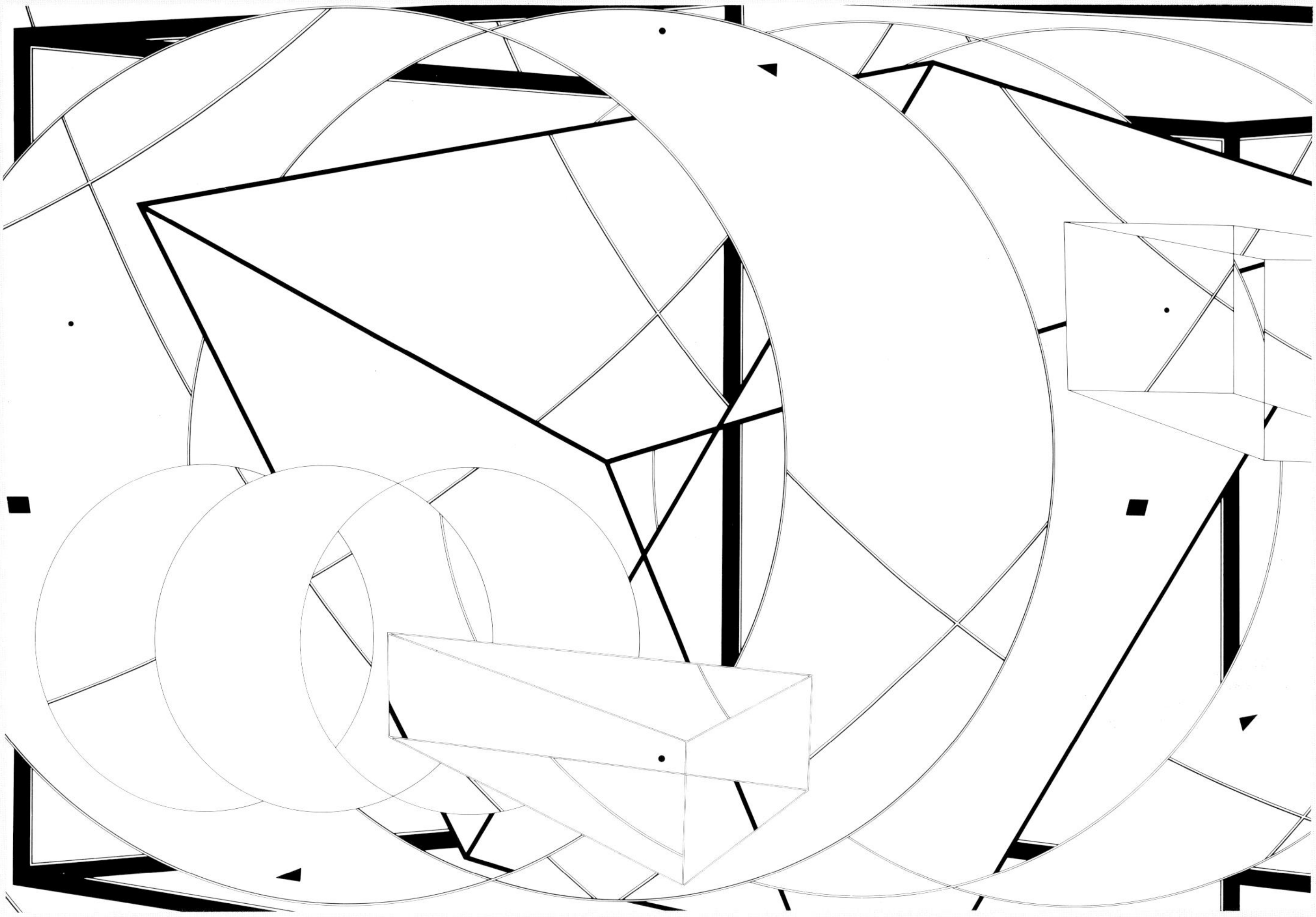

73

74

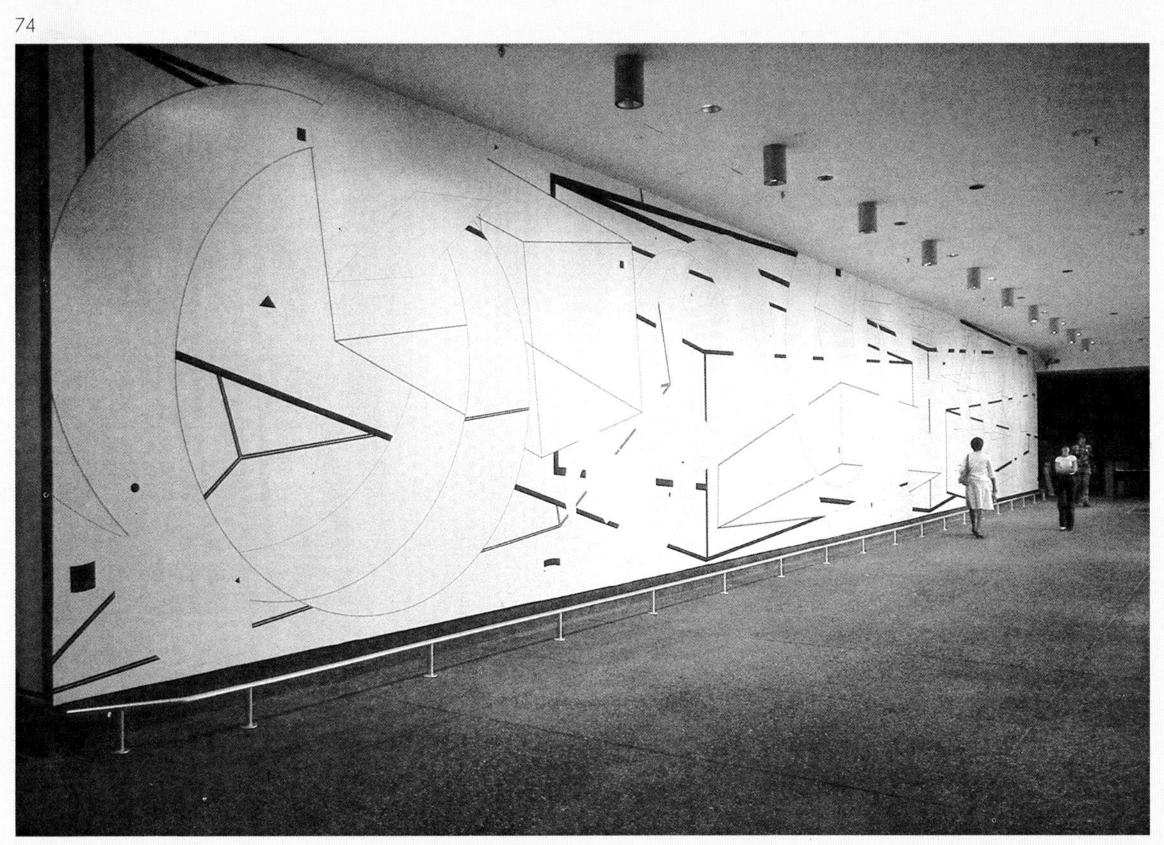

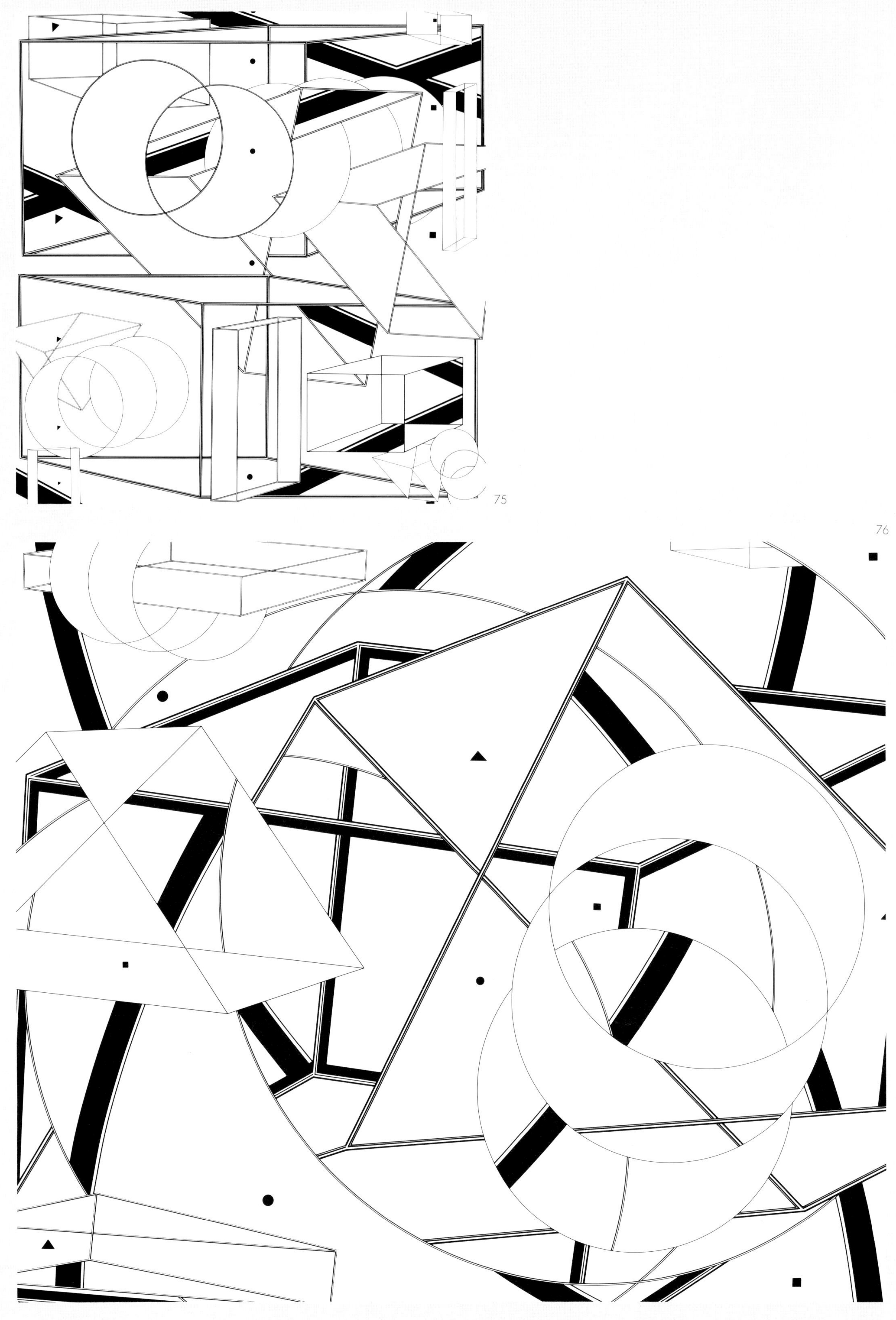

75

76

75. **Inversion VII,** 1977.
Acrylic on canvas, 48×48 in. (122×122 cm).
Collection of Tomoyuki Fugisawa, Tokyo.

76. **Inversion VIII,** 1977.
Acrylic on canvas, 60×72 in. (152.5×183 cm).
Mr. and Mrs. Paul W. Hoffmann, Naperville, Illinois.

77. **Inversion X,** 1977.
Acrylic on canvas, 72×96 in. (183×343.8 cm).
Collection of Mr. and Mrs. Harry W. Anderson, Atherton, California.

77

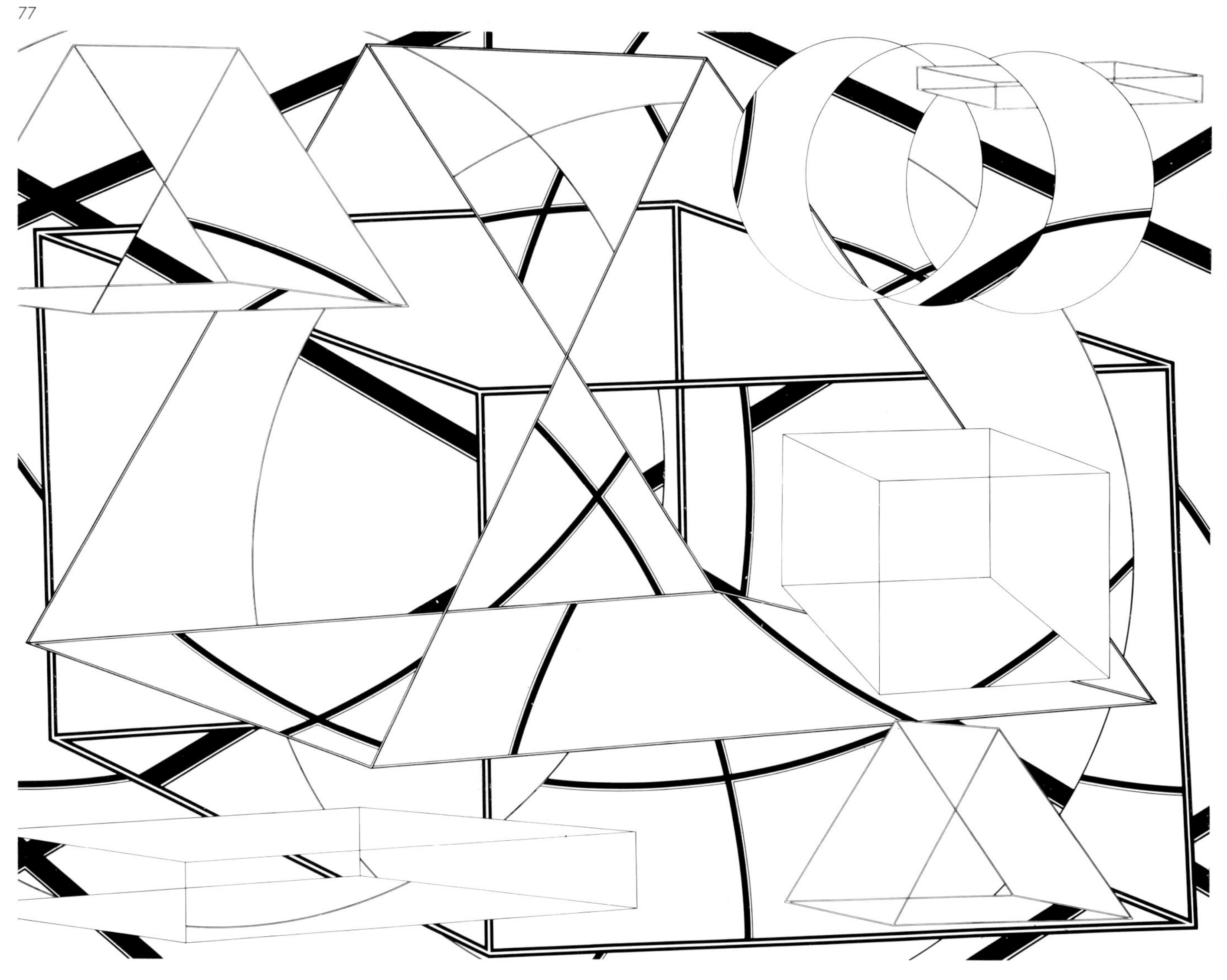

78. **Inversion XI,** 1977.
Acrylic on canvas, 72×96 in. (183×343.8 cm).
Collection of Sydney and Frances Lewis Foundation, Richmond, Virginia.

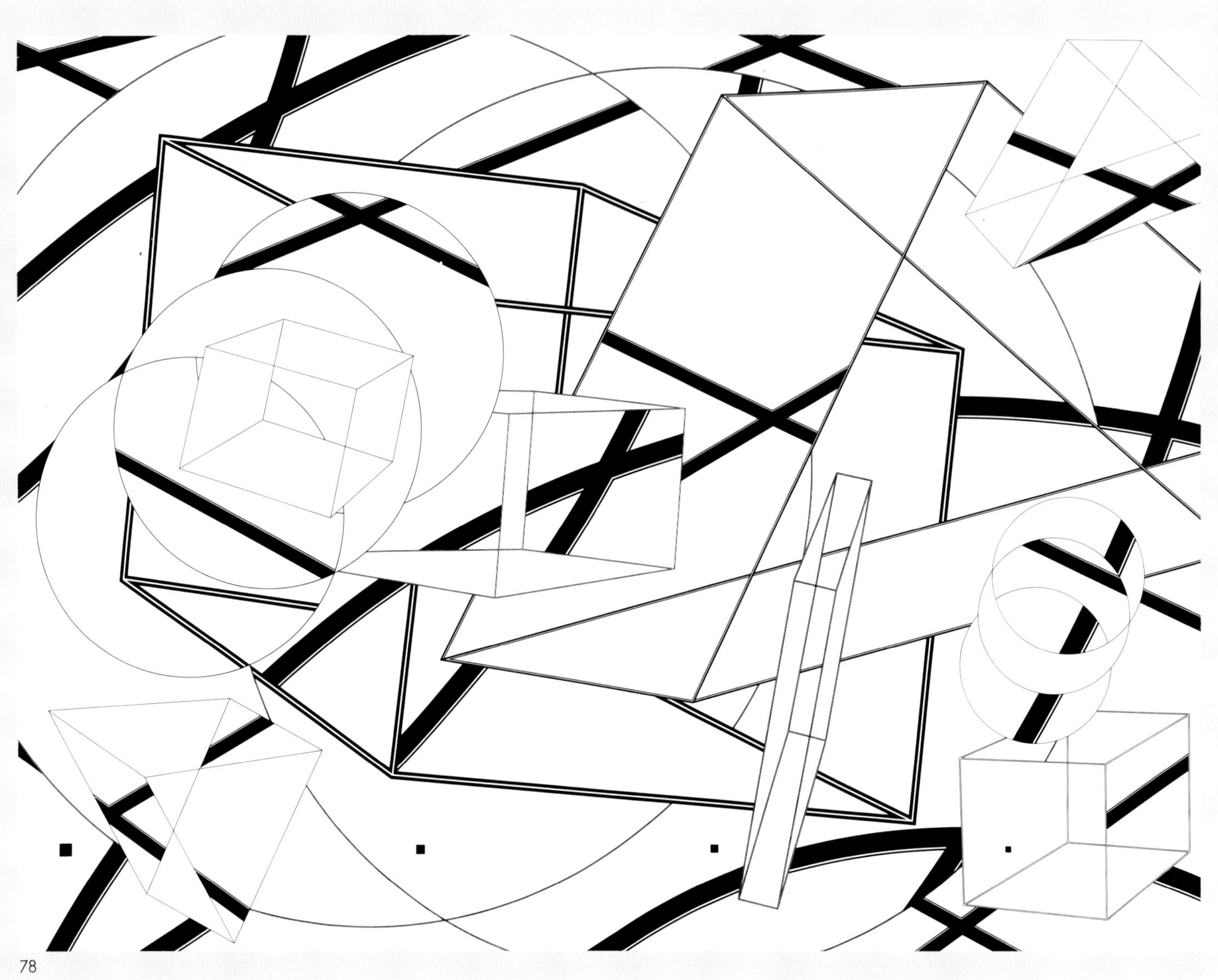

79. **Inversion XIV,** 1978.
Acrylic on canvas, 60×60 in. (152.4×152.4 cm).
Collection of Mr. and Mrs. Edward Merrin, New York.

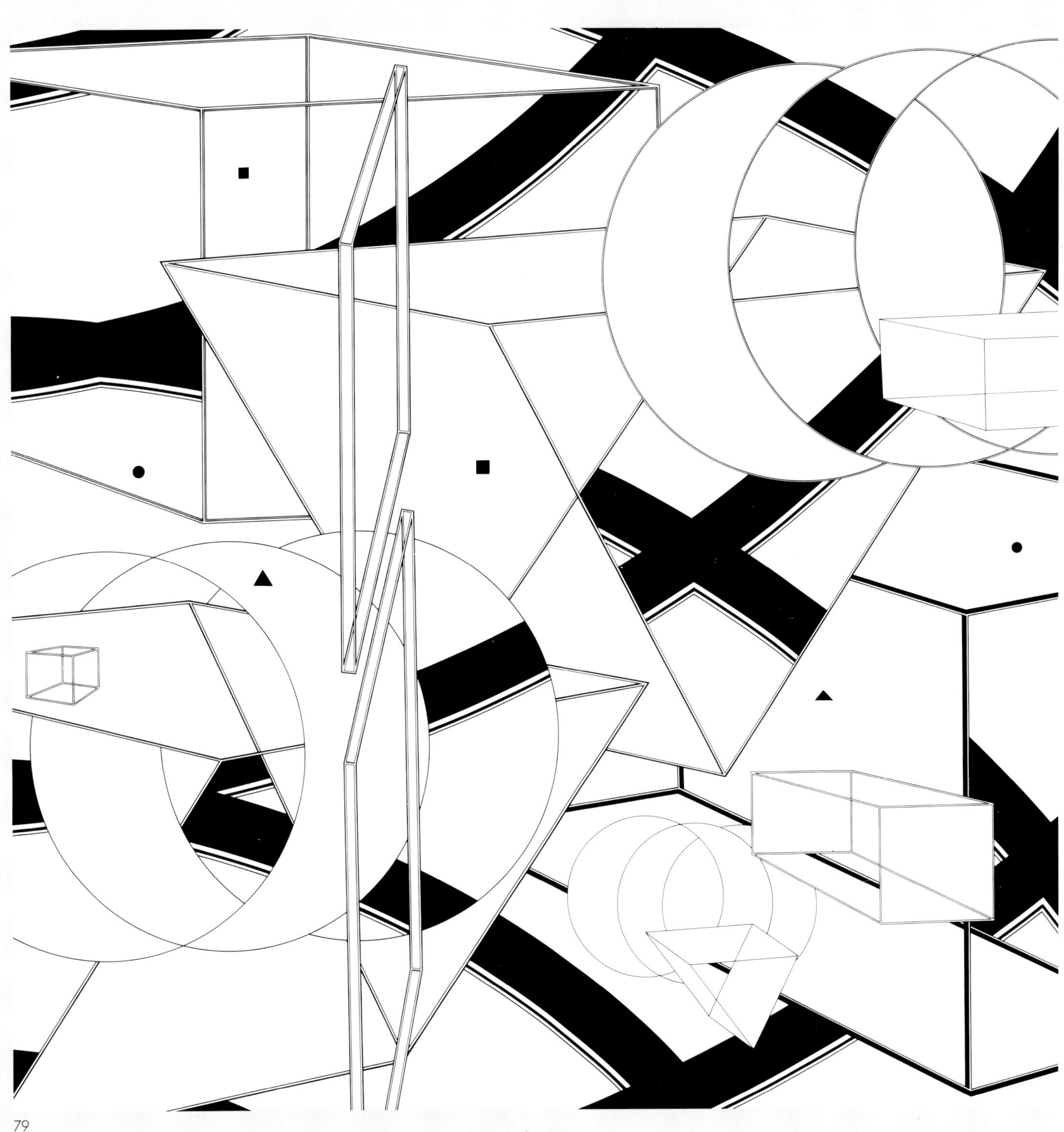

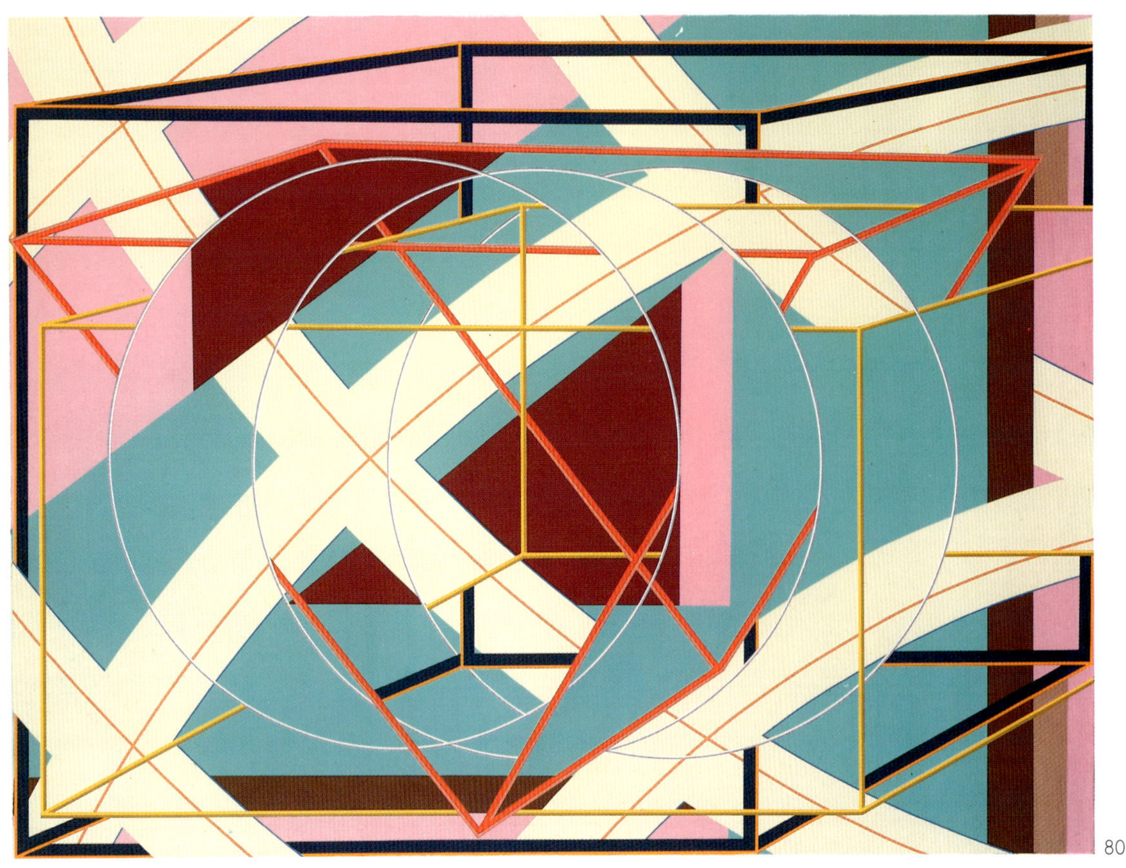

80

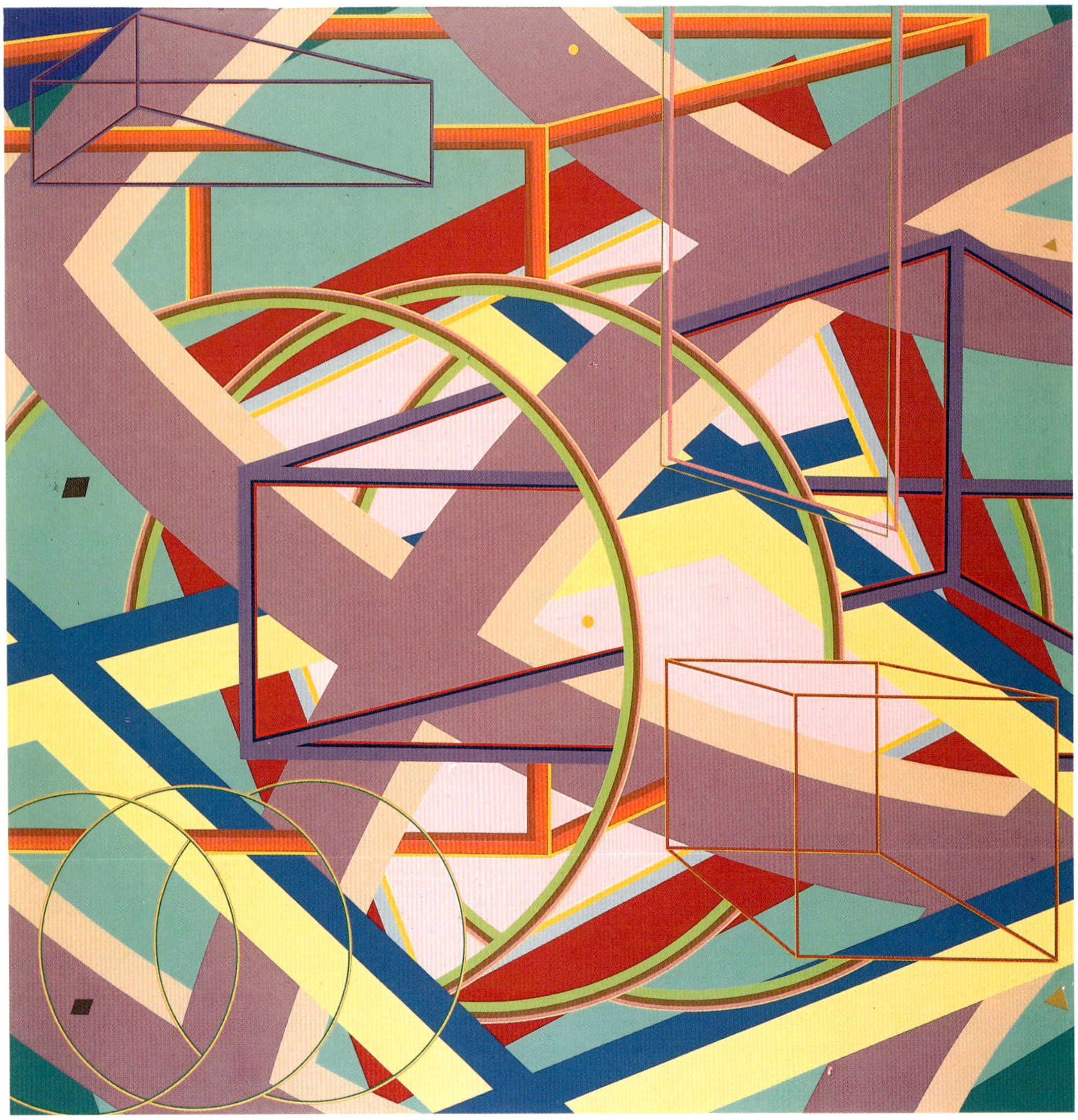

81

80. **B-G-1,** 1978.
Acrylic on canvas, 36×48 in. (91.5×122 cm).
Collection of John S. Hilson, New York.

81. **B-G-3,** 1978.
Acrylic on canvas, 84×84 in. (213.4×213.4 cm).
Collection of Sydney and Frances Lewis, Richmond, Virginia.

82. **C-B-1,** 1978.
Acrylic on canvas, 72×84 in. (183×213.4 cm).
Collection, The Museum of Modern Art, New York,
The Riklis Collection of McCrory Corporation (fractional gift).

83. **C-O-1,** 1978.
Acrylic on canvas, 72×84 in. (183×213.4 cm).
Collection of Mr. and Mrs. Seymour Malamed, New York.

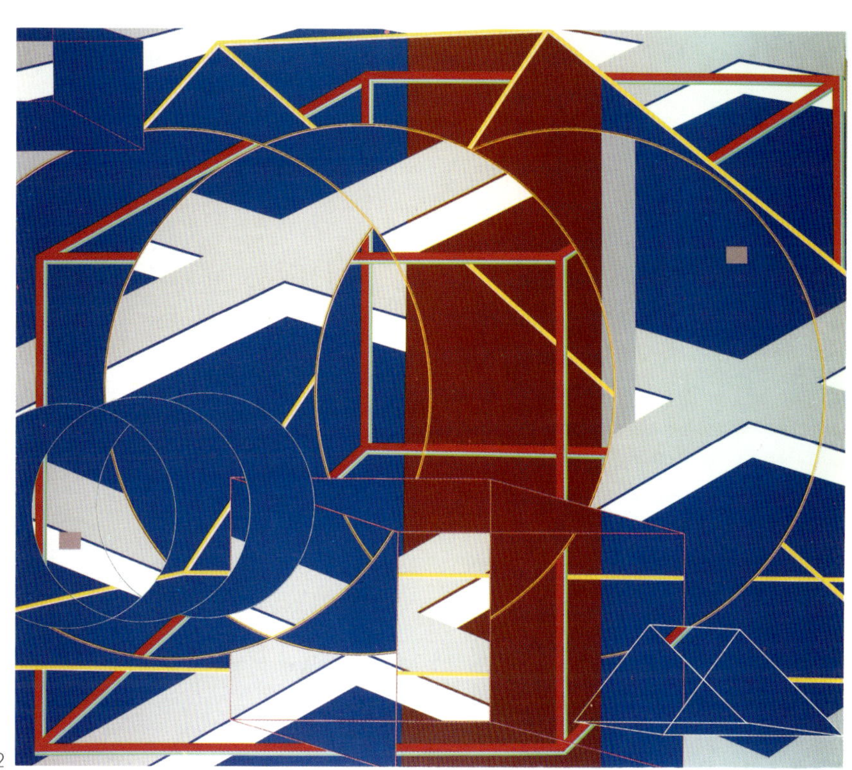

82

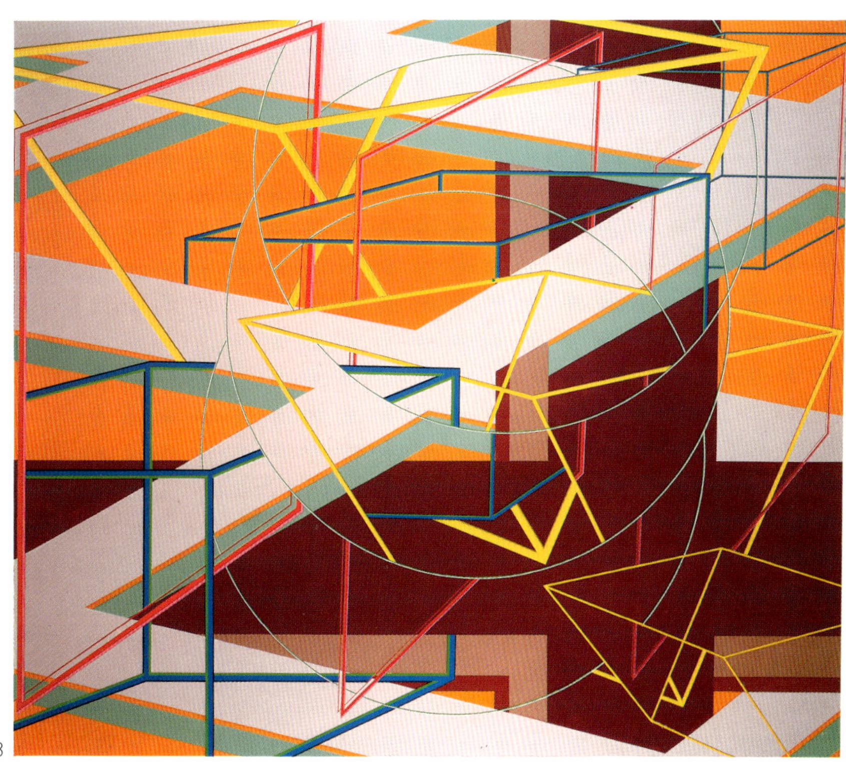

83

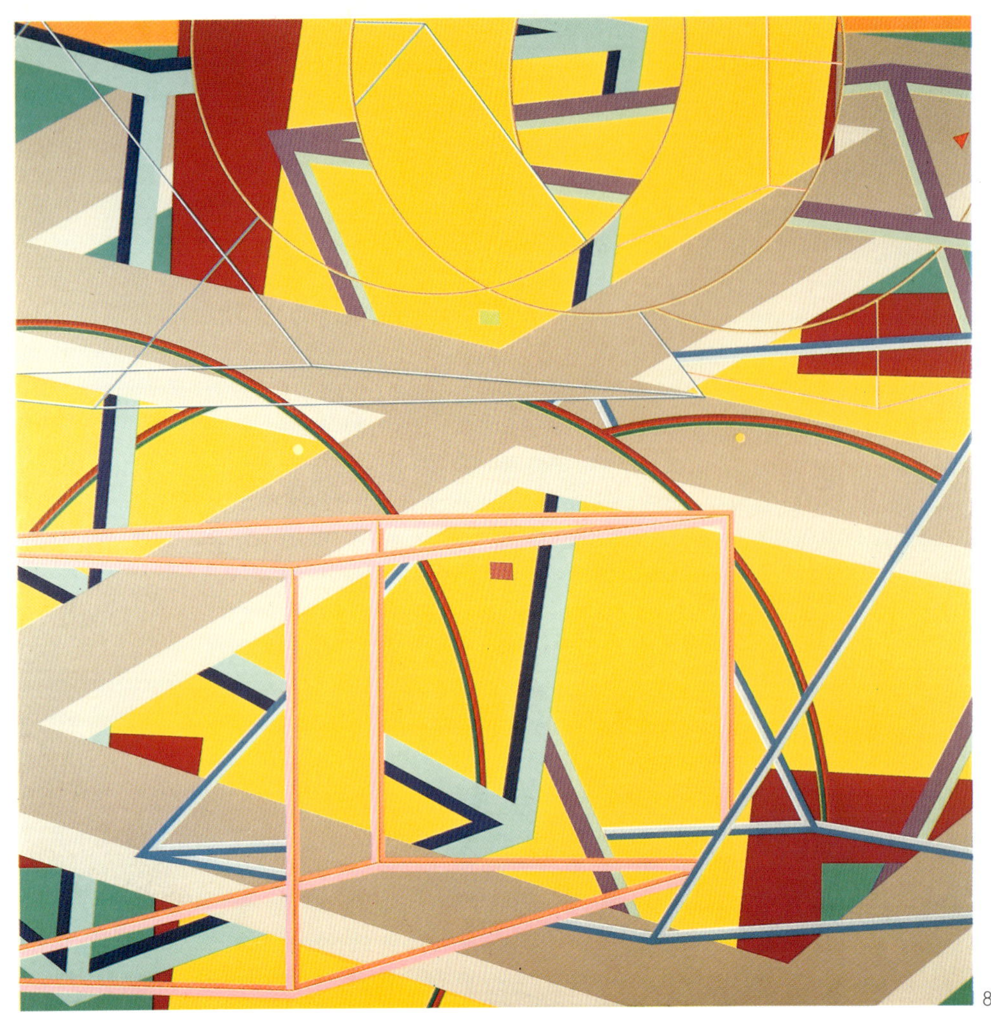
84

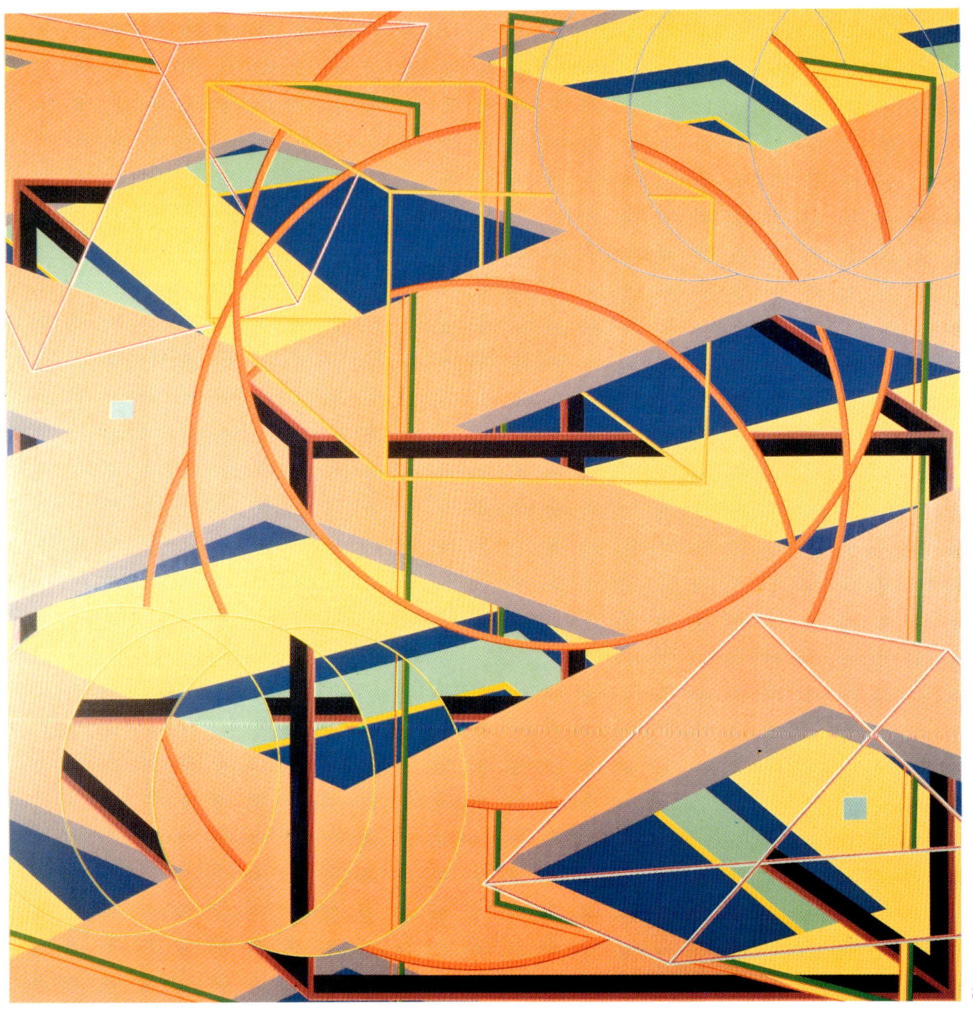
85

84. **C-Y-1,** 1978.
Acrylic on canvas,
114×114 in. (289.5×289.5 cm).
Albright-Knox Art Gallery, Buffalo, New York
(Gift of Seymour H. Knox).

85. **C-B-B-1,** 1978.
Acrylic on canvas,
84×84 in. (213.4×213.4 cm).
Collection of Mr. and Mrs. Bagley Wright,
Seattle.

86. **B-C,** 1979.
Acrylic on canvas,
84×84 in. (213.4×213.4 cm).
Private collection.

87. **C-G-1,** 1978.
Acrylic on canvas,
60×60 in. (152.4×152.4 cm).
Collection of Briga Lapiner, Perth, Australia.

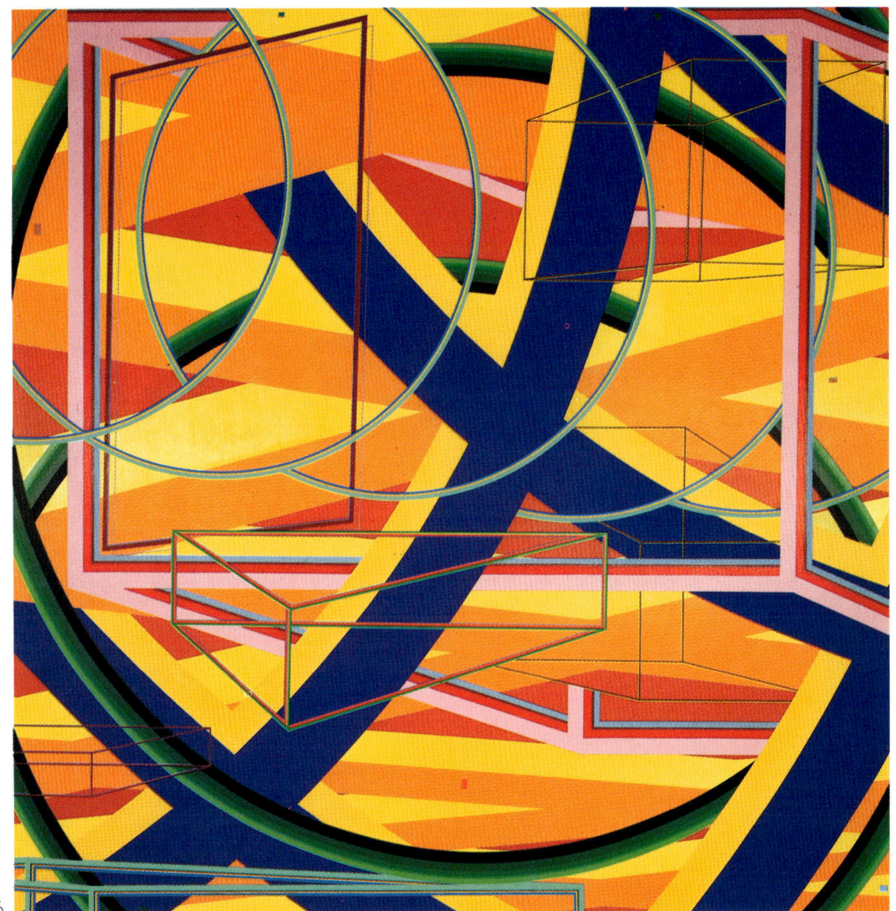

86

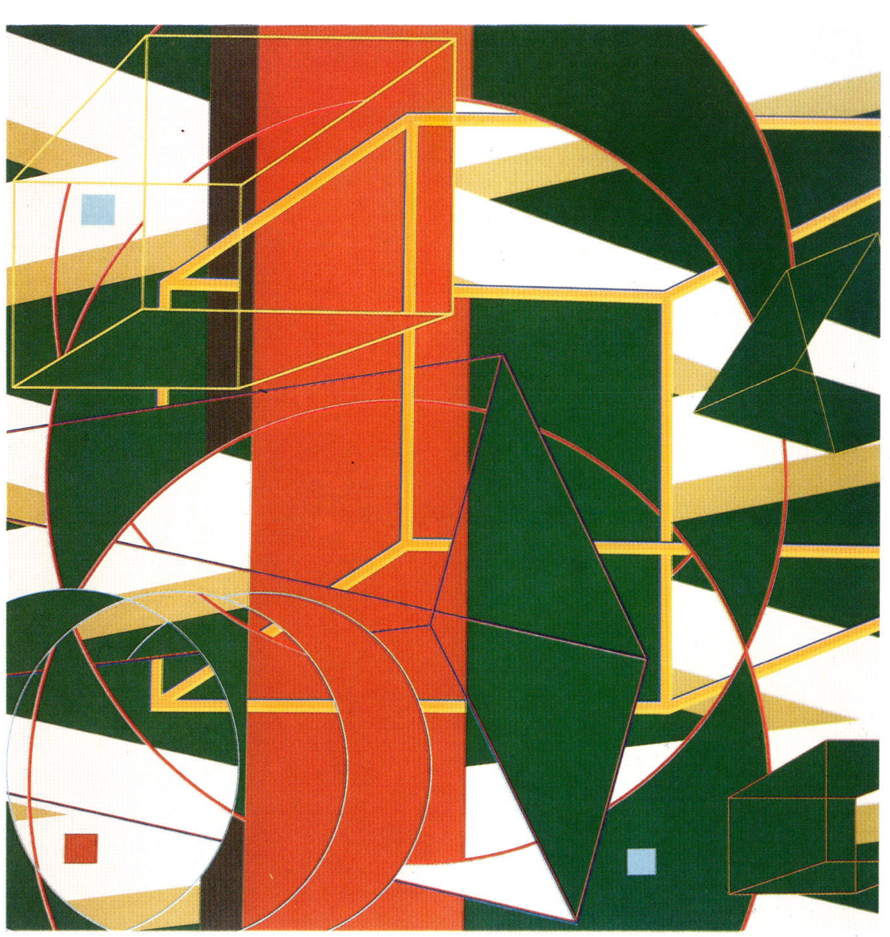

87

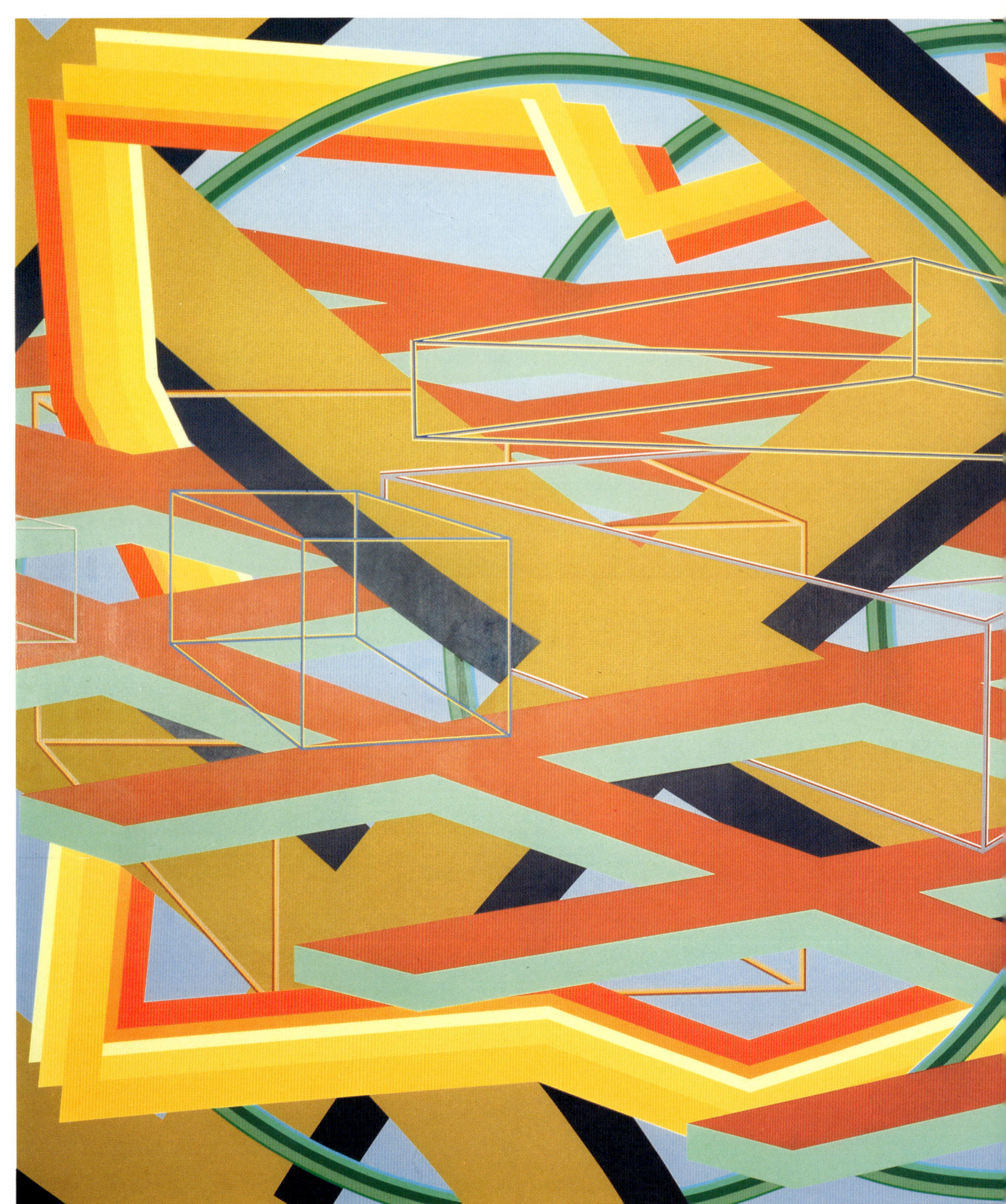

88. **D-C,** 1979.
Acrylic on canvas, 96×168 in. (243.8×426.7 cm).
Dallas Museum of Fine Arts (Matching grants from the National Endowment for the Arts, the 500, Inc., and the General Acquisitions Fund).

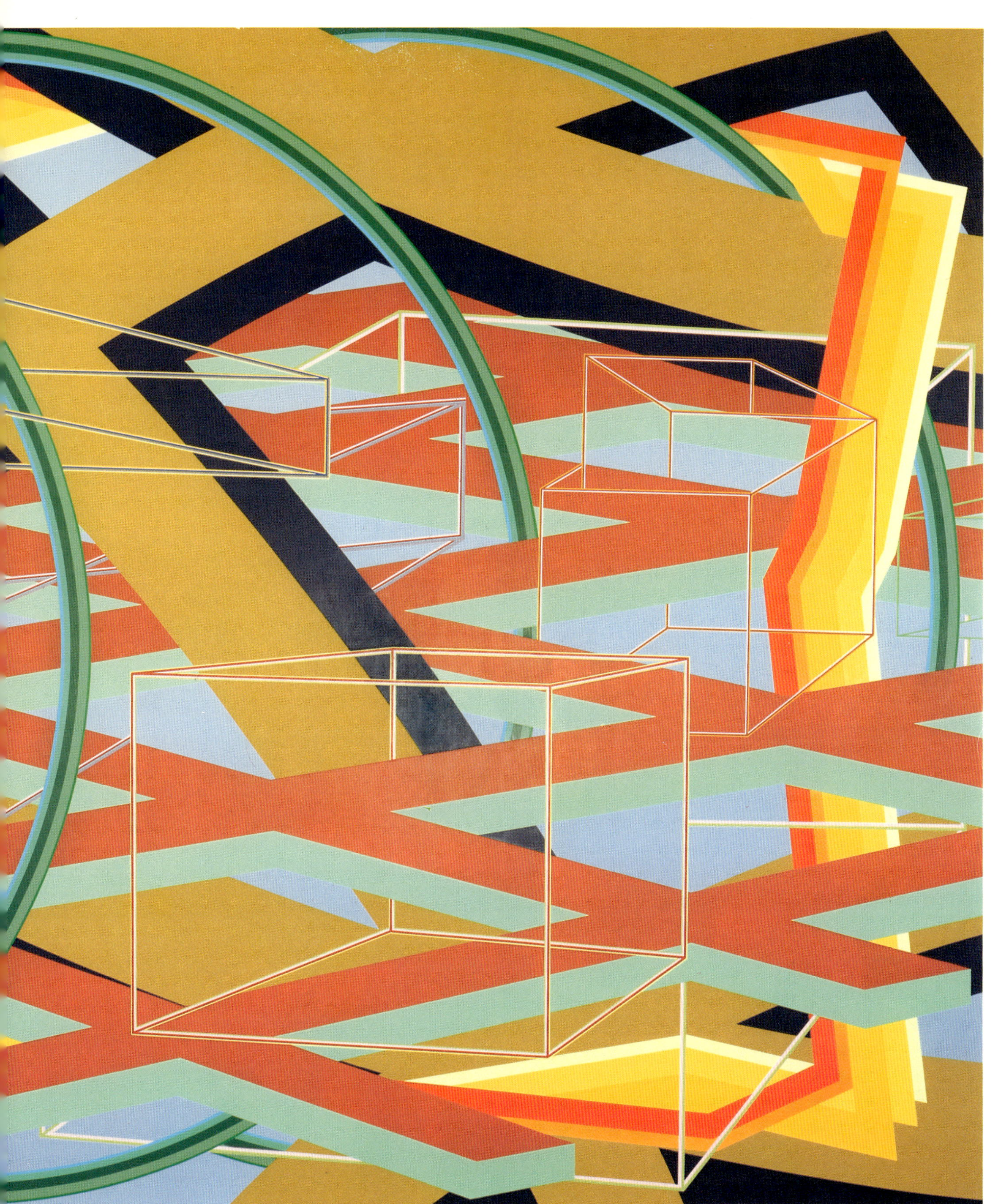

89. **P-R-J,** 1979.
Acrylic on canvas, 114×114 in. (289.5×289.5 cm).
Collection of Mr. and Mrs. Barry A. Berkus, Santa Barbara, California.

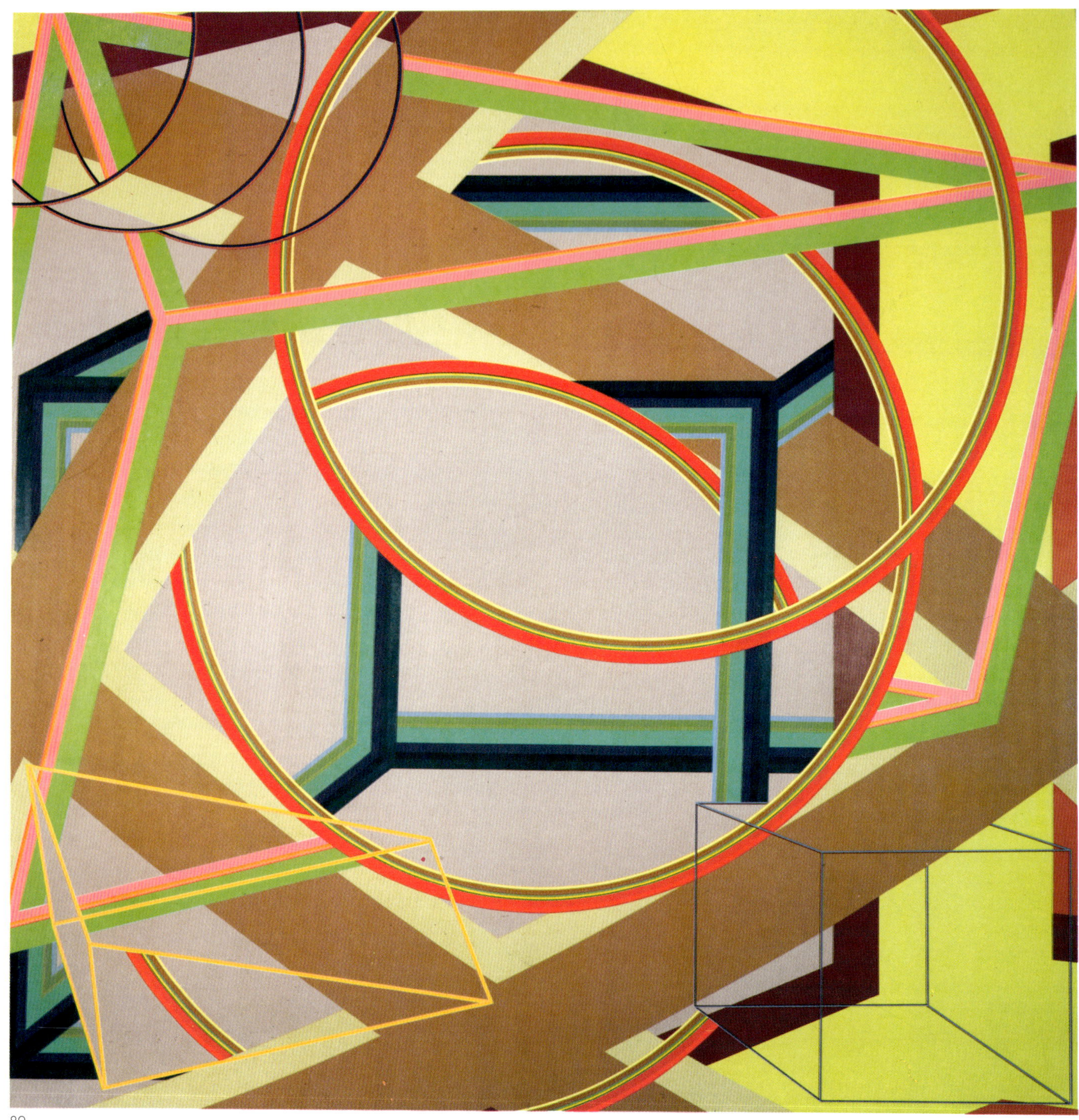

89

90. **Flow I,** 1980.
Acrylic on canvas, 82×120 in. (208.2×304.8 cm).
Private collection.

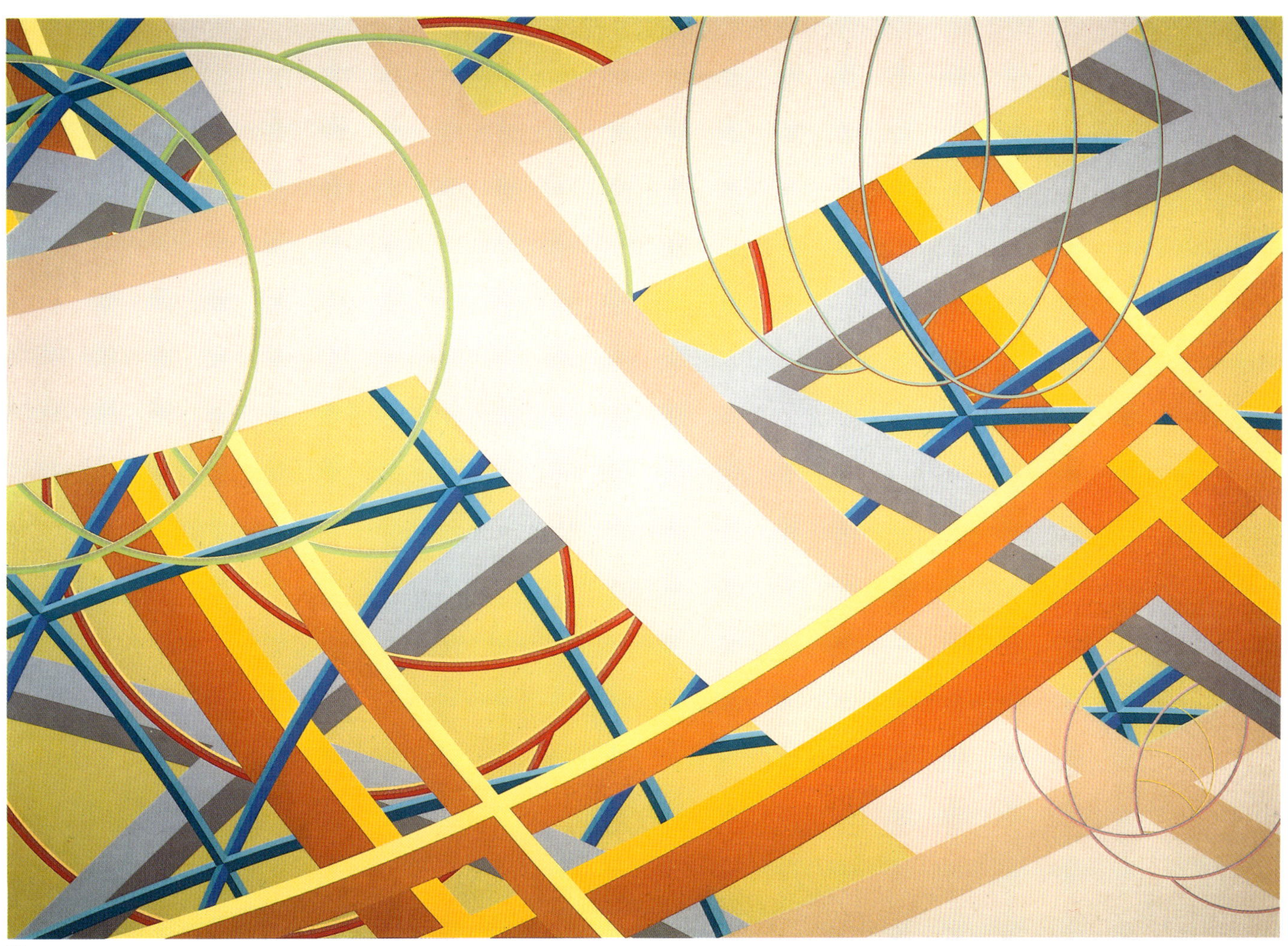

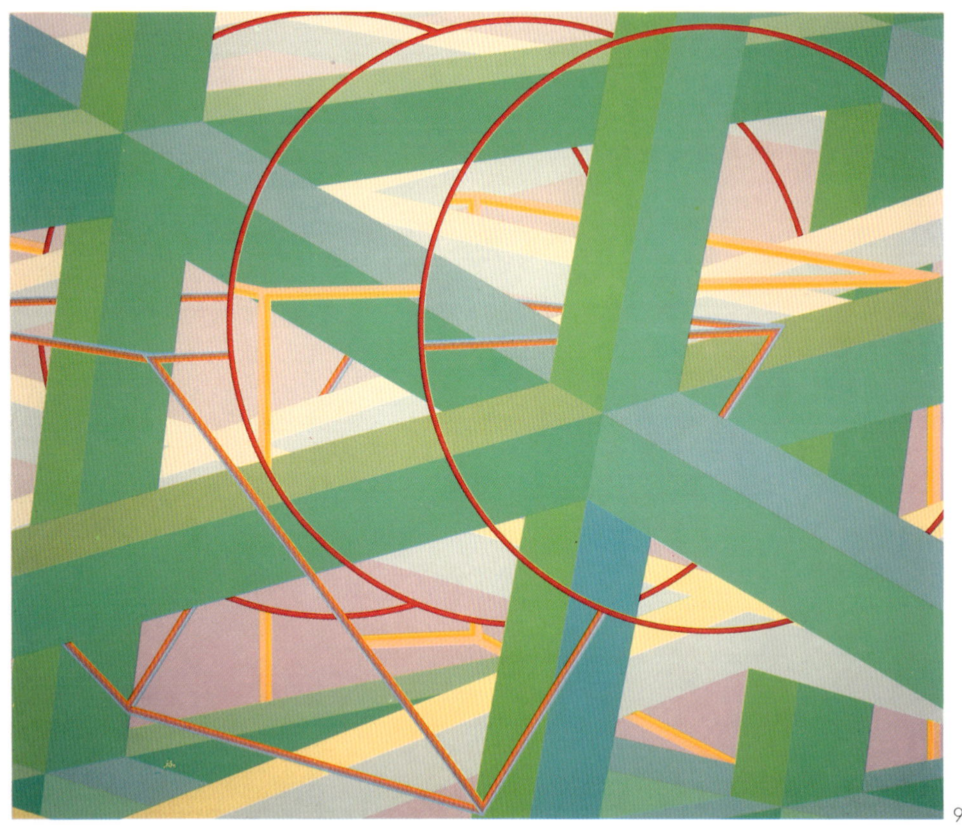

91

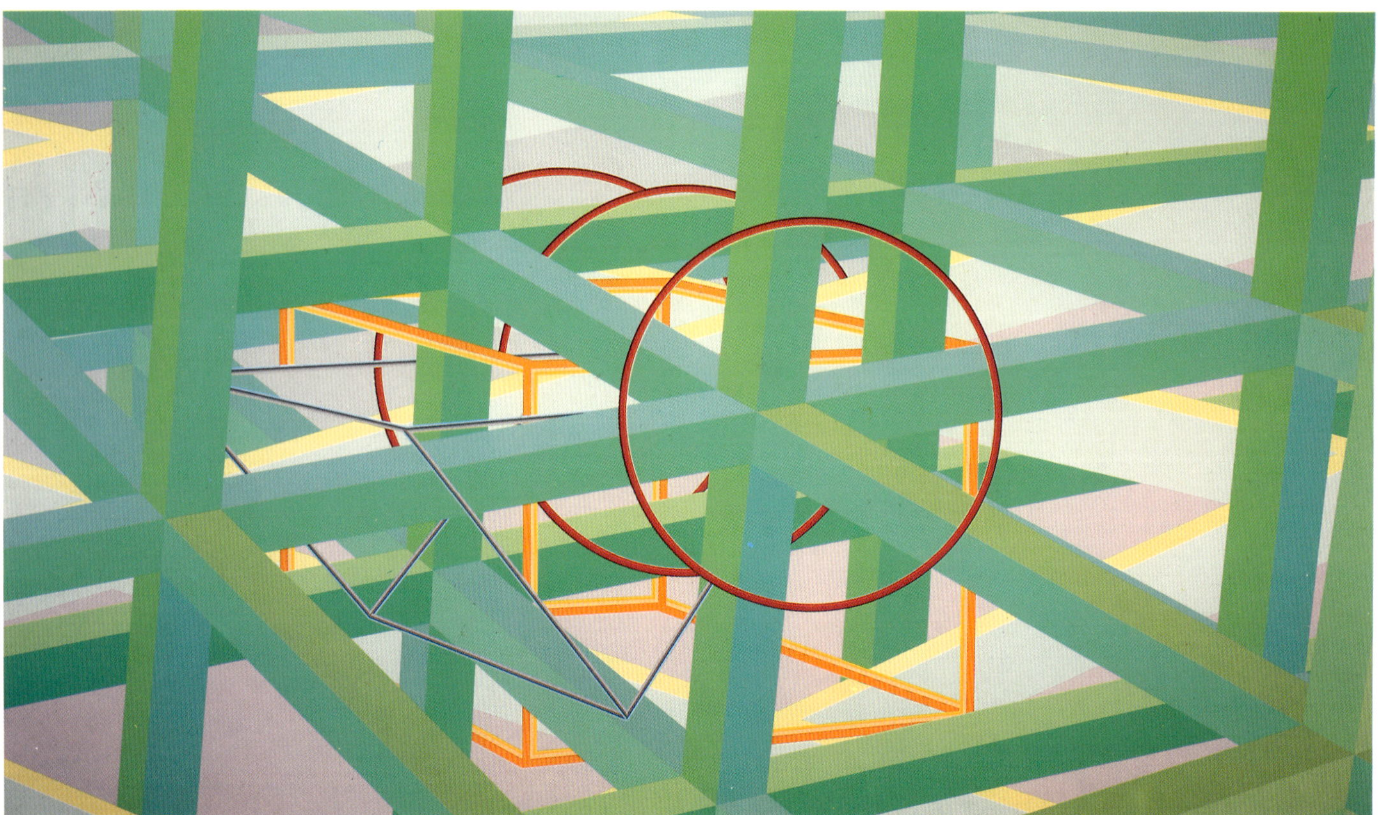

92

91. **Venetian II,** 1980.
Acrylic on canvas, 96×168 in. (243.8×426.7 cm).
Collection of Mr. and Mrs. Richard Hedreen, Bellevue, Washington.

92. **Venetian I,** 1980.
Acrylic on canvas, 60×72 in. (152.4×183 cm).
Collection of Mr. and Mrs. Robert Lazarus, Jr., Columbus, Ohio.

93. **Bruges I,** 1980.
Acrylic on canvas, 60×60 in. (152.4×152.4 cm).
Collection of Ophelia and William Rudin, New York.

94. **Bruges II,** 1981.
Acrylic on canvas, 84×84 in. (213.4×213.4 cm).
The Santa Barbara Museum of Art, California
(Gift of Carol L. Valentine).

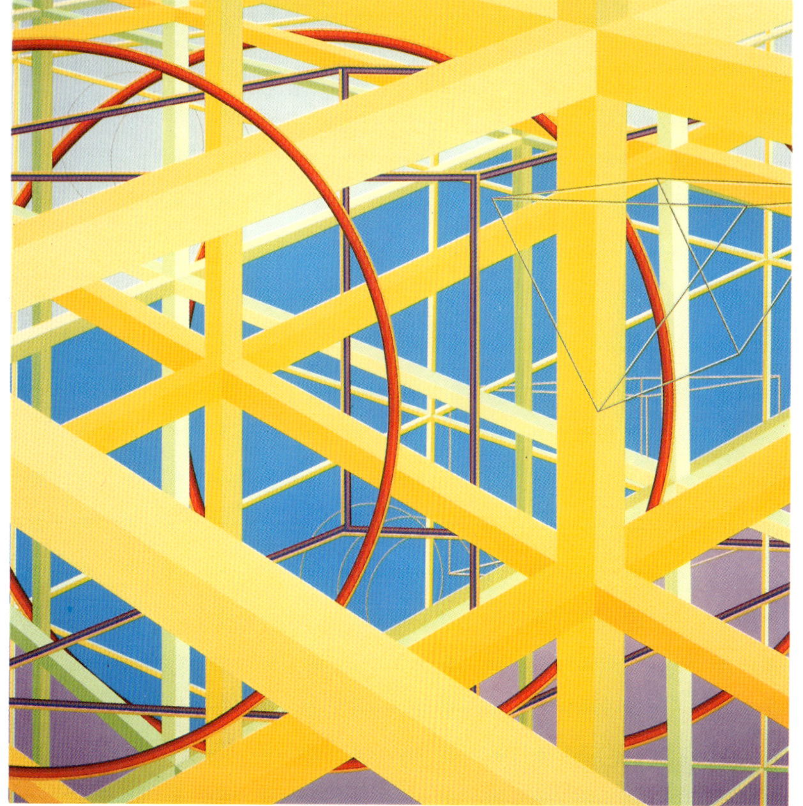

93

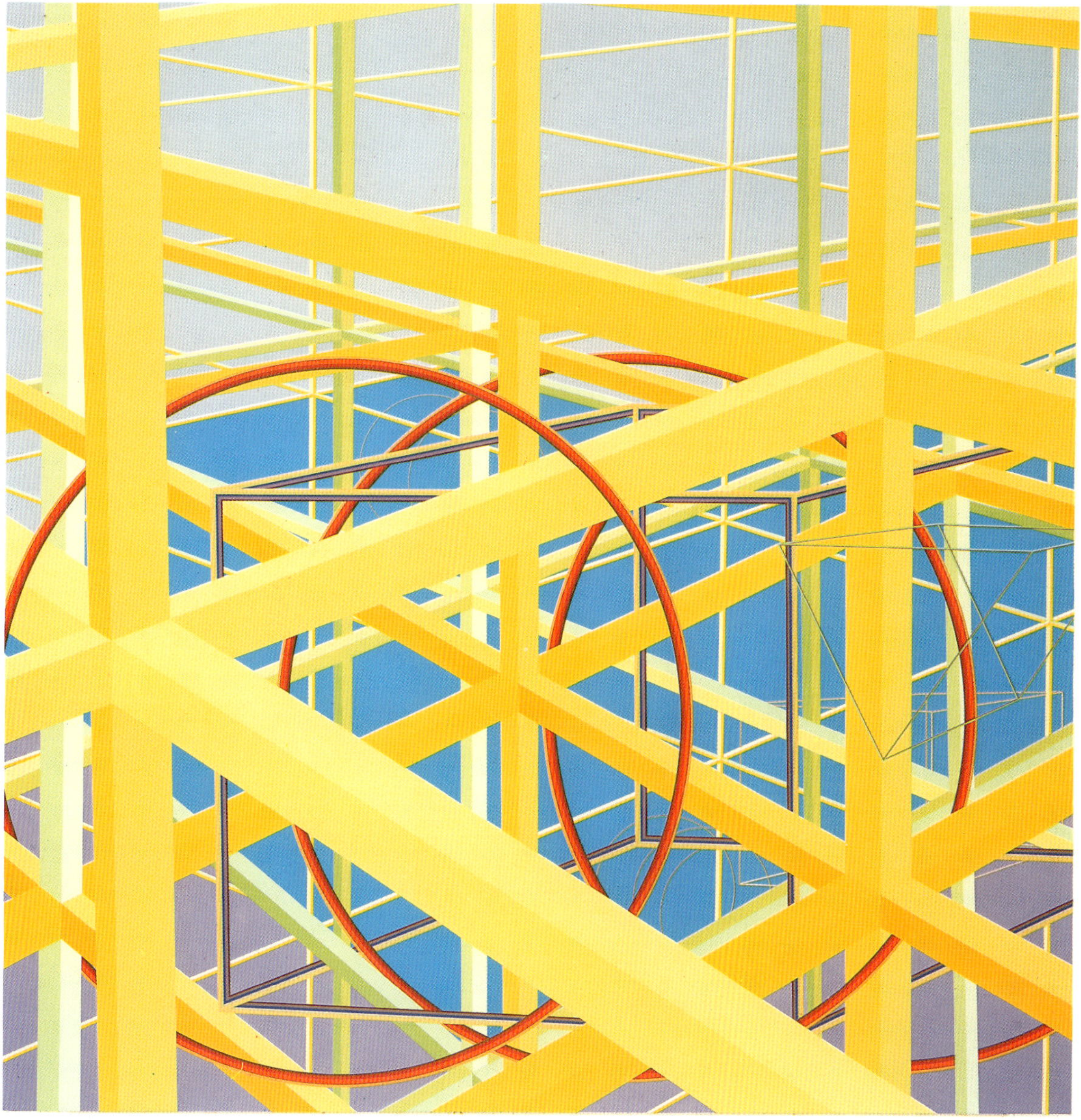

94

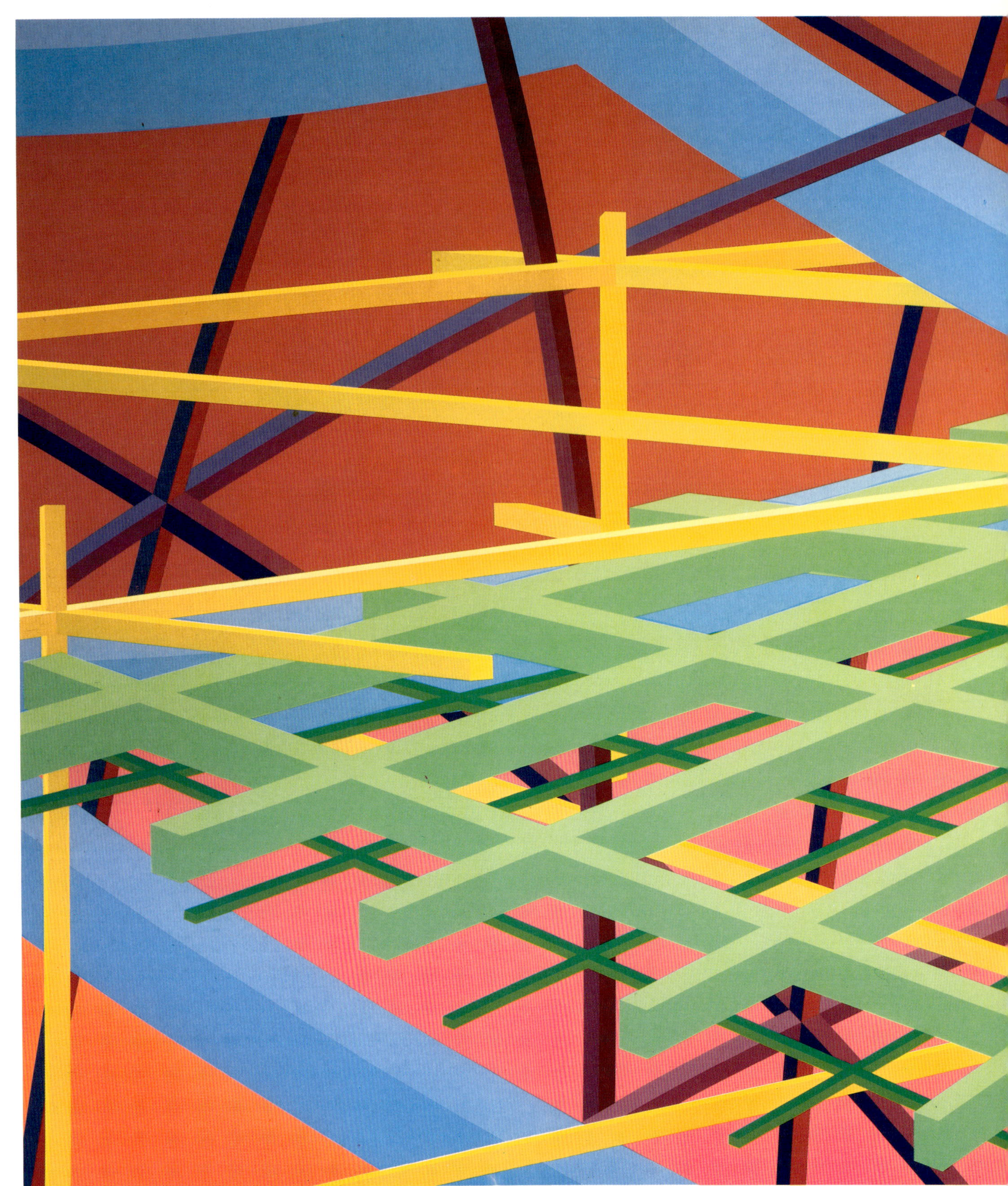

95

95. **M's Passage,** 1980.
Acrylic on canvas, 114×192 in. (289.5×487.7 cm).
Collection of Mara Held, New York.

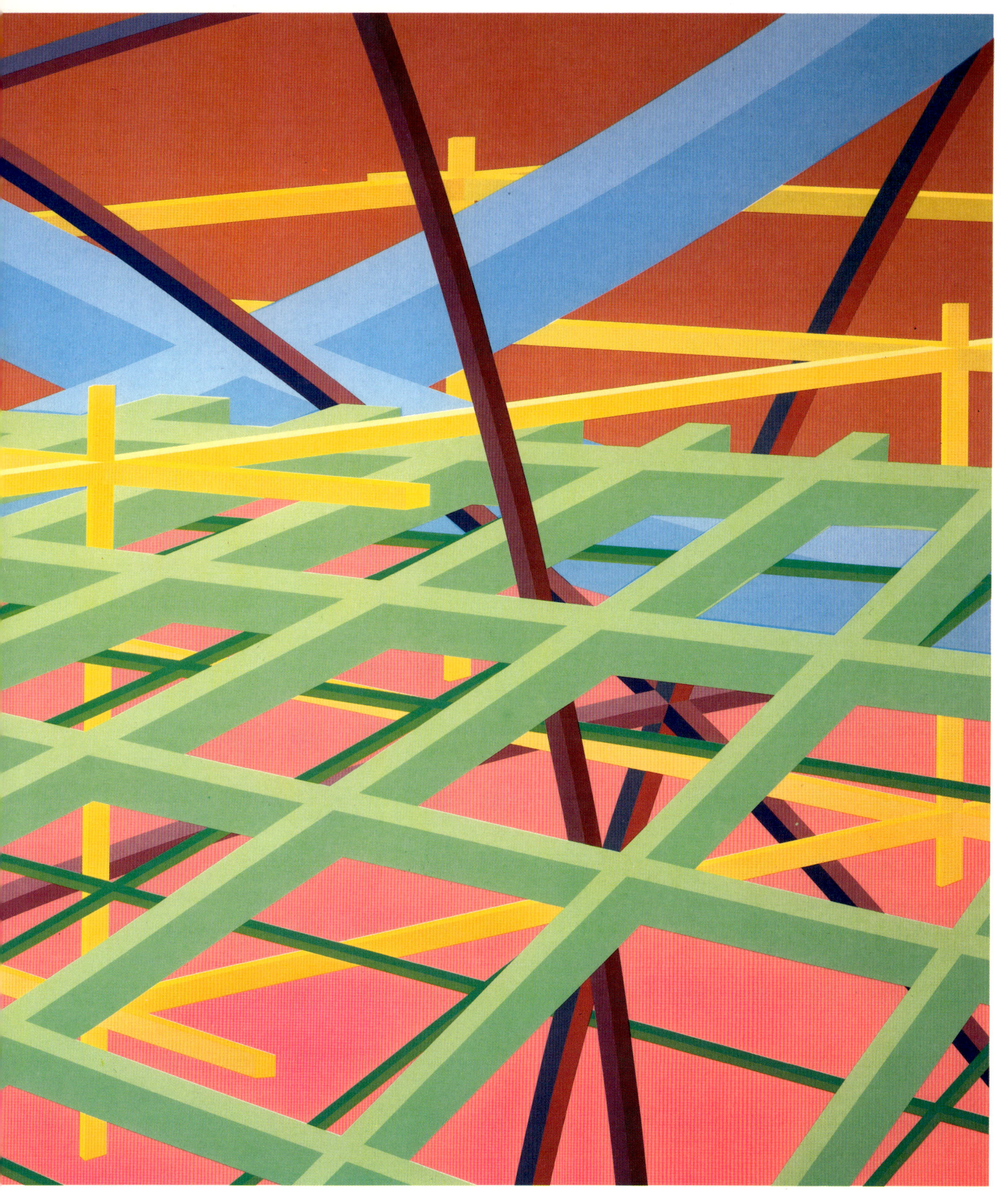

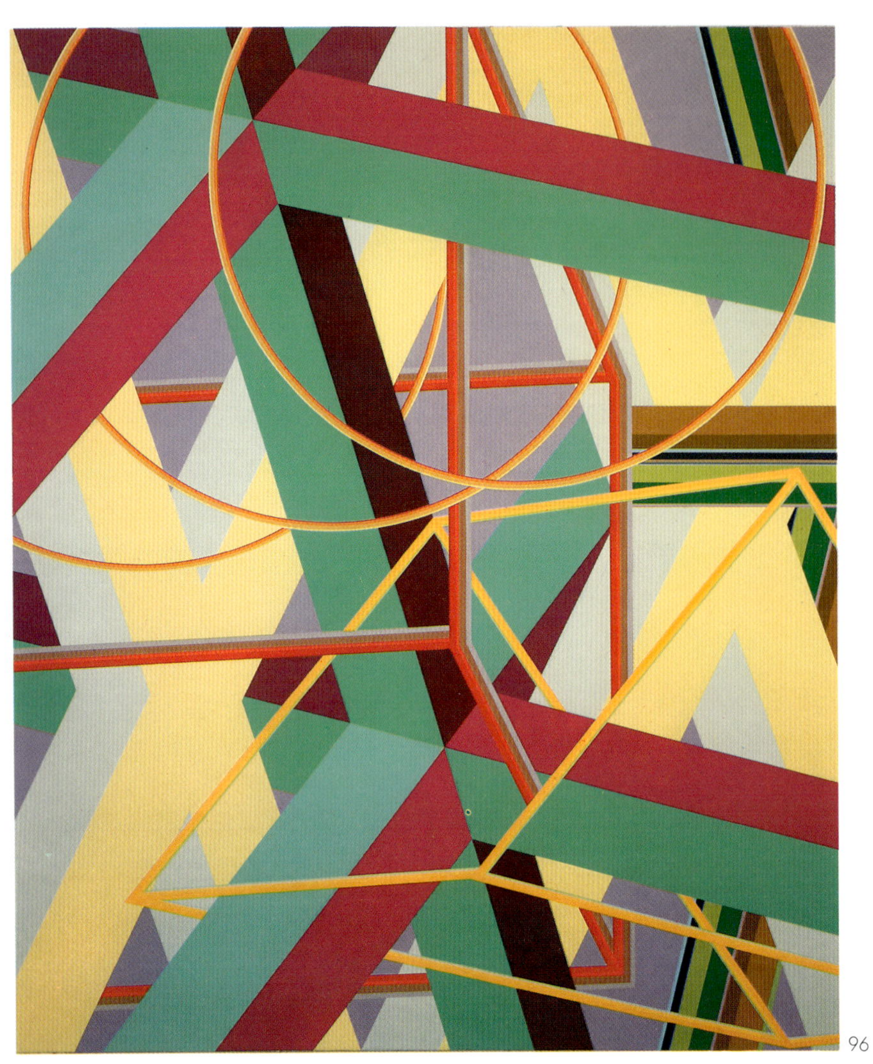

96

97

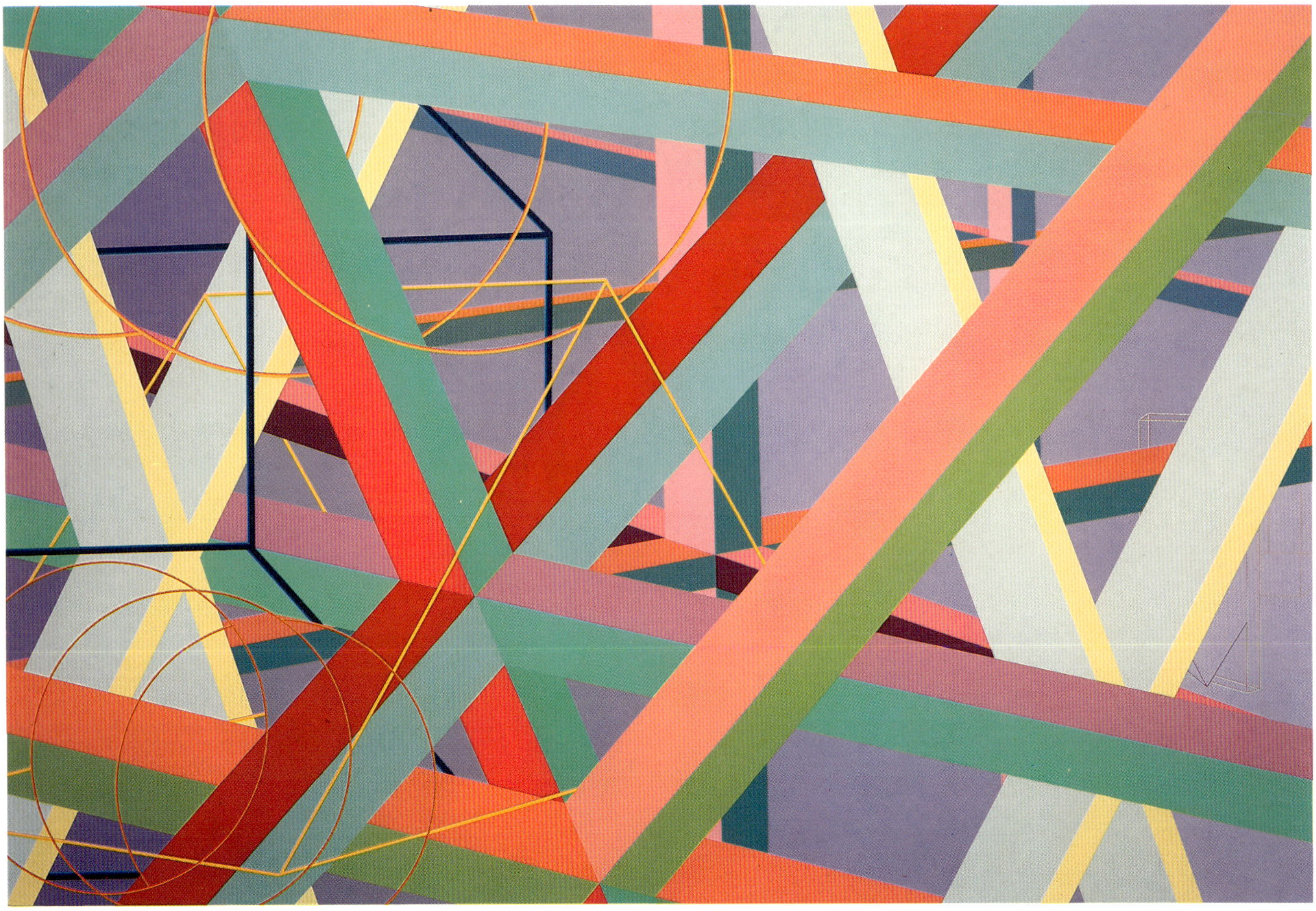

96. **Florentine I,** 1980.
Acrylic on canvas, 72×60 in. (183×152.4 cm).
The Brett Mitchell Collection, Inc., Cleveland.

97. **Florentine IV,** 1980.
Acrylic on canvas, 72×108 in. (183×274.3 cm).
Collection of Wayne Anderson, Paris.

98. **Florentine V,** 1980.
Acrylic on canvas, 72×108 in. (183×274.3 cm).
Collection of Fried, Frank, Harris, Shriver & Jacobson, New York.

98

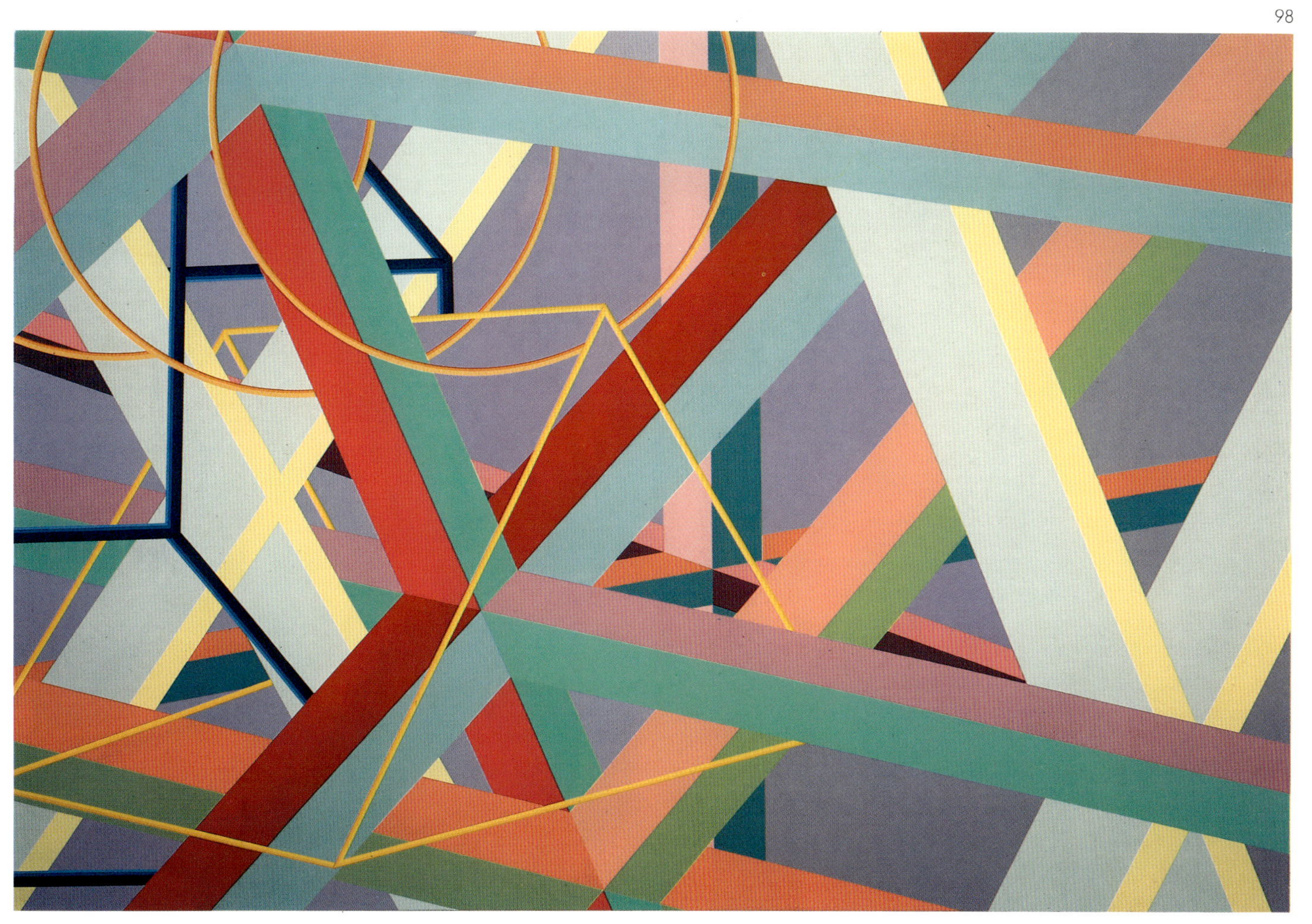

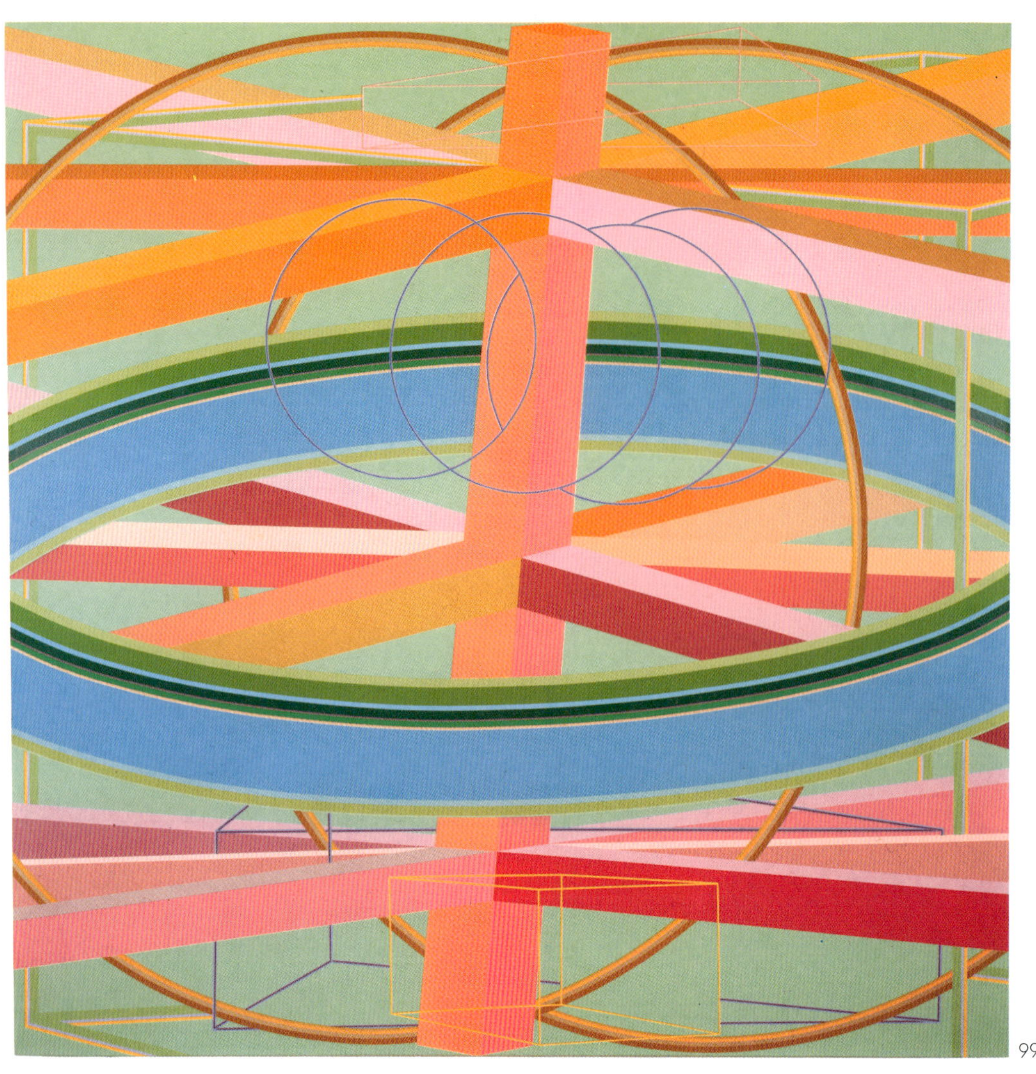

99

100

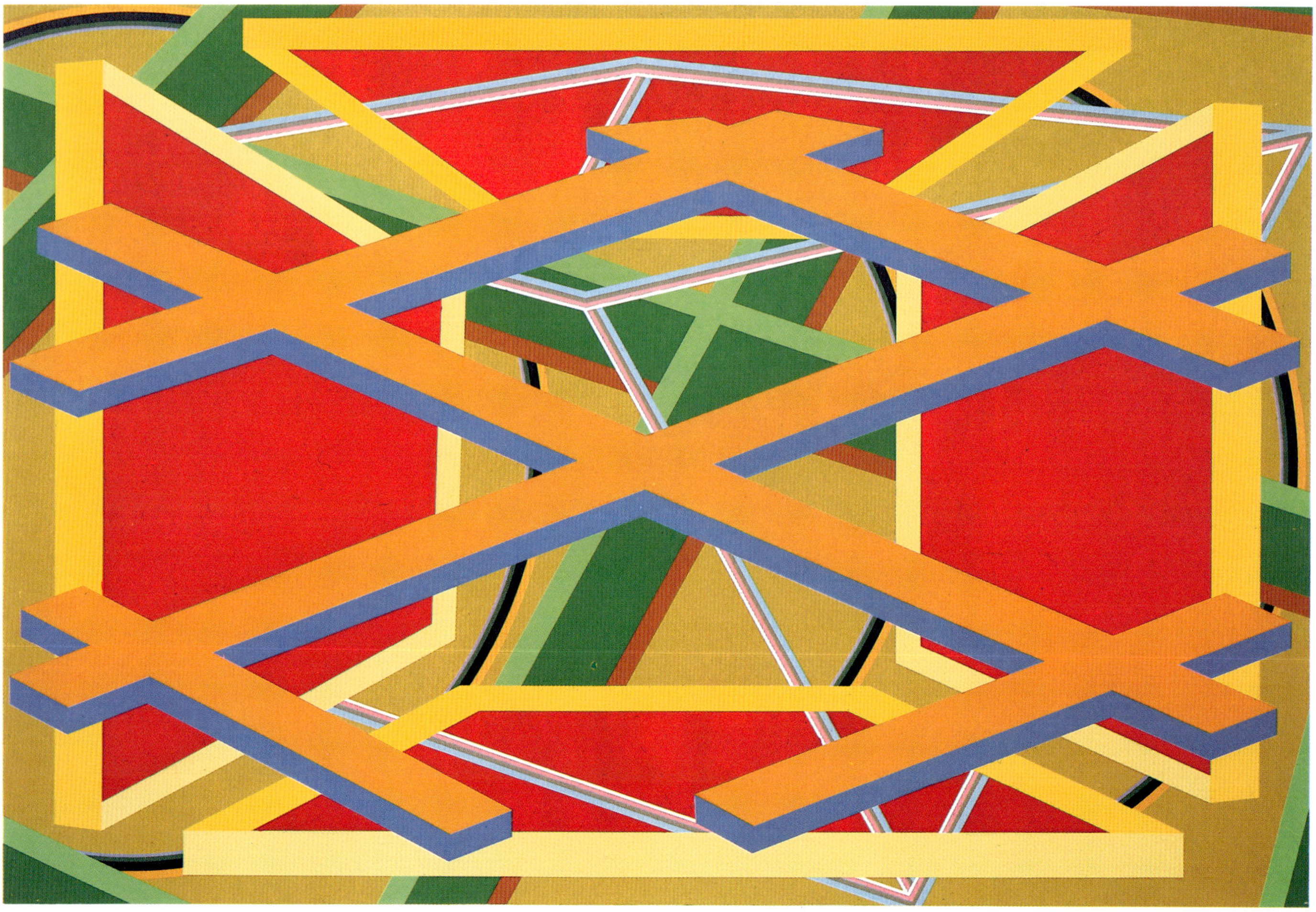

99. **Padua II,** 1981.
Acrylic on canvas, 84×84 in. (213.4×213.4 cm).
Collection of the artist.

100. **X-Square,** 1981.
Acrylic on canvas, 72×108 in. (183×274.3 cm).
Fondation Verranem, Brussels.

101. **Hadrian's Court I,** 1982.
Acrylic on canvas, 84×72 in. (213.4×183 cm).
Collection of Mr. and Mrs. Harry W. Anderson, Atherton, California.

101

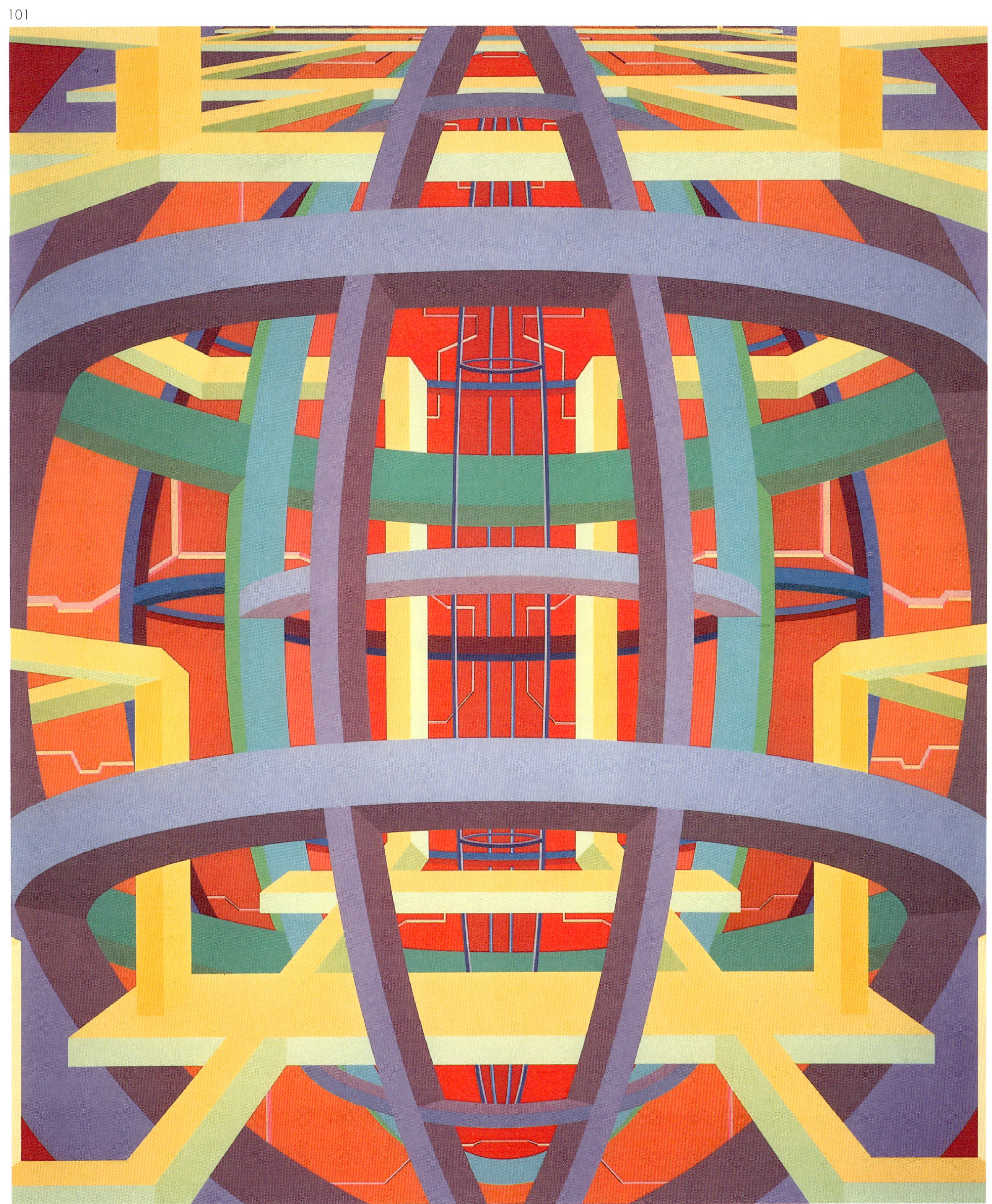

102. **Rome II,** 1982.
Acrylic on canvas, 108×216 in. (274.3×548.5 cm).
Delaware Art Museum, Wilmington, Delaware.

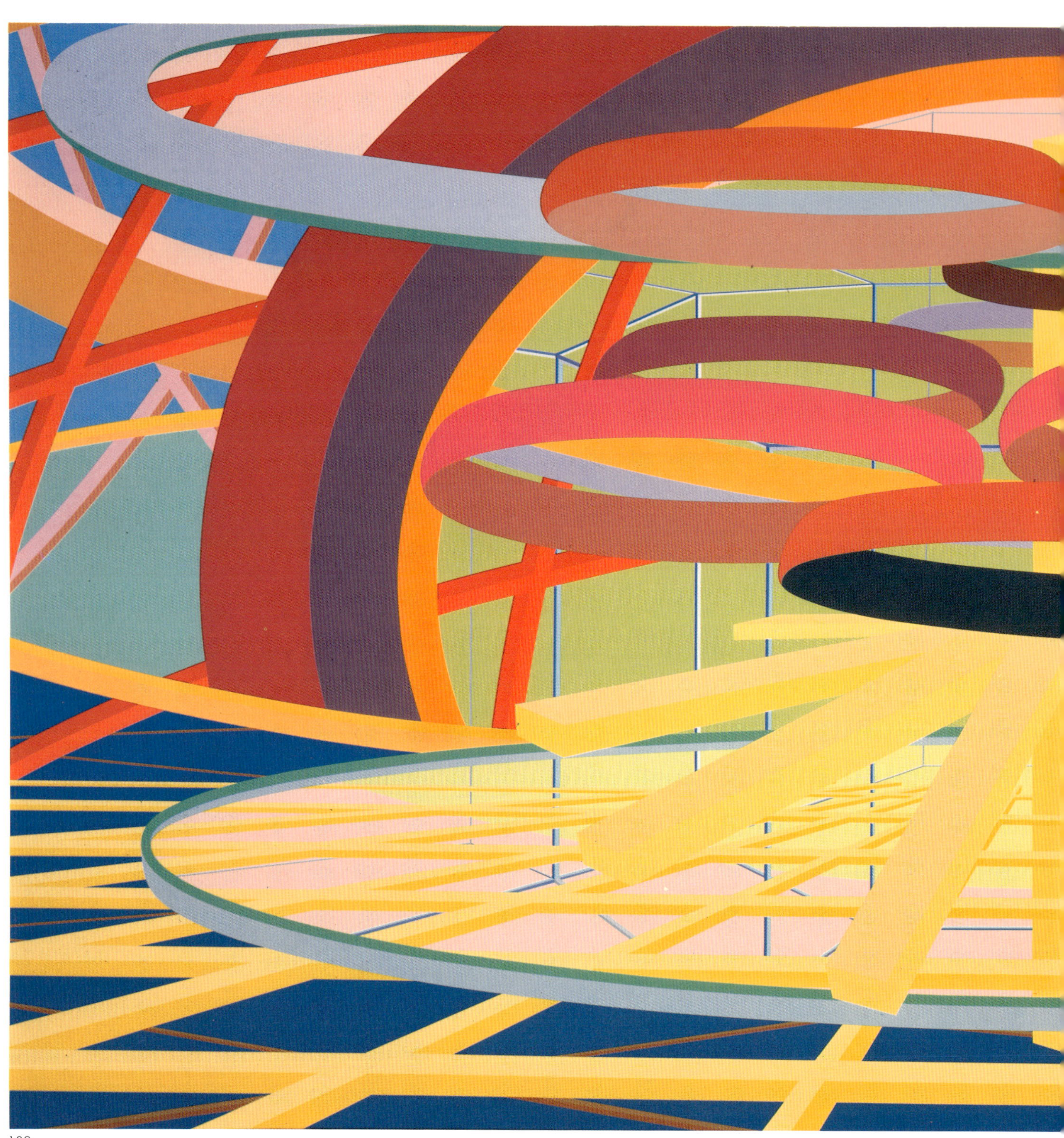

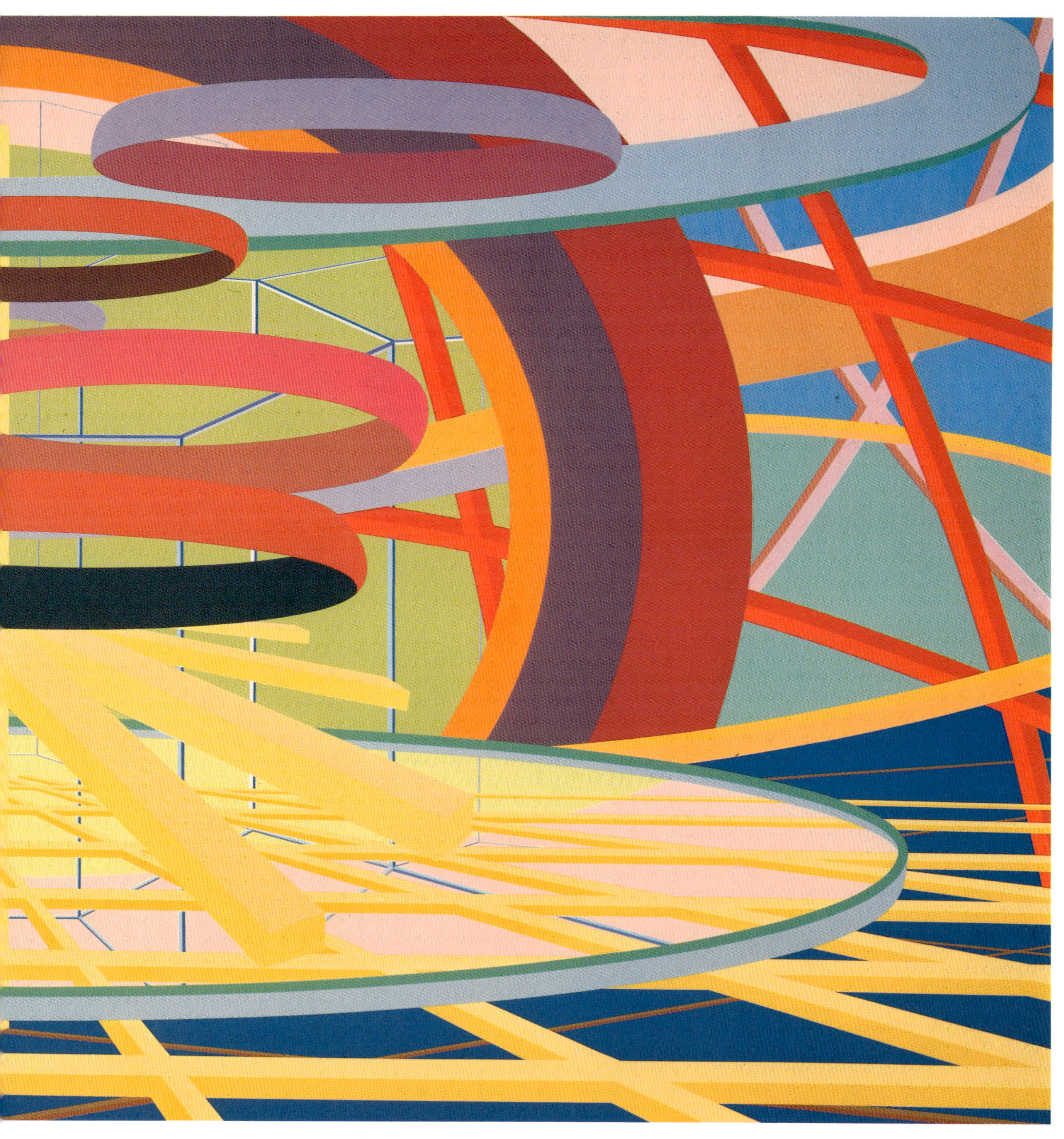

103. **Thalassa Circled,** 1982.
Acrylic on canvas, 60×72 in. (152.4×183 cm).
Collection of the Exxon Corporation, New York.

104. **Thalassa Circled IV,** 1983.
Acrylic on canvas, 48×60 in. (122×152.4 cm).
Collection of Mr. and Mrs. Matthew C. Strauss Rancho,
Santa Fe, California.

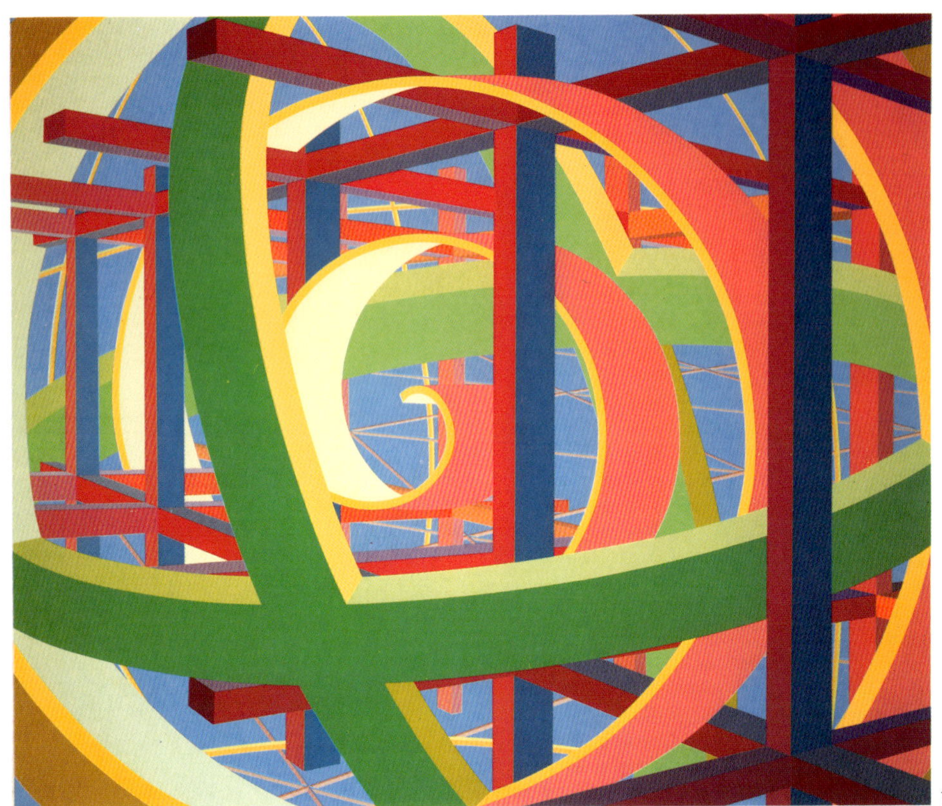

103

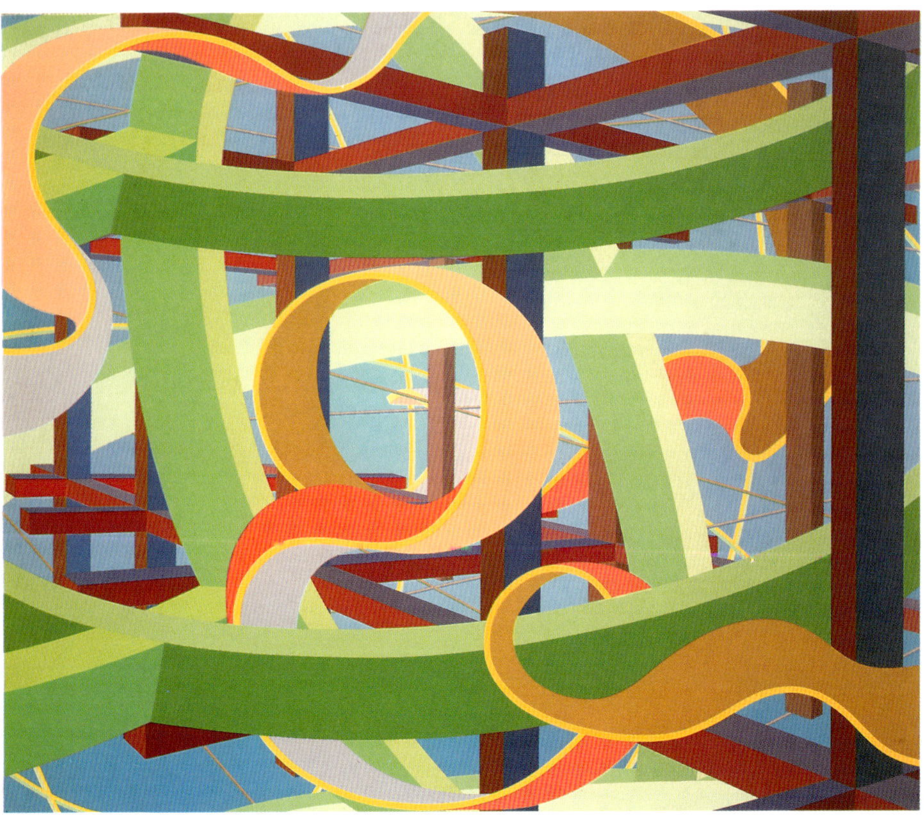

104

105. **Piero's Piazza,** 1982.
Acrylic on canvas, 96×144 in. (243.8×365.8 cm).
Albright-Knox Art Gallery, Buffalo, New York (Gift of Seymour H. Knox).

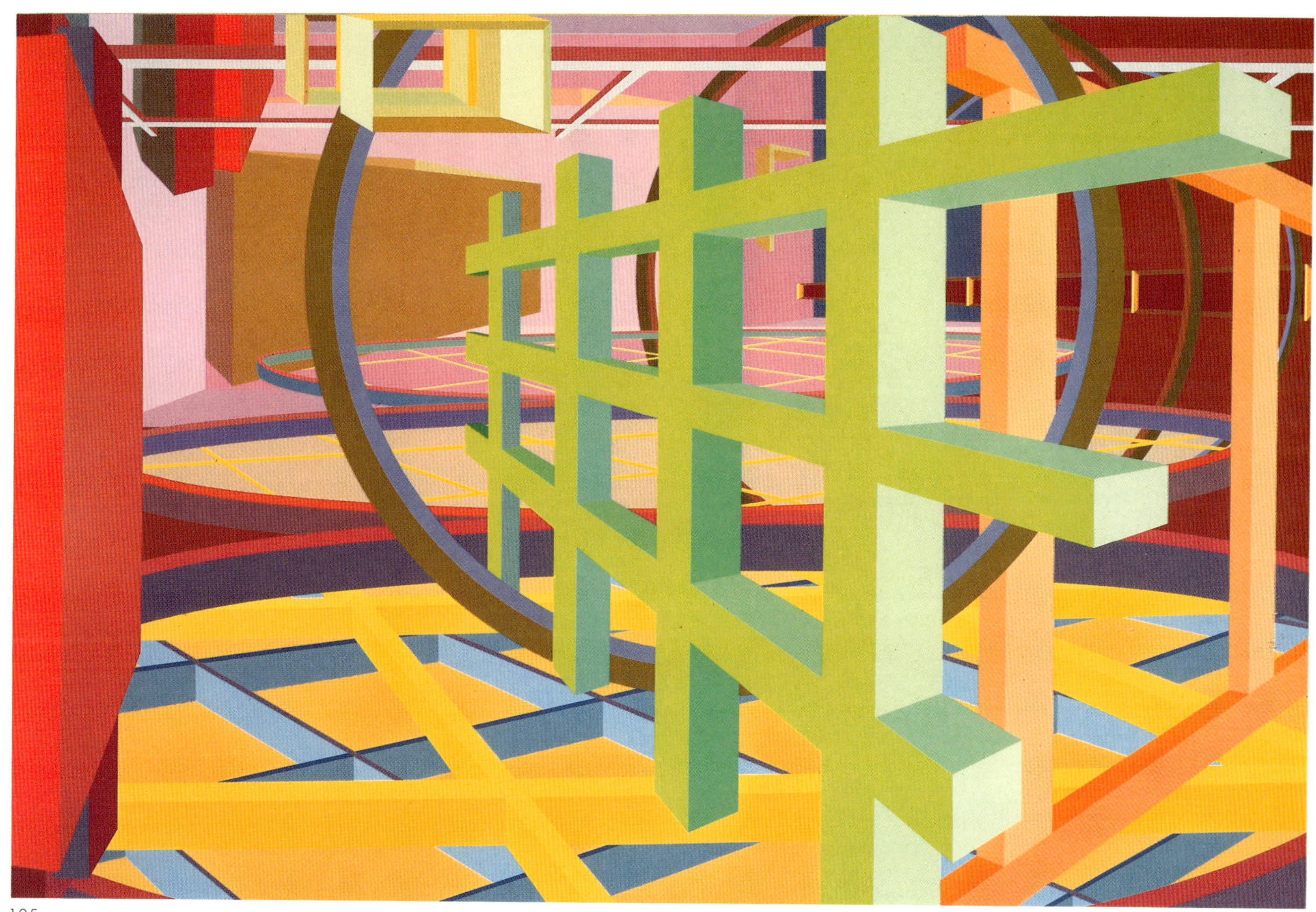
105

106. **Trajan's Edge I,** 1982.
Acrylic on canvas, 84×72 in. (213.4×183 cm).
Collection of Mr. and Mrs. Irving Sands,
Akron, Ohio.

107. **Trajan's Edge III,** 1983.
Acrylic on canvas, 108×108 in.
(274.3×274.3 cm).
Private collection.

108. **Herculaneum III,** 1983.
Acrylic on canvas, 84×84 in. (213.4×213.4 cm).
Collection of Martin and Linda Weissman,
Bloomfield Hills, Michigan.

109. **Vorcex I,** 1983.
Acrylic on canvas, 84×84 in. (213.4×213.4 cm).
The Brett Mitchell Collection, Inc., Cleveland.

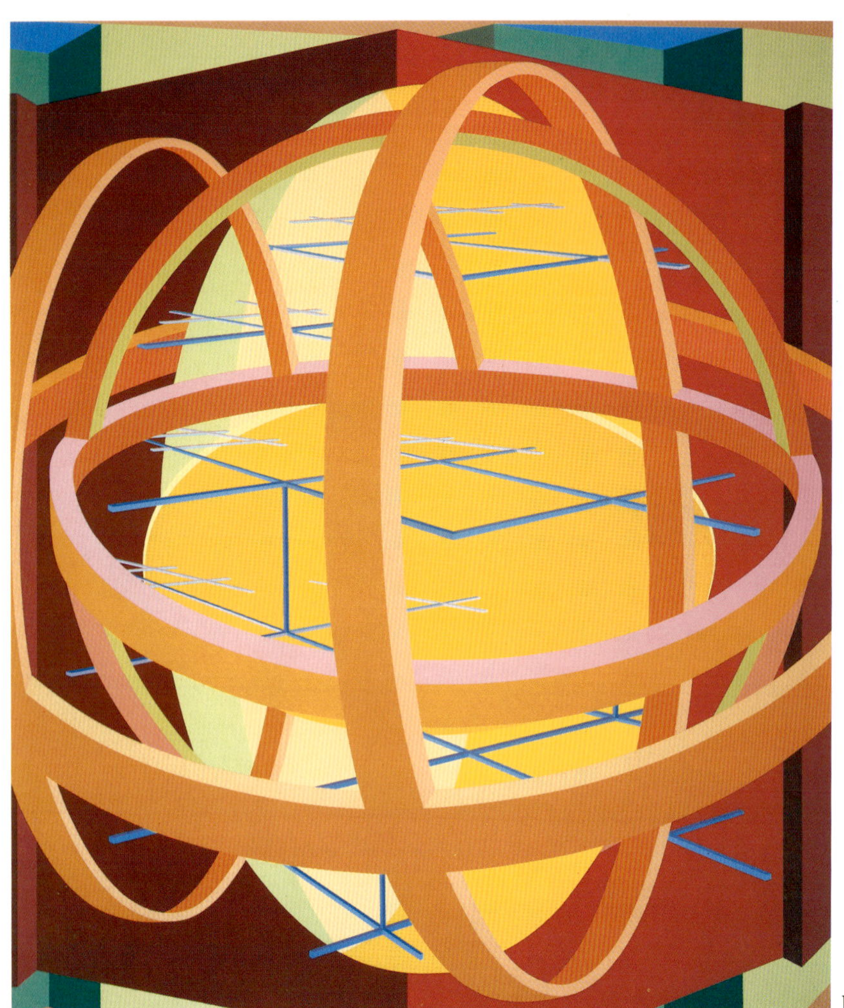

106

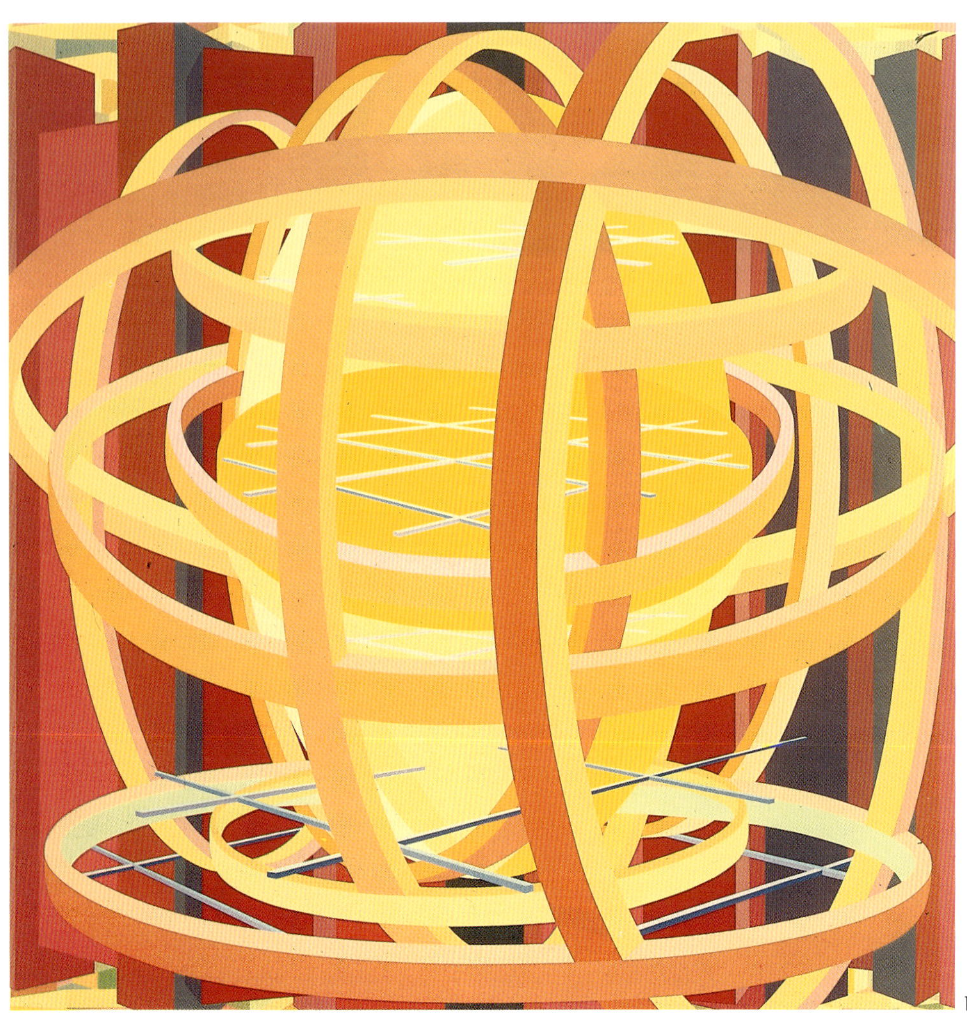

107

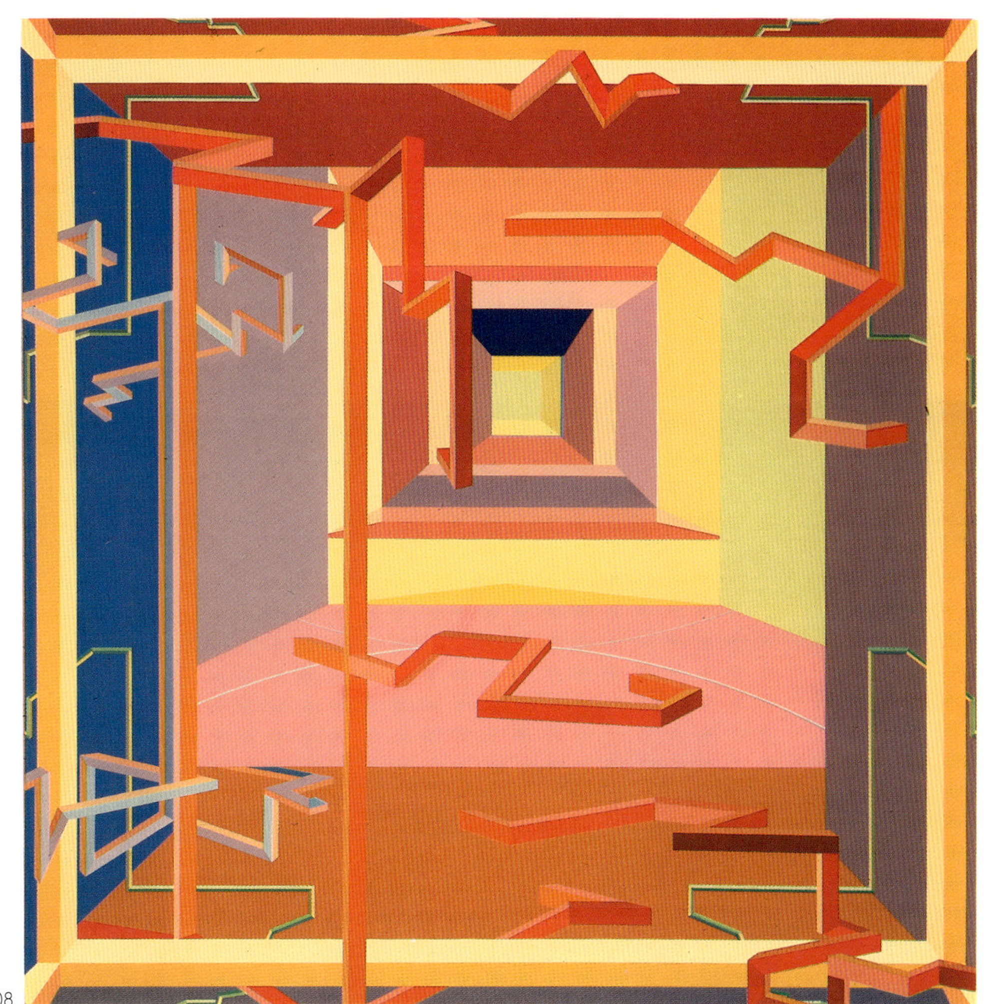
108

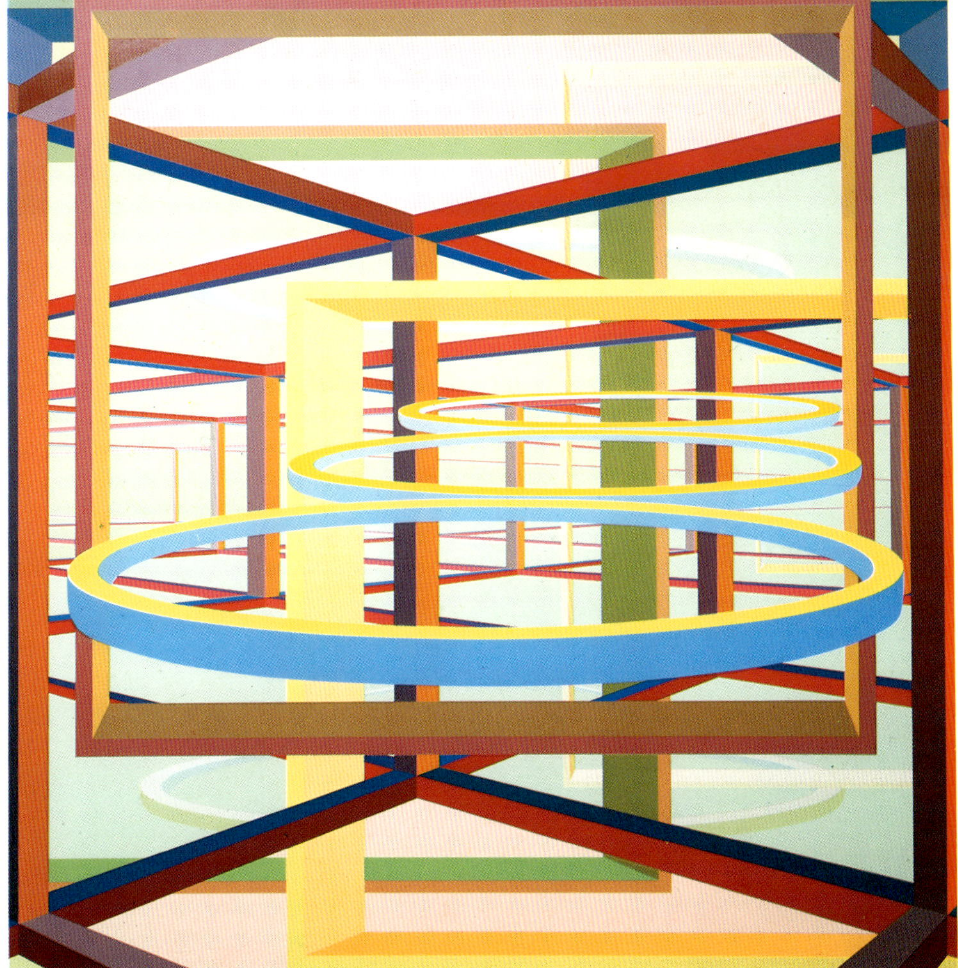
109

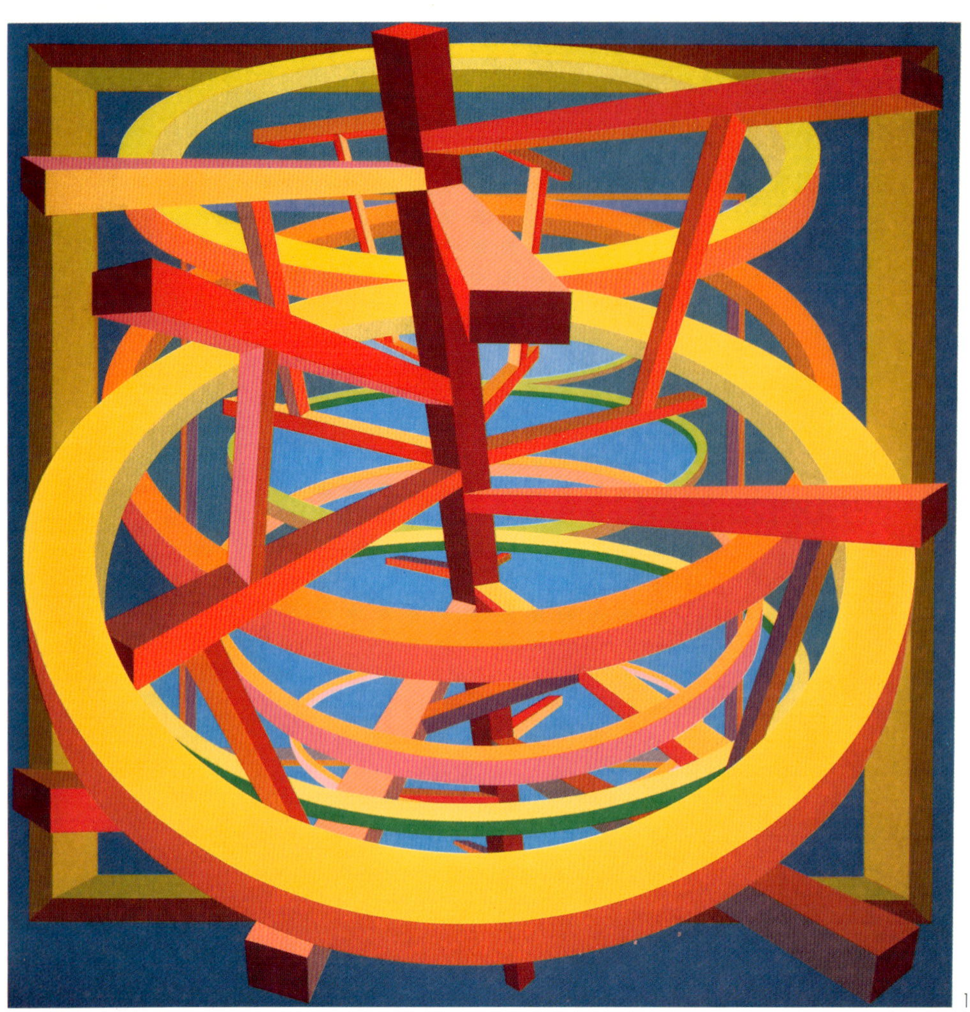

110

110. **Pisa II,** 1983.
Acrylic on canvas,
84×84 in. (213.4×213.4 cm).
Collection of Dr. and Mrs. Joel Bernstein, Deerfield, Illinois.

111. **Vorcex III,** 1984.
Acrylic on canvas,
84×84 in. (213.4×213.4 cm).
Collection of Gary Ellis, Houston, Texas.

112. **Mantegna's Edge** (mural), 1983.
Acrylic on canvas,
174×634 in. (4.40×16 m).
Collection of Southland Financial Corporation, Dallas.

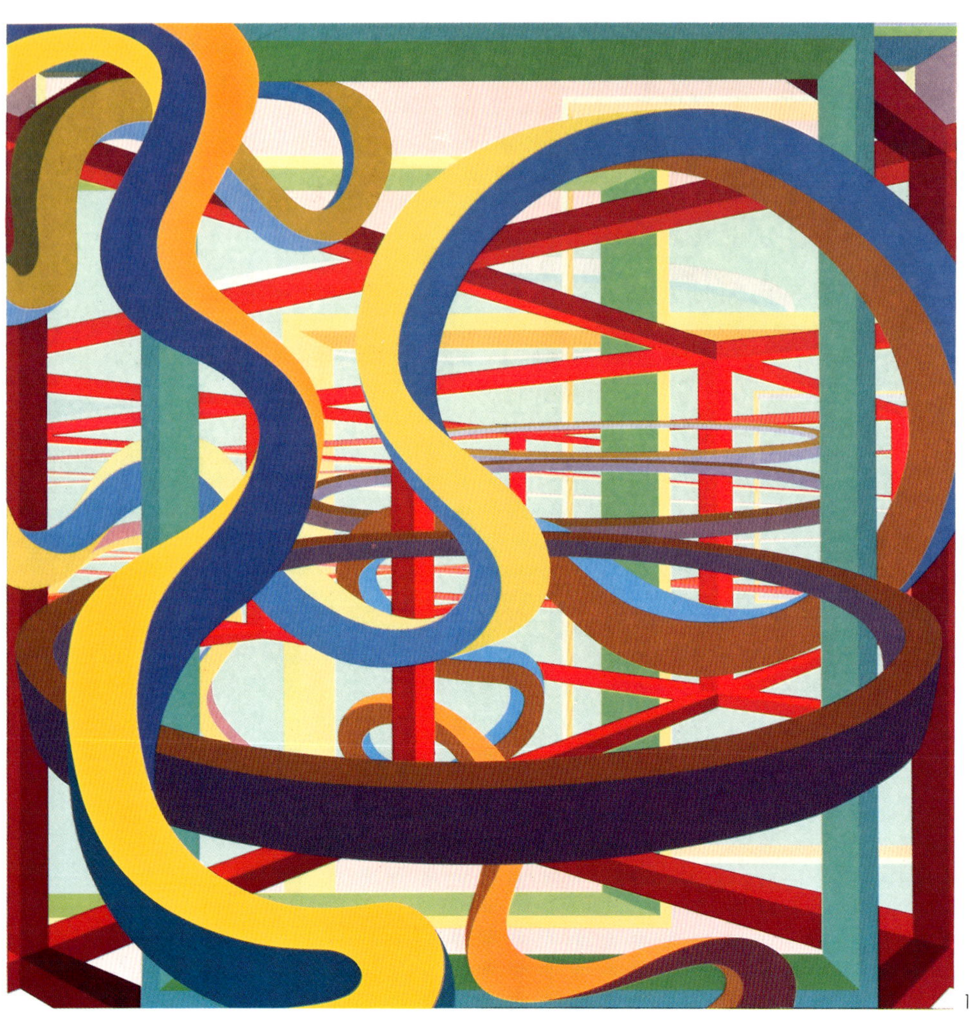

111

11

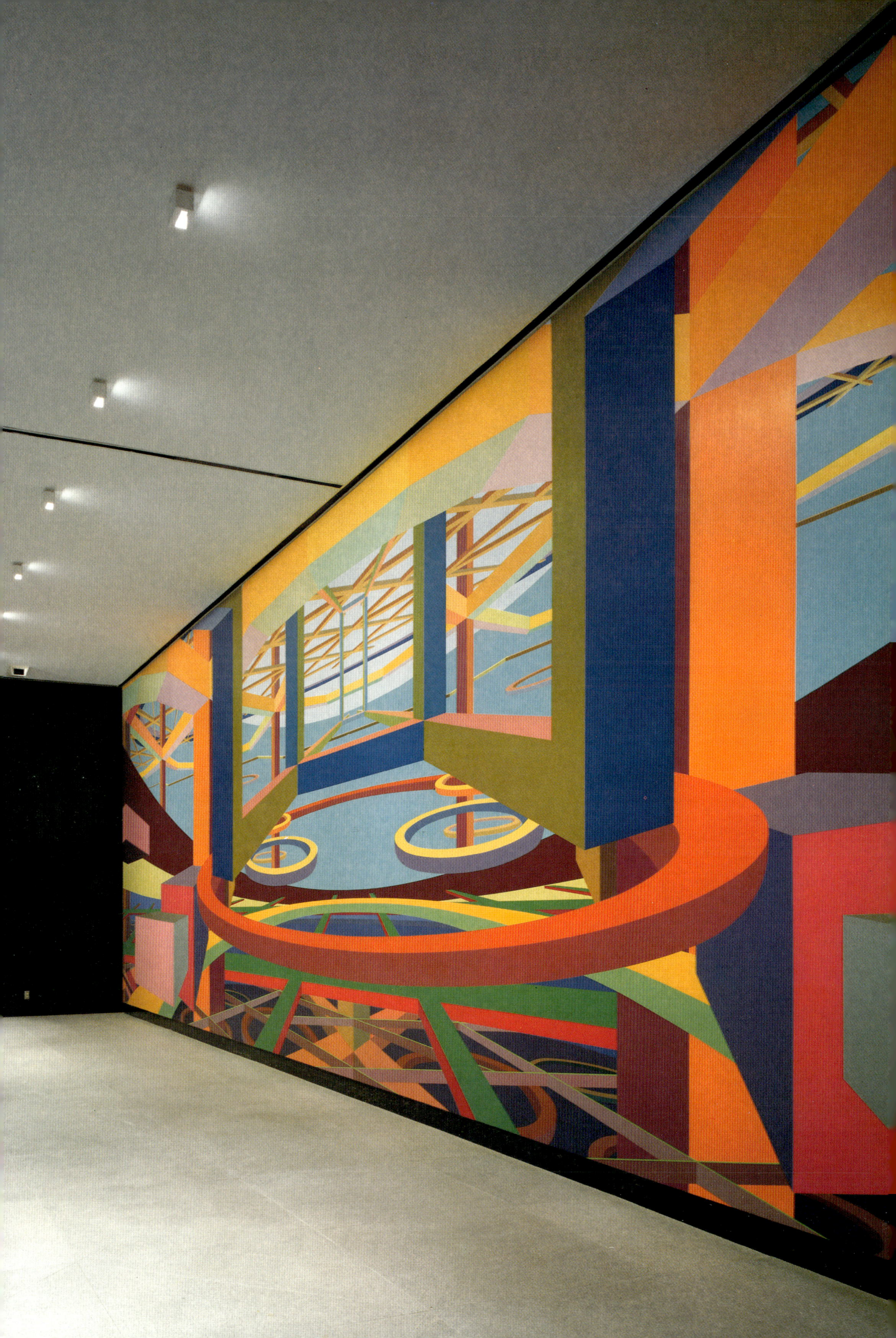

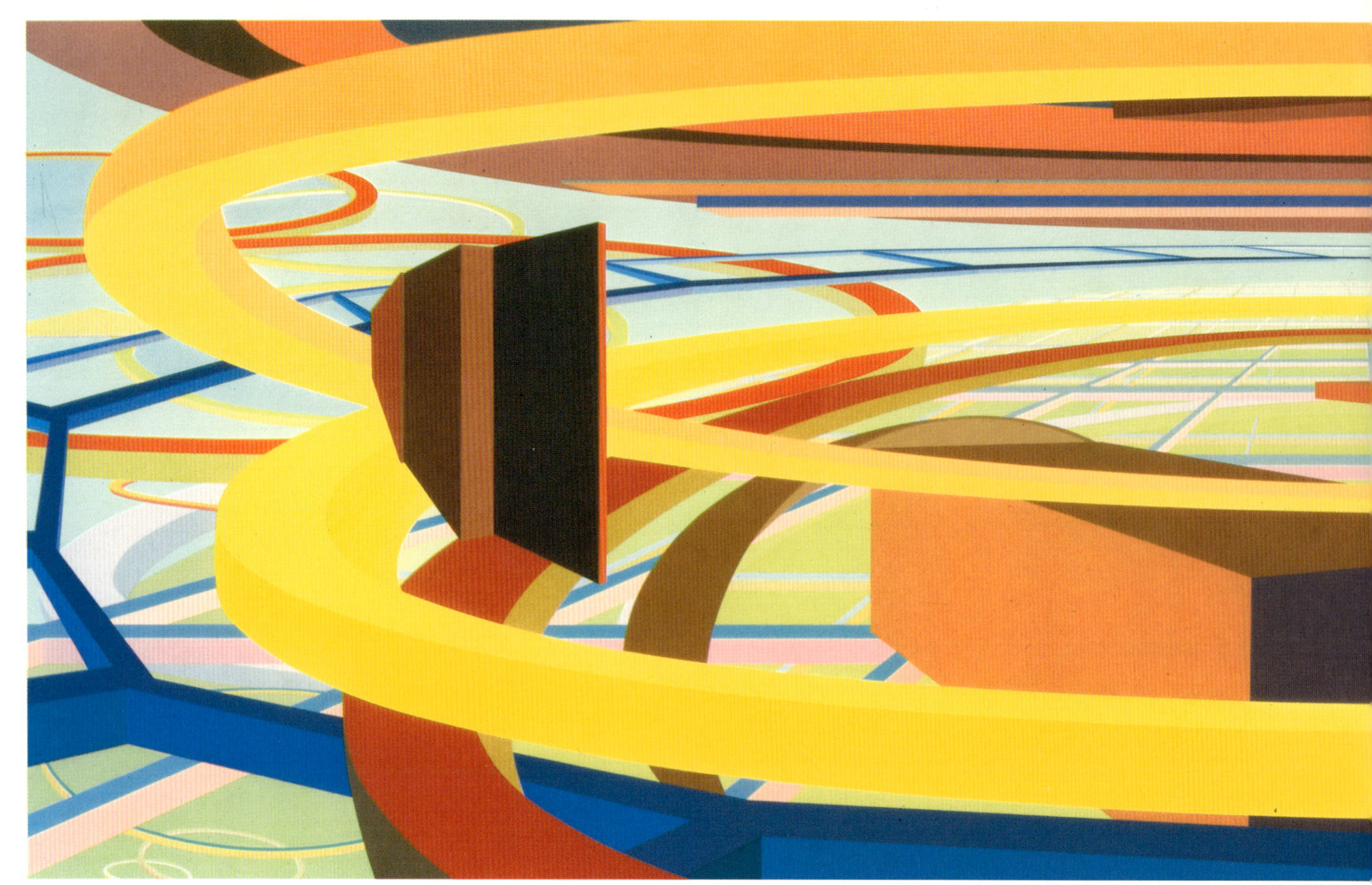

113

113. **The First Circle,** 1985.
Acrylic on canvas, 60×198 in. (152.4×503 cm).
André Emmerich Gallery, New York.

114. **Pan North IV,** 1985.
Acrylic on canvas, 72×84 in. (183×213.4 cm).
Collection of Mr. N. Riklis, Beverly Hills, California.

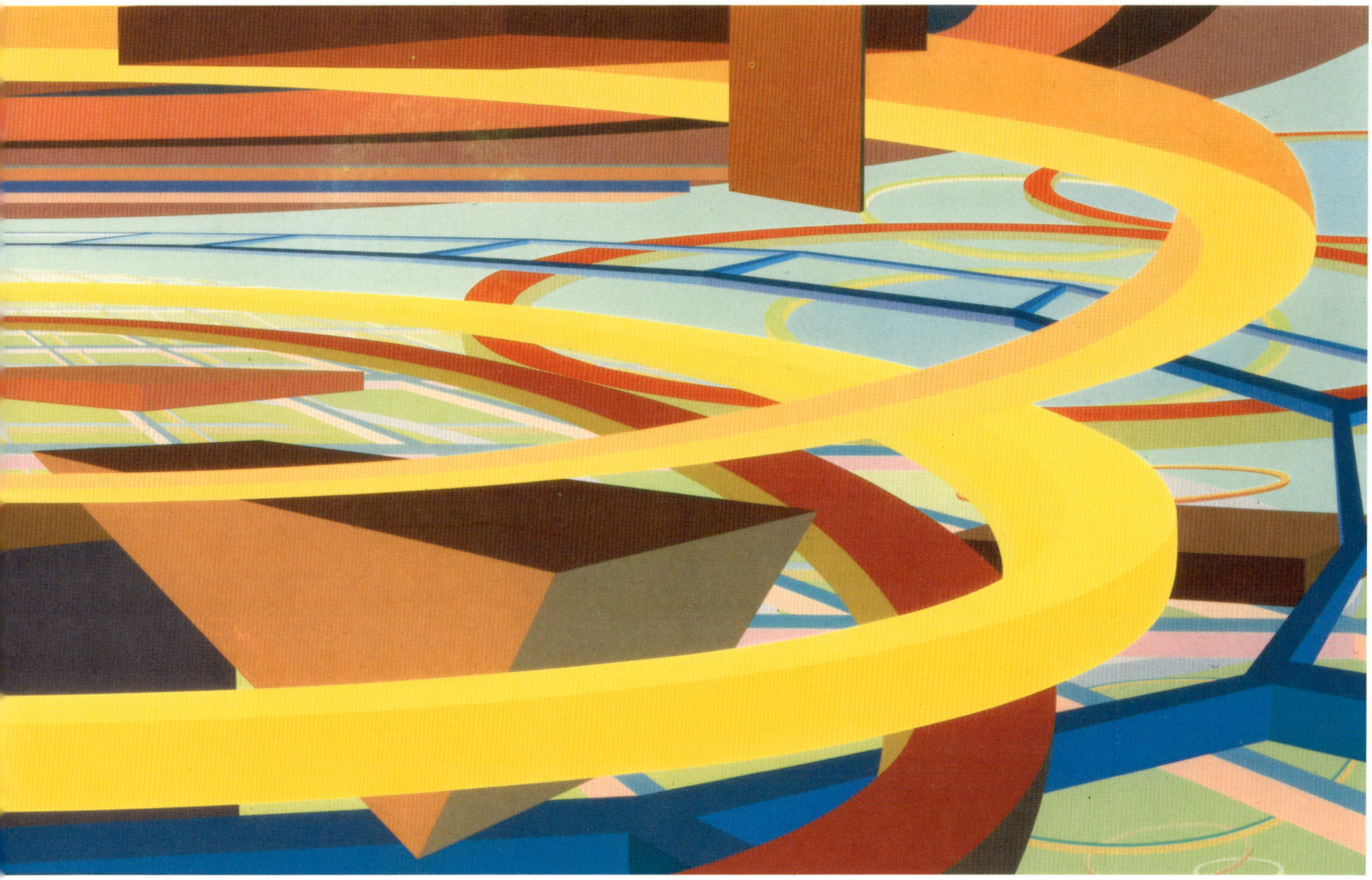

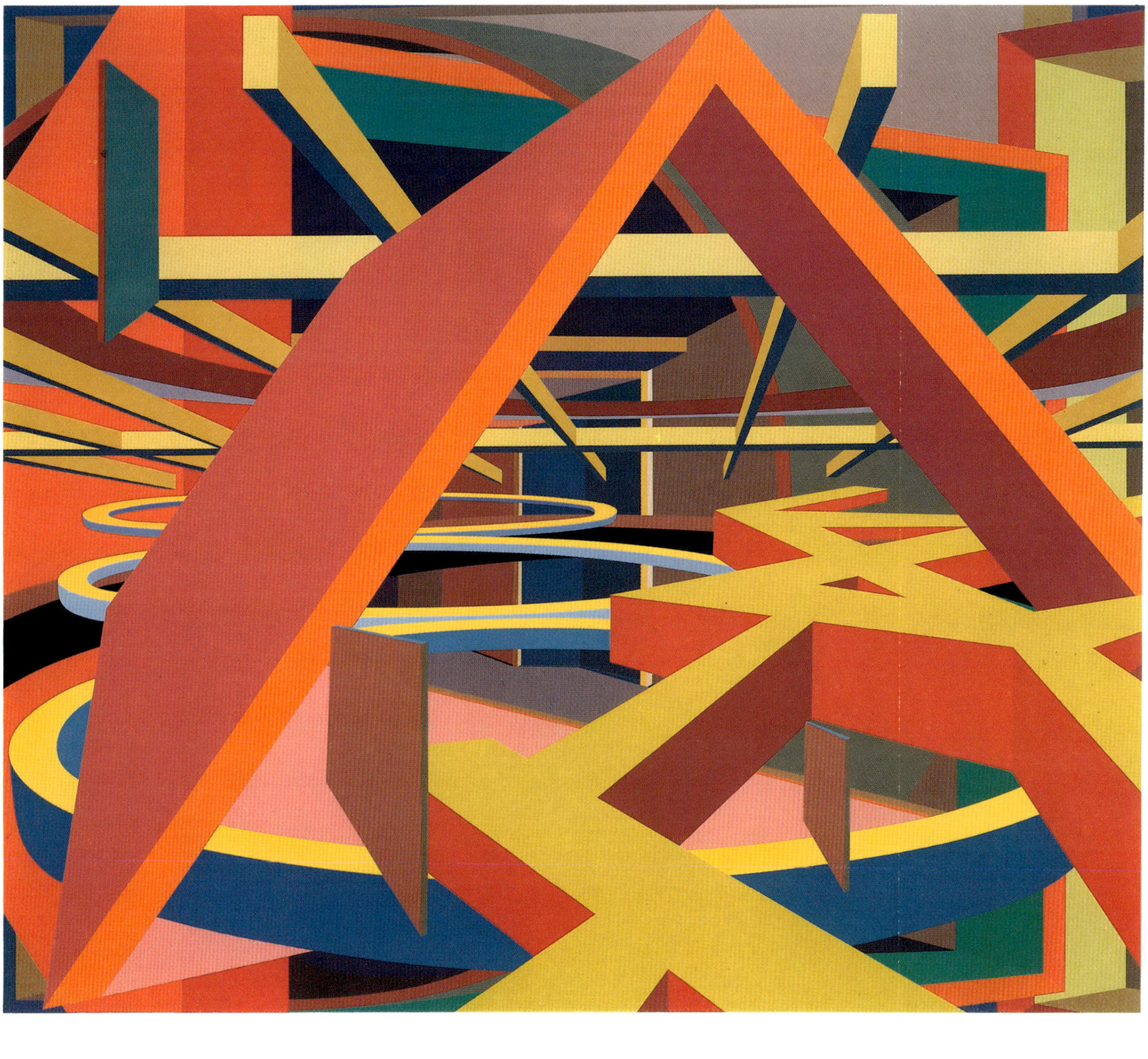

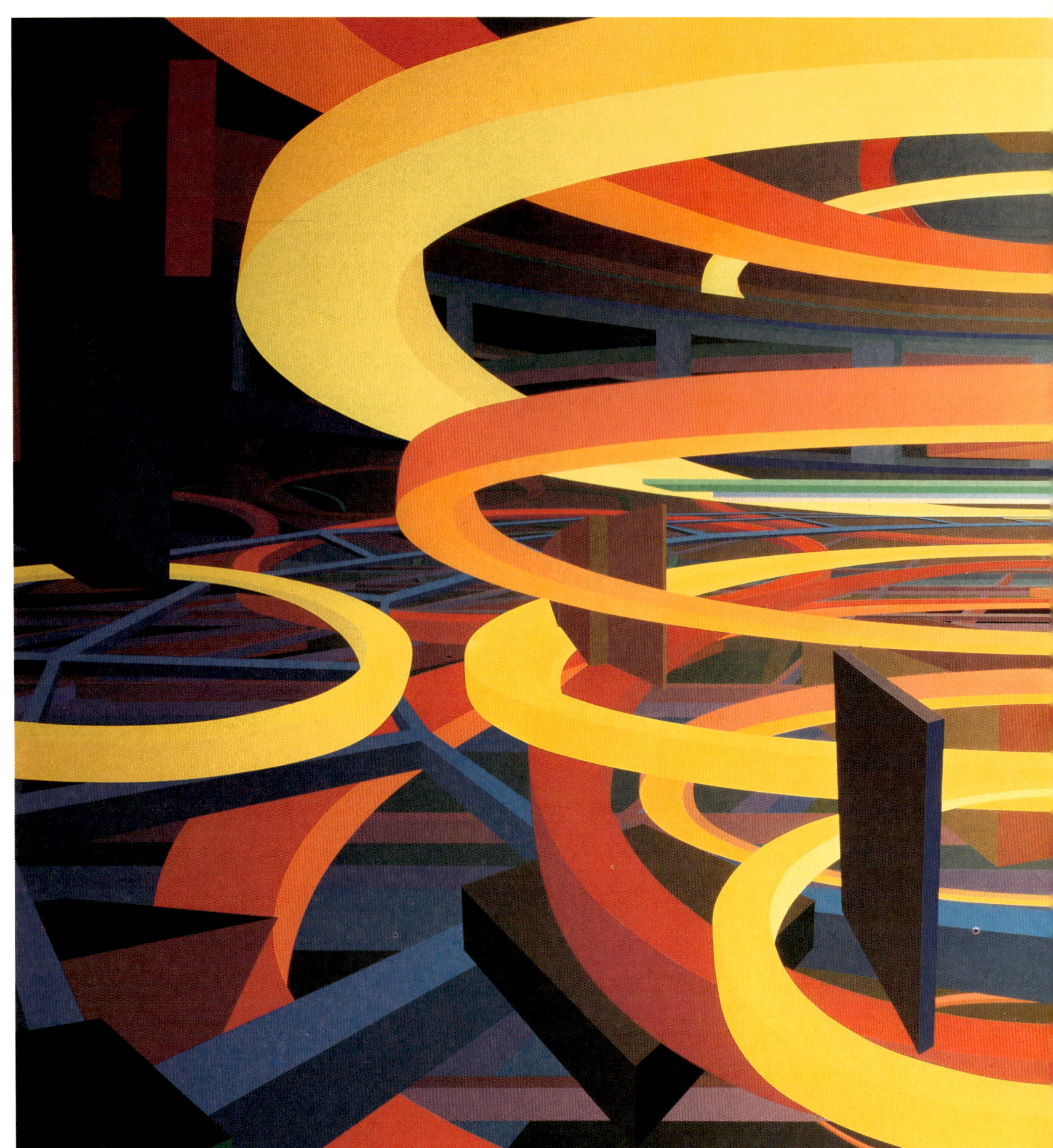

115

115. **The Third Circle,** 1986.
Acrylic on canvas, 168×300 in. (426.7×762 cm).
Collection of Larry Silverstein, New York.

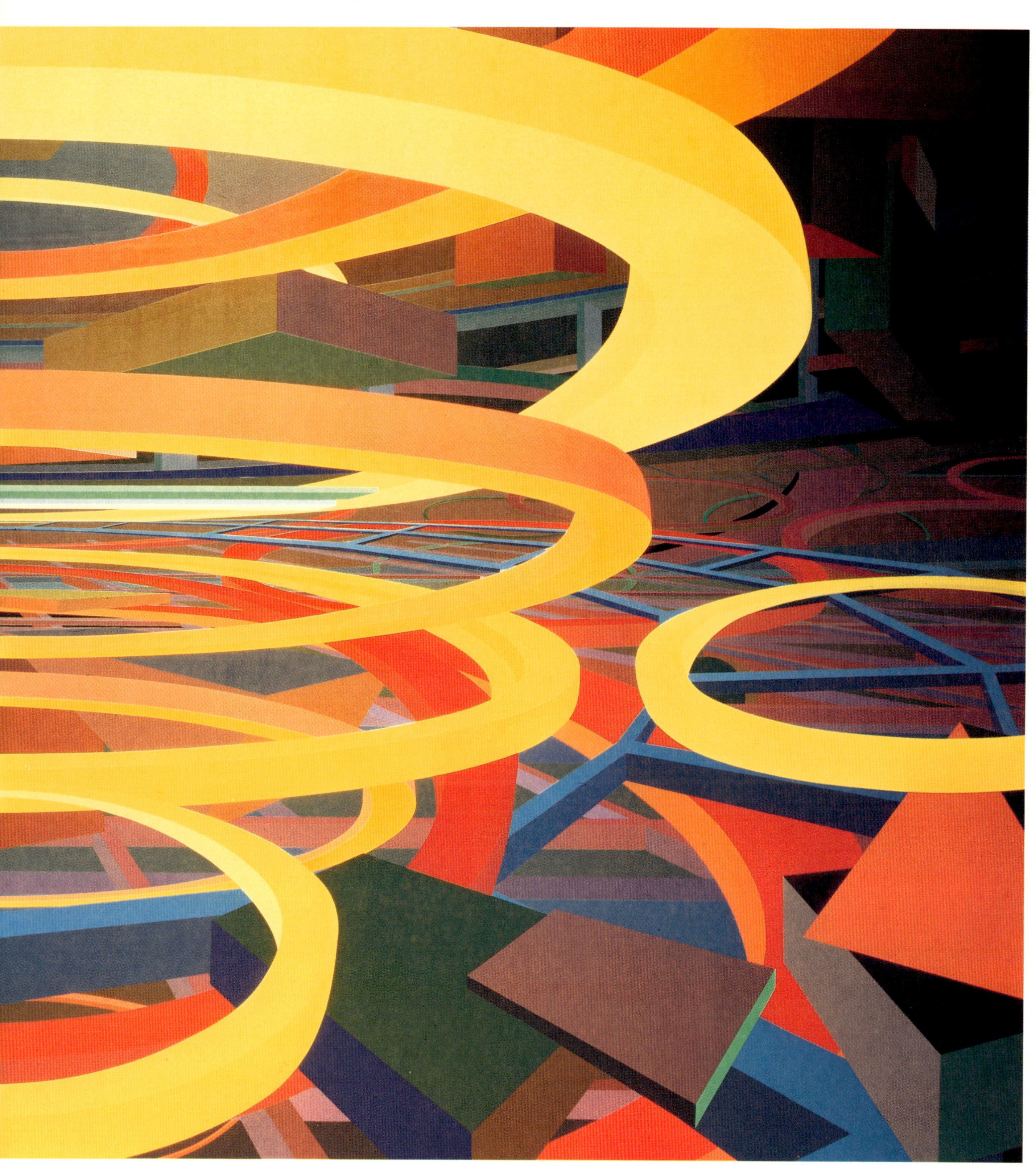

116. **Pan North XI,** 1987.
Acrylic on canvas, 108×168 in. (274.3×426.7 cm).
Collection of Charles Benenson, Greenwich, Connecticut.

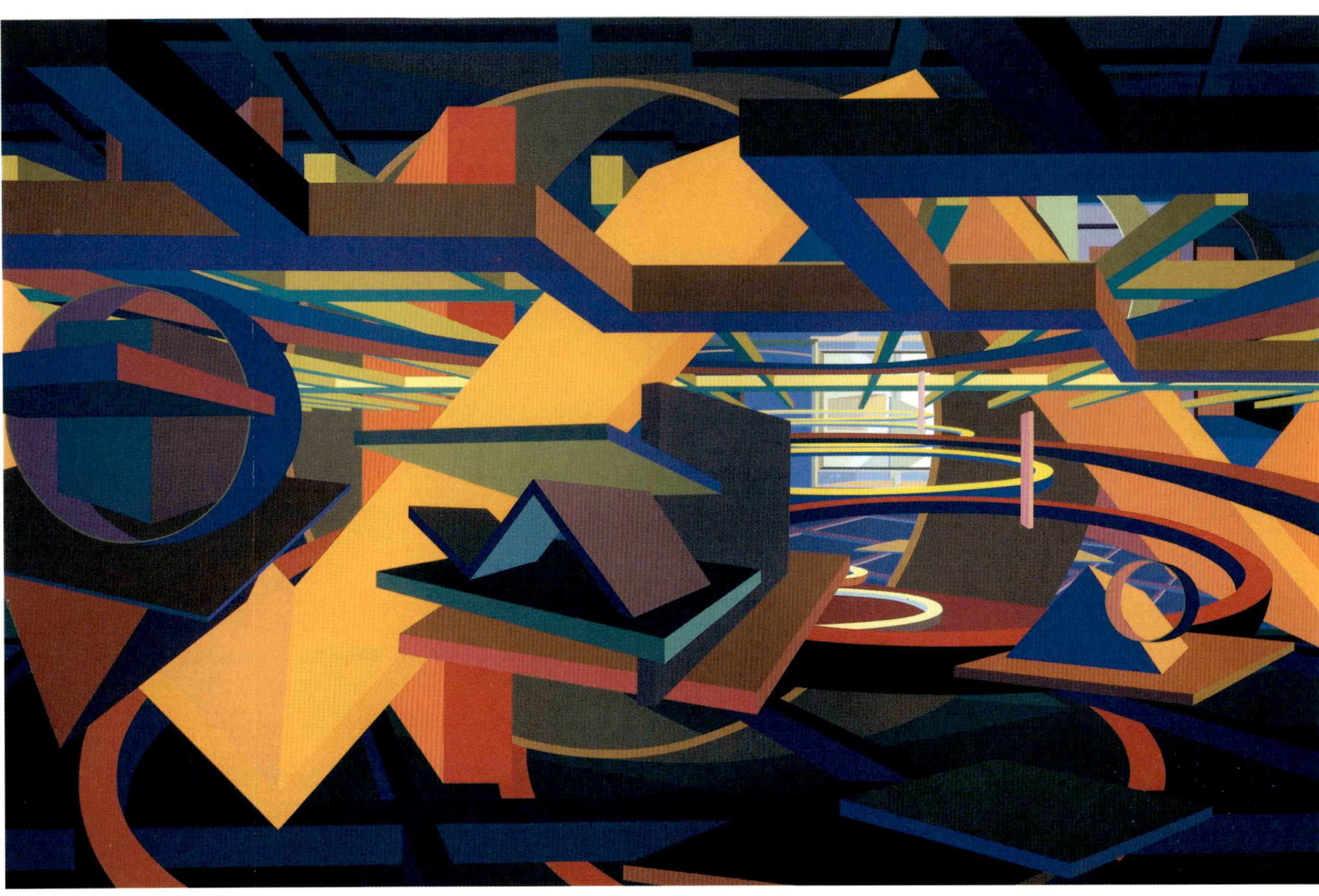

116

117. **East End,** 1987.
Acrylic on canvas, 96×144 in. (243.8×365.8 cm).
Private collection, San Francisco.

118. **Nectarus II,** 1987.
Acrylic on canvas, 84×60 in. (213.4×152.4 cm).
Collection of Kitty B. Weese, Chicago.

119. **Sea of Tranquility II,** 1987.
Acrylic on canvas, 72×120 in. (183×274.3 cm).
Private collection, Detroit.

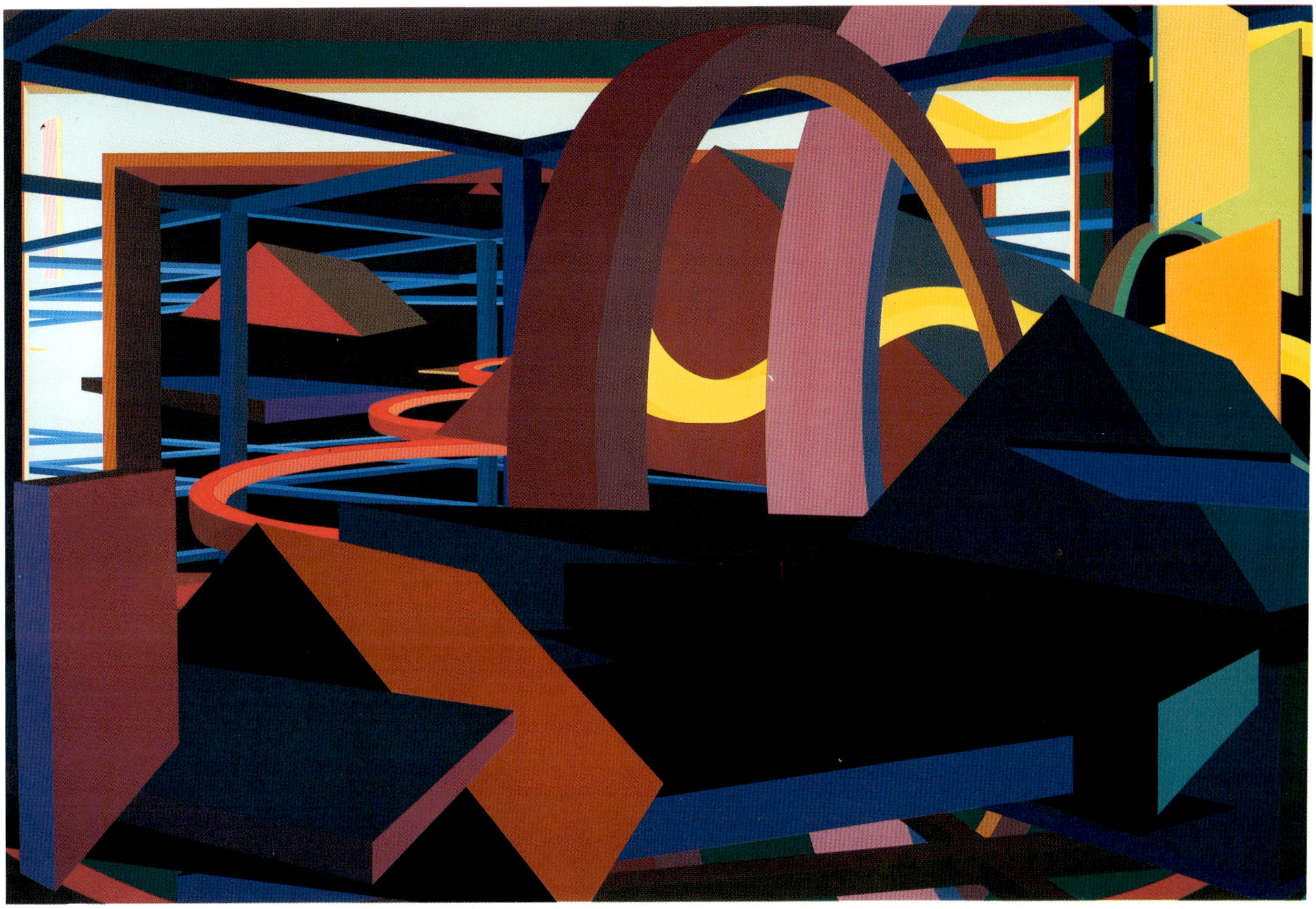

117

118

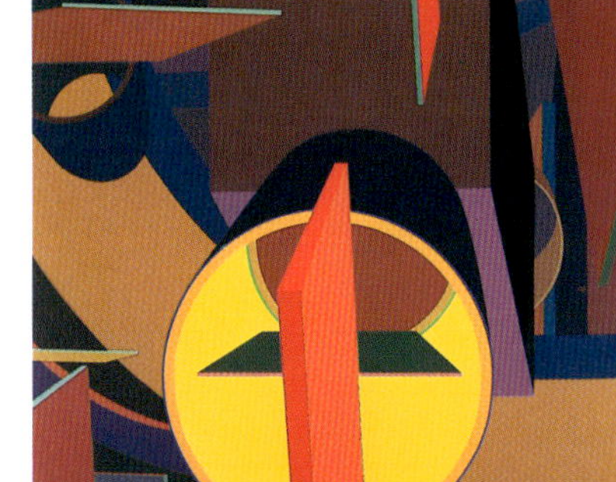

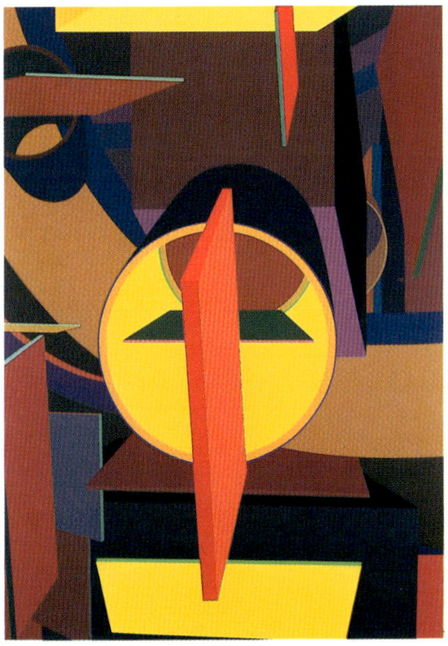

119

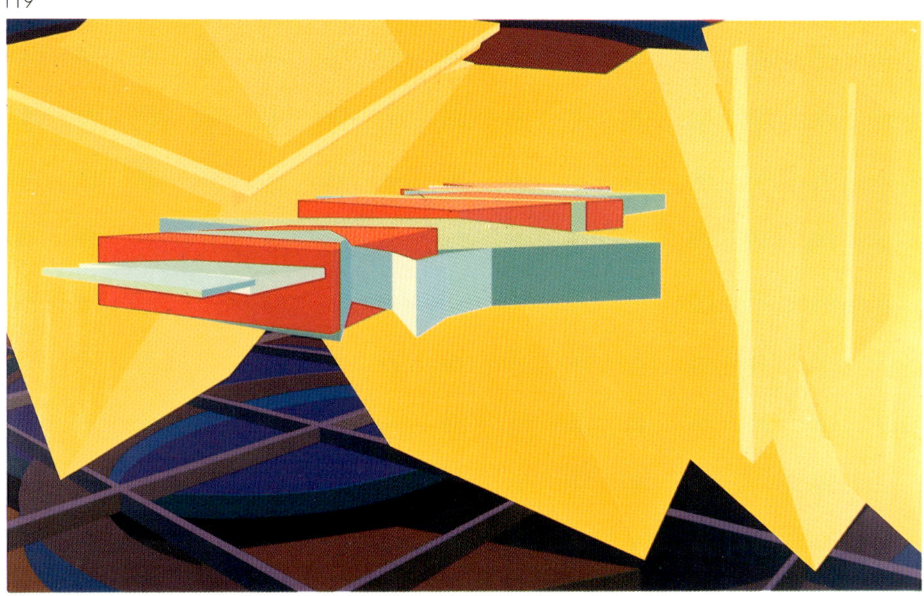

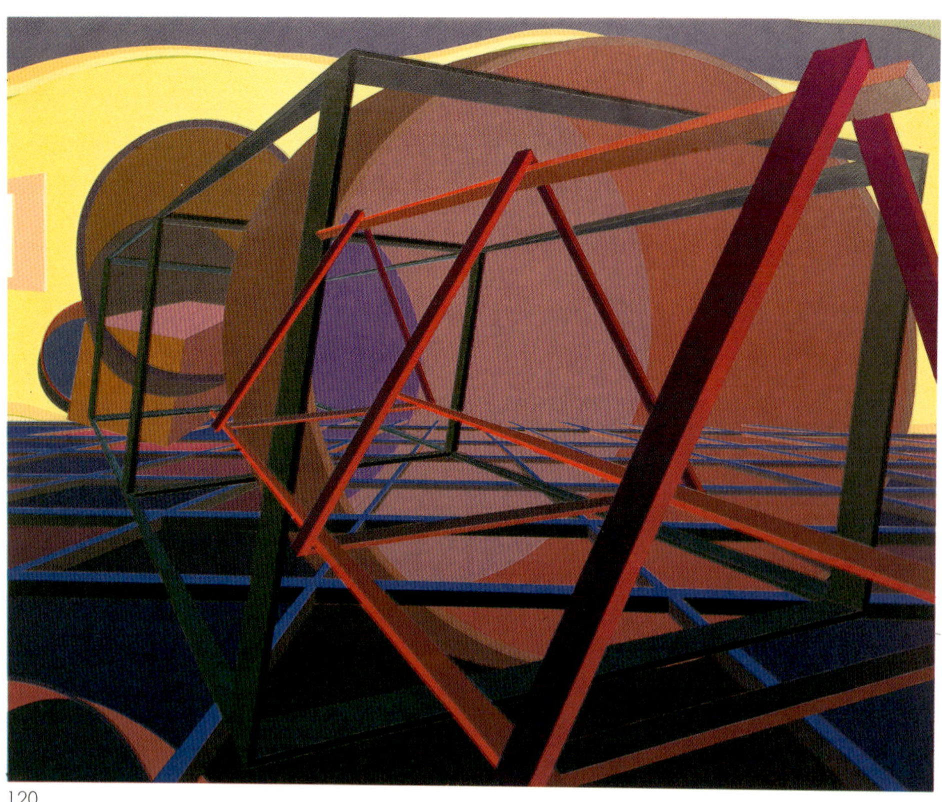

120

120. **Vaporium,** 1987.
Acrylic on canvas,
48×60 in. (122×152.4 cm).
Collection of Mr. James Halperin,
Kings Point, New York.

121. **Vaporium II,** 1987.
Acrylic on canvas,
60×84 in. (152.4×213.4 cm).
Collection of Mr. Walter Netsch, Jr.,
Chicago.

122. **Vaporium VI,** 1988.
Acrylic on linen,
84×84 in. (213.4×213.4 cm).
R. Crosby Kemper Foundation,
Kansas City, Missouri.

123. **Vaporium VII,** 1988.
Acrylic on linen,
96×144 in. (243.8×365.8 cm).
André Emmerich Gallery, New York.

121

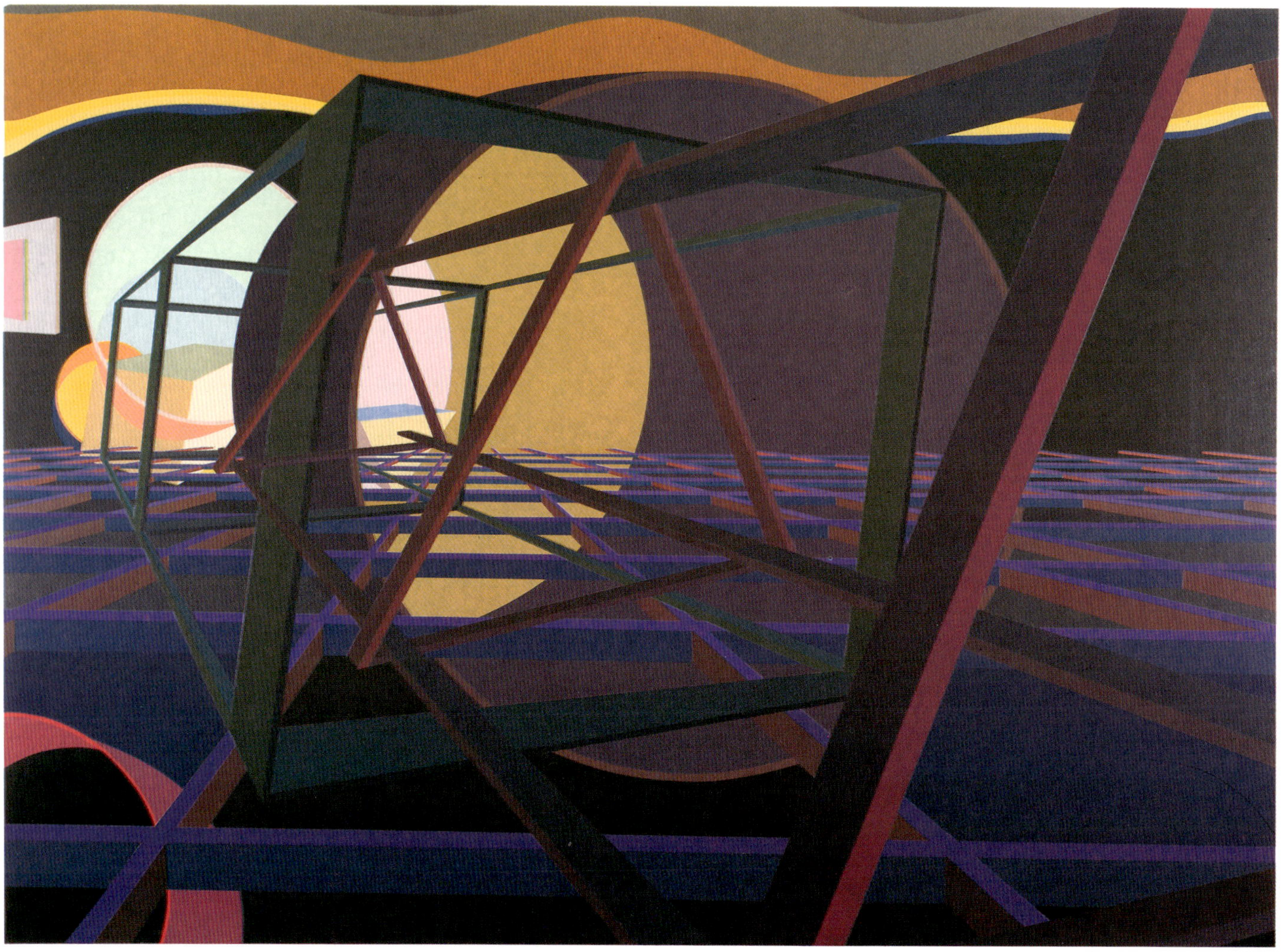

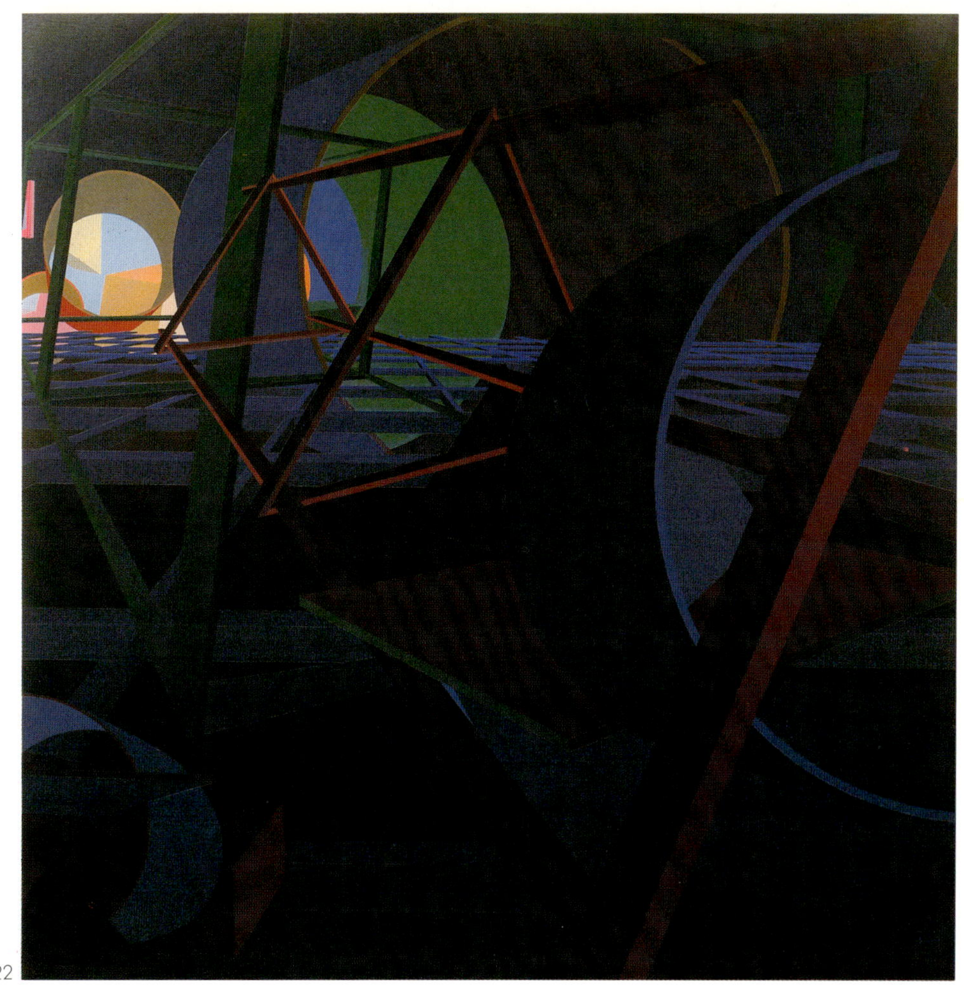

122

123

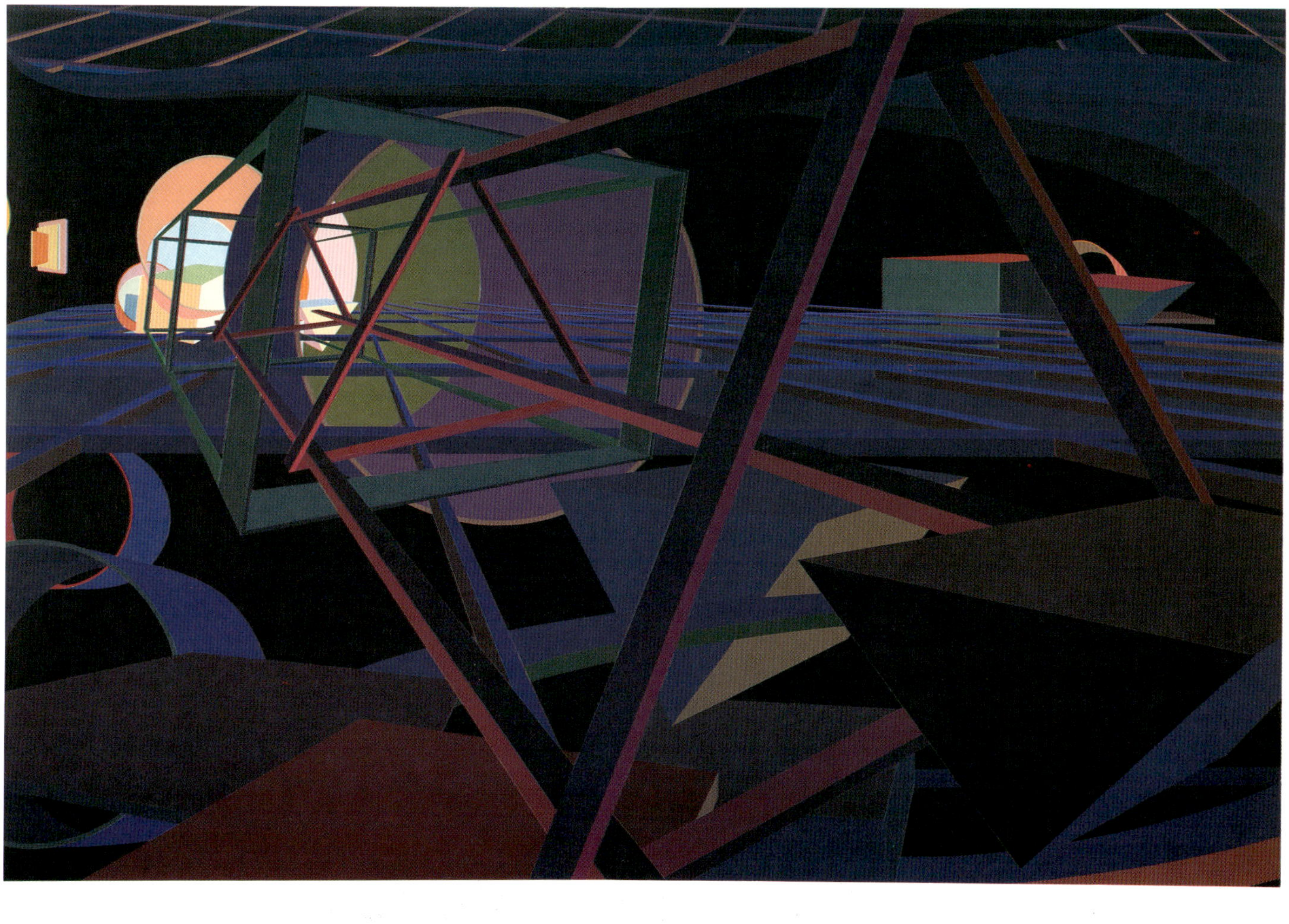

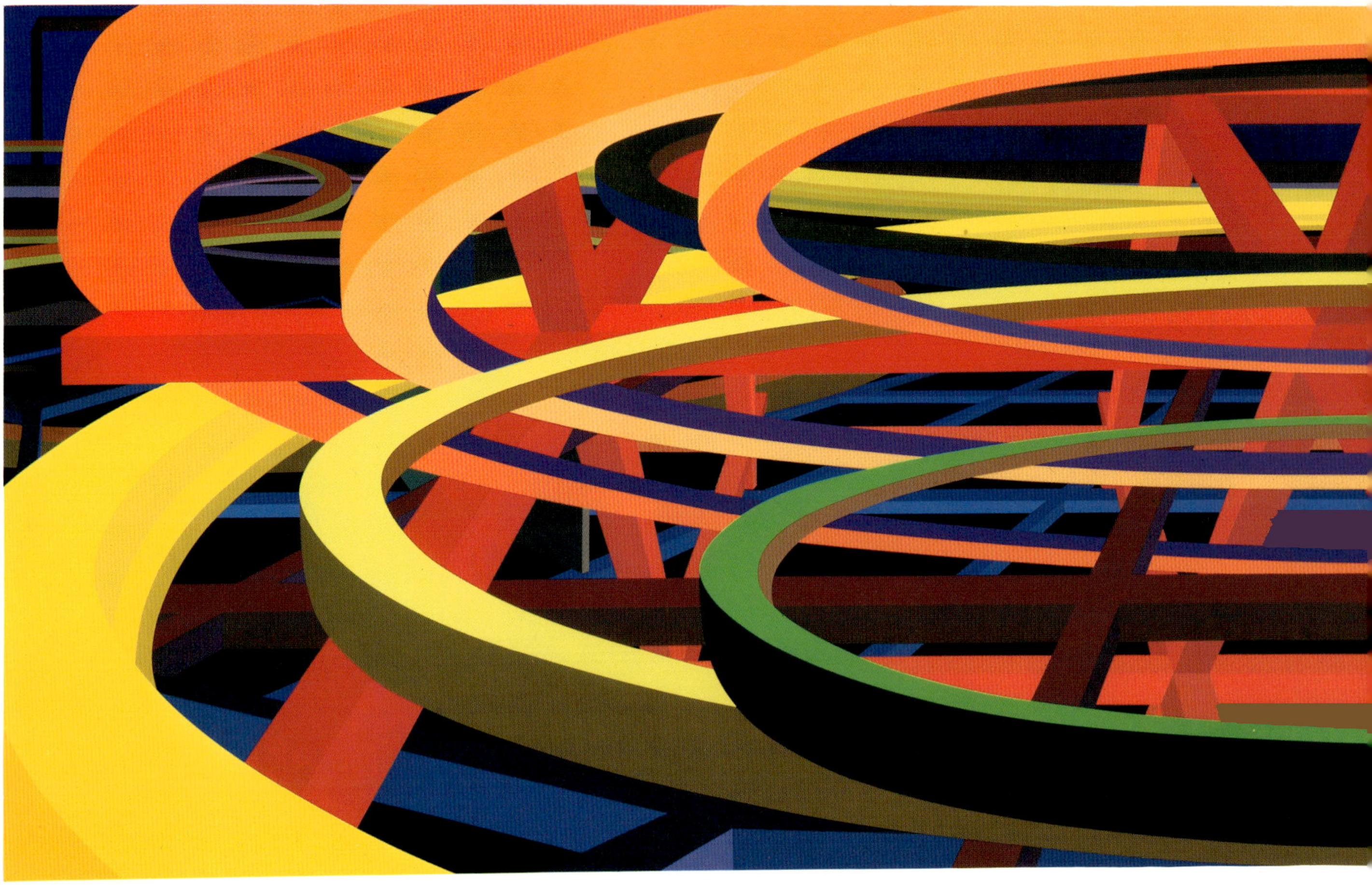

124

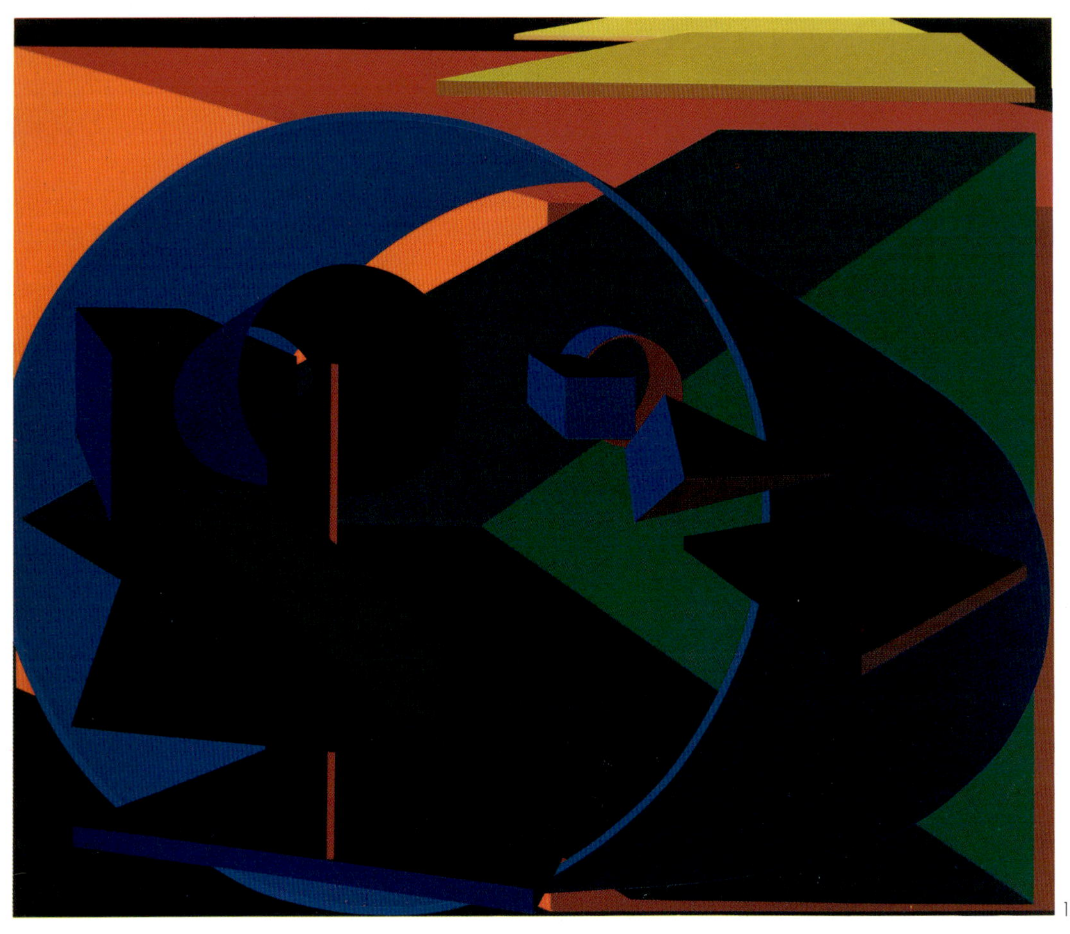

125

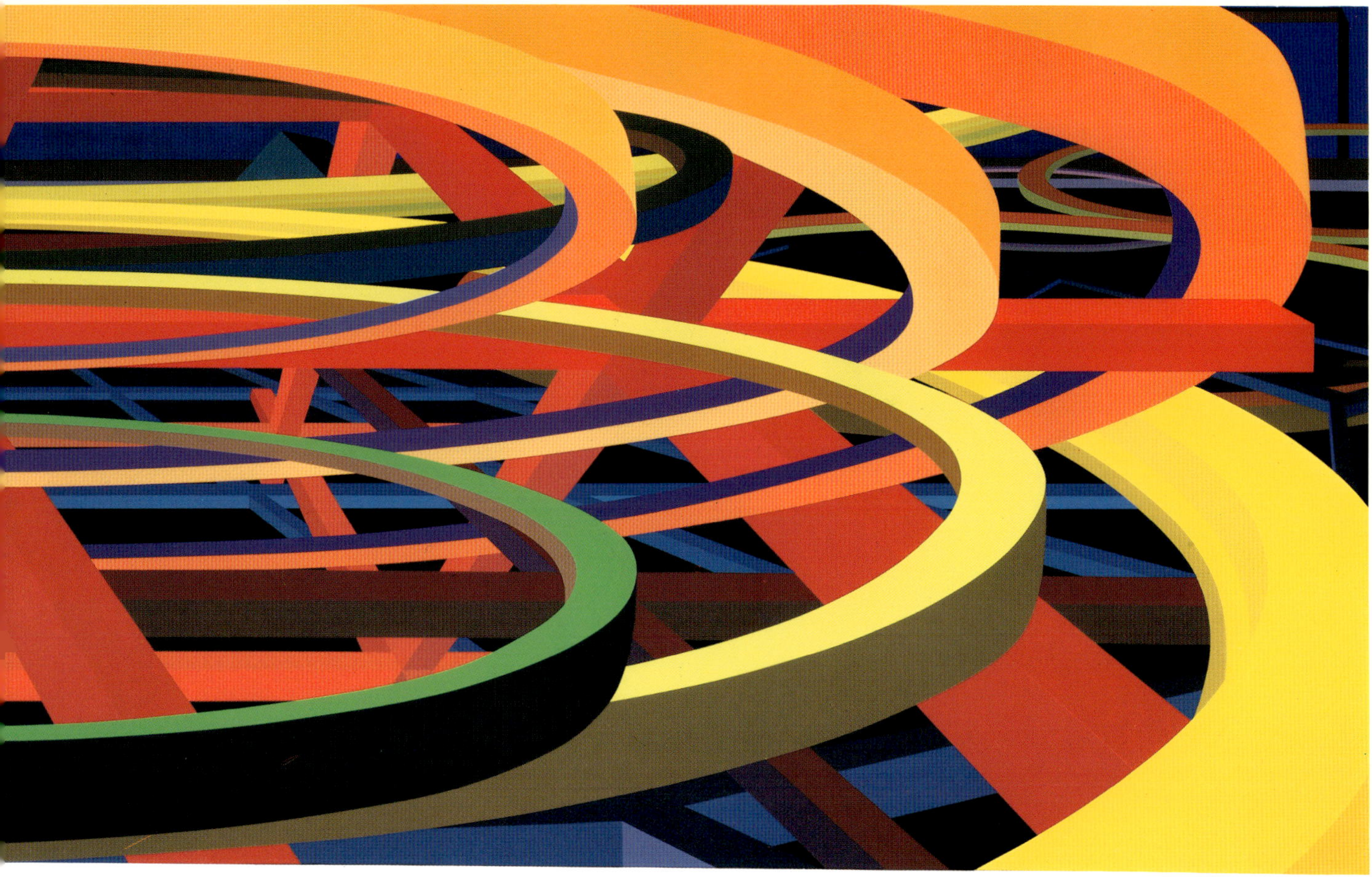

124. **Second Circle,** 1987.
Acrylic on canvas, 60×192 in. (152.4×487.7 cm).
John Berggruen Gallery, San Francisco, California.

125. **Fathom Mark I,** 1988.
Acrylic on canvas, 60×72 in. (152.4×183 cm).
John Berggruen Gallery, San Francisco, California.

126. **Fathom Mark II,** 1988.
Acrylic on linen, 48×48 in. (122×122 cm).
Collection of Jack and Noreen Rounick, Gladwynne, Pennsylvania.

127. **Fathom Mark III,** 1988.
Acrylic on linen, 36×36 in. (91.5×91.5 cm).
Collection of Carol Rivin, Beverly Hills, California.

126

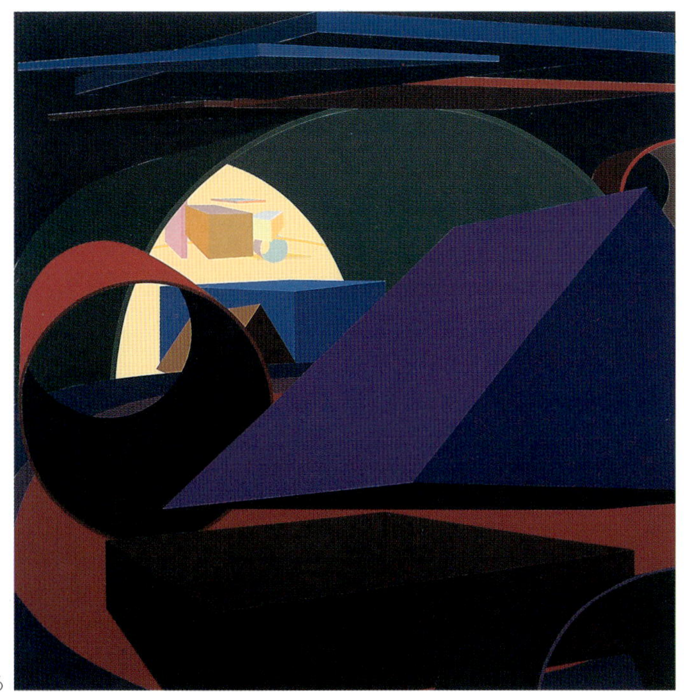

127

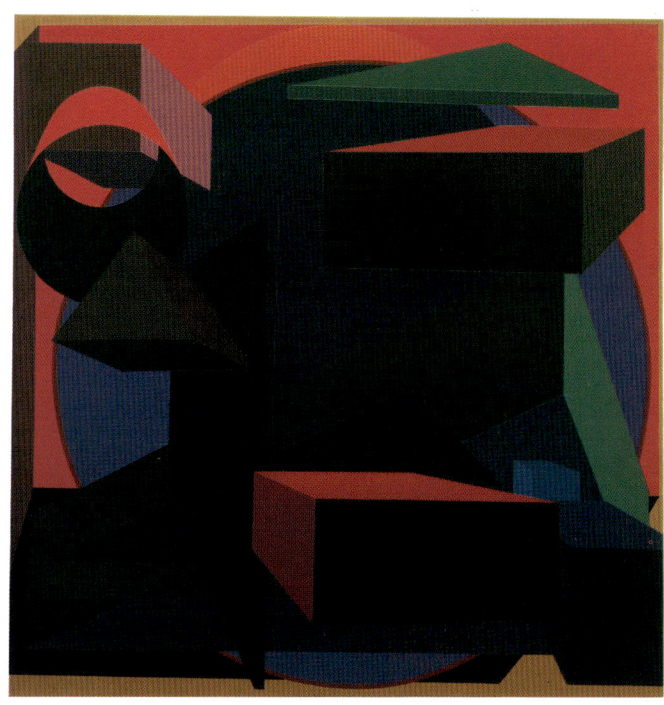

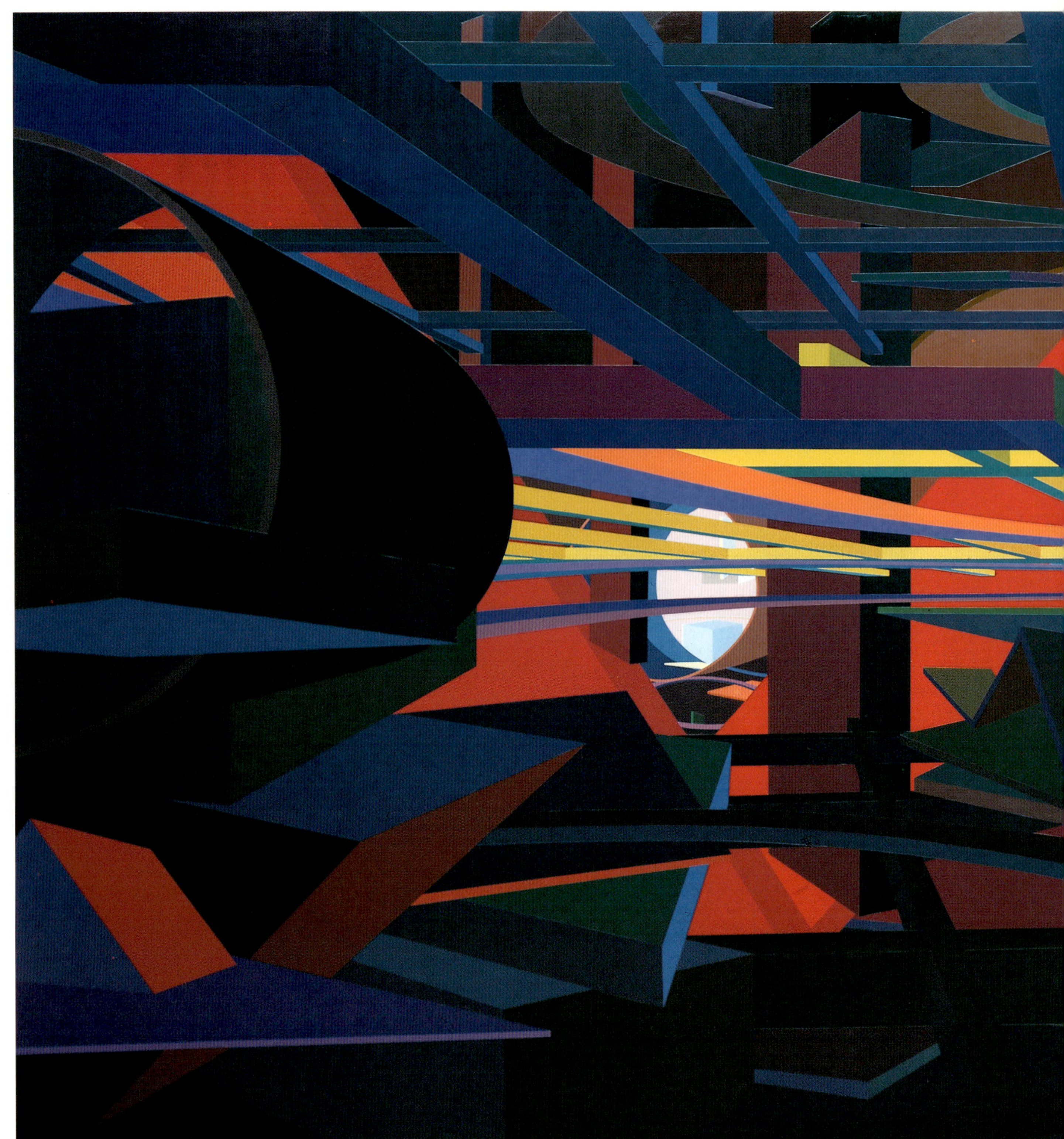

128

128. **Pan North XII,** 1988.
Acrylic on canvas, 168×300 in. (426.7×762 cm).
André Emmerich Gallery, New York.

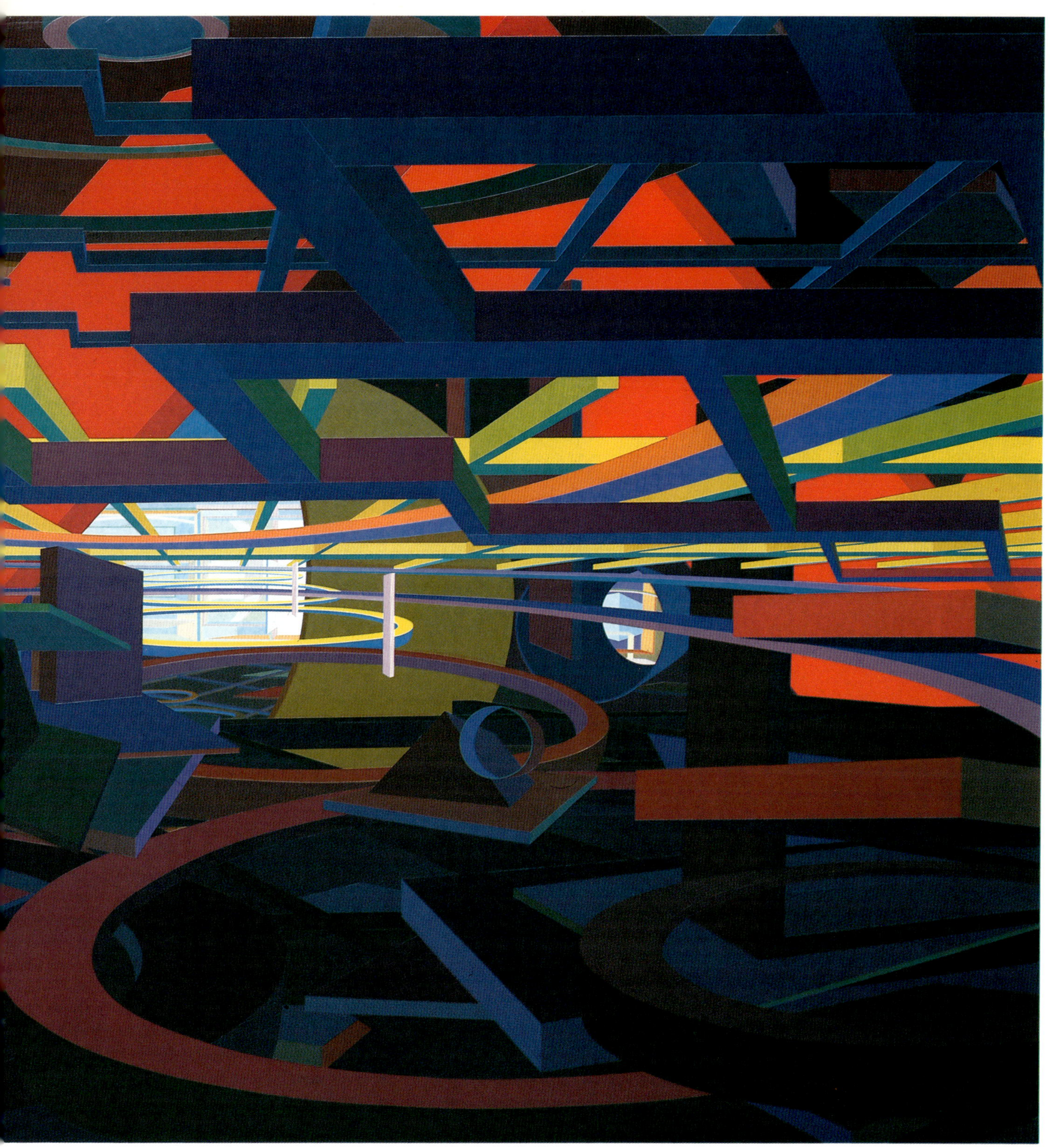

129. **Roberta's Trip IV,** 1988.
Acrylic on linen,
108×216 in. (274.3×548.5 cm).
André Emmerich Gallery,
New York.

130. **Fathom Mark XV,** 1989.
Acrylic on canvas,
60×72 in. (152.4×183 cm).
Collection of Professor
Alain Dubois, Lausanne.

131. **Quattro Centric III,** 1989.
Acrylic on canvas,
48×48 in. (122×122 cm).
Collection of Dr. and
Mrs. Kenneth Gitlin,
Bloomfield Hills, Michigan.

132. **Fathom Mark X,** 1989.
Acrylic on canvas,
48×48 in. (122×122 cm).
Collection of Andrea Fine,
Toronto, Ontario.

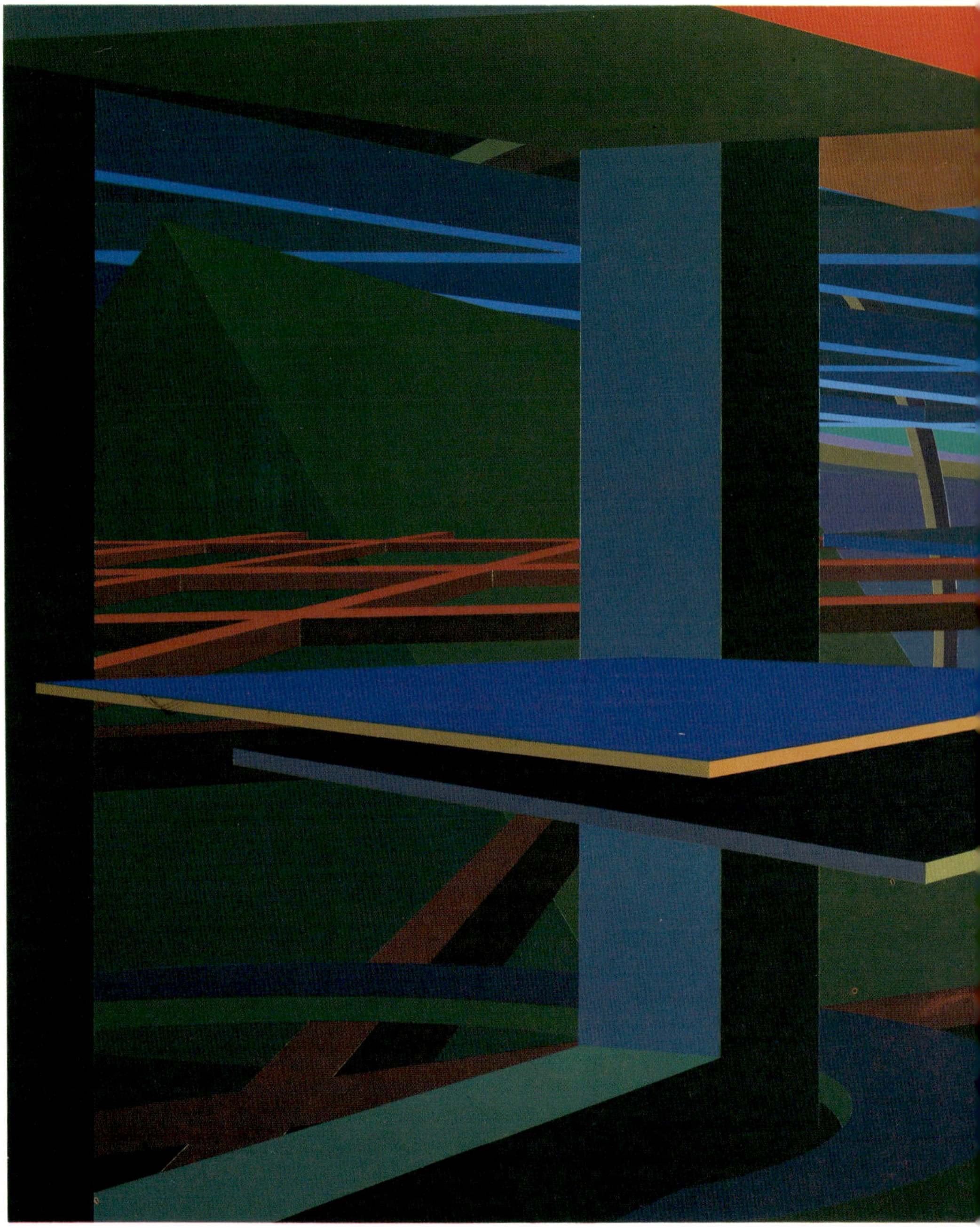

129

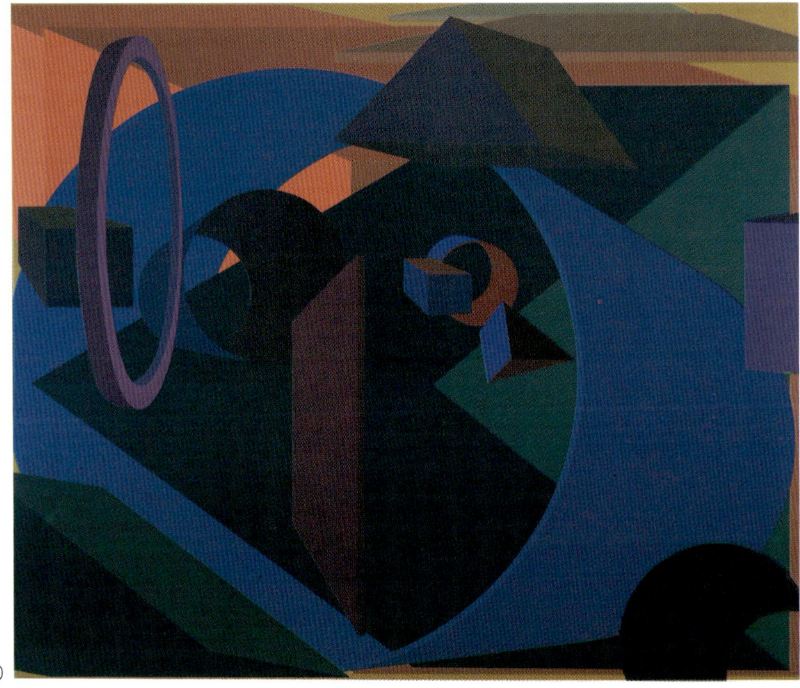

130

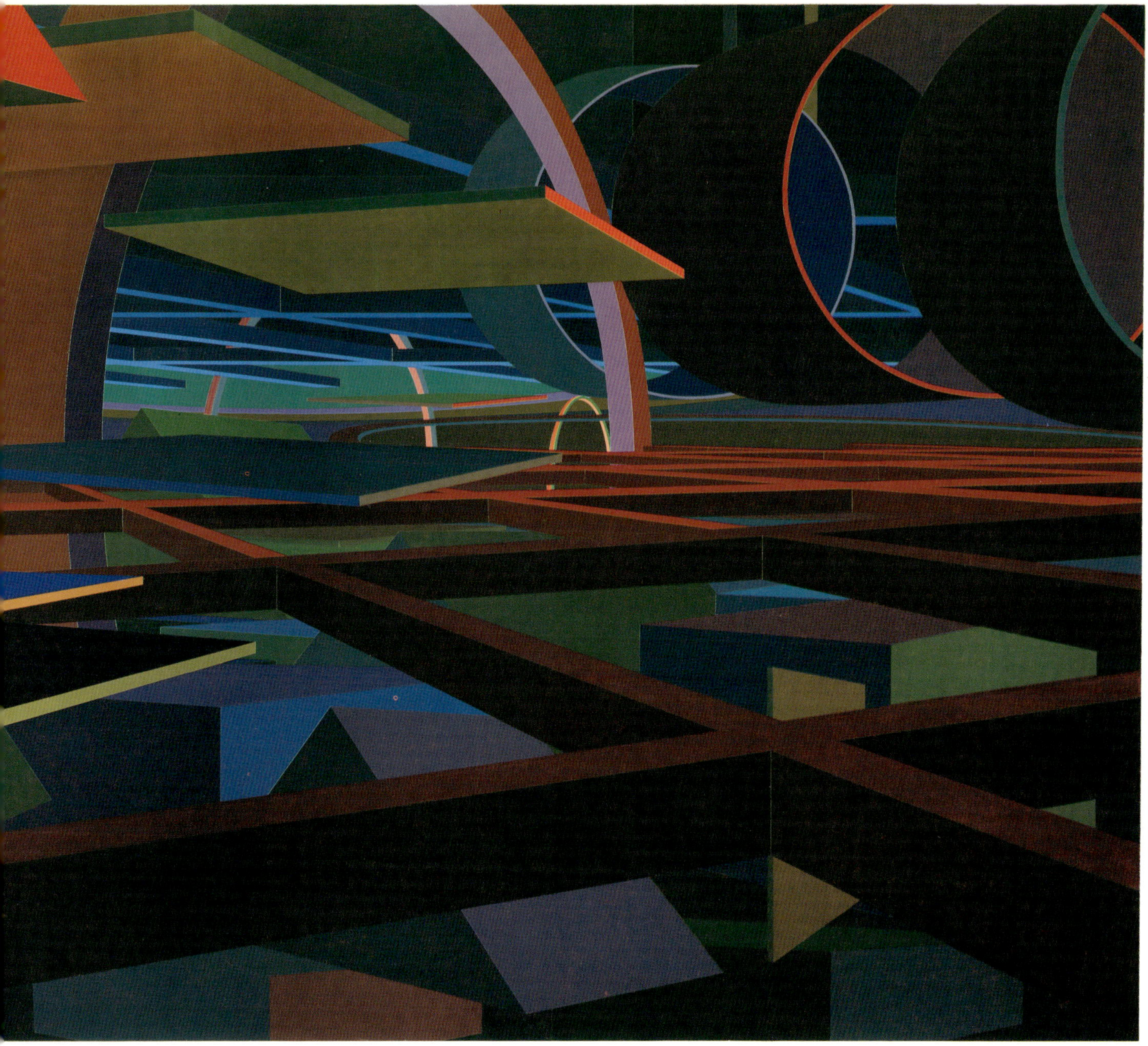

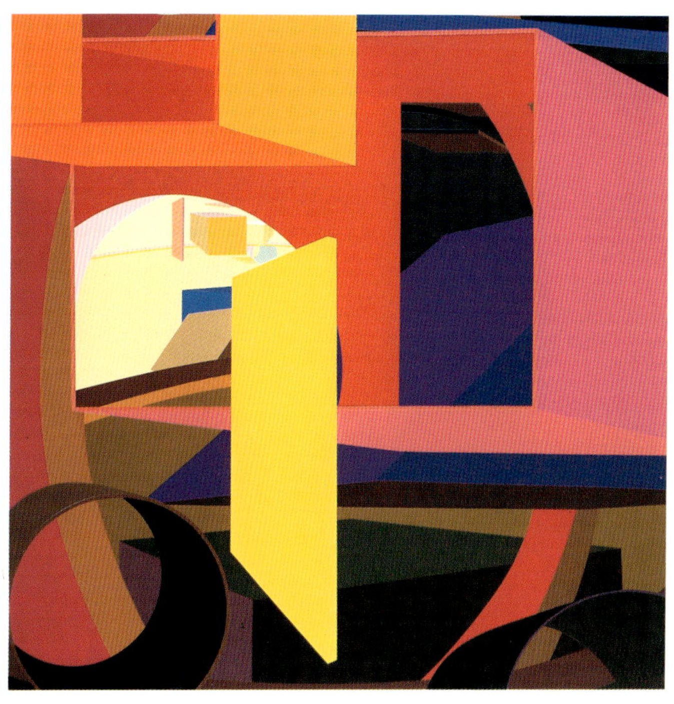

131

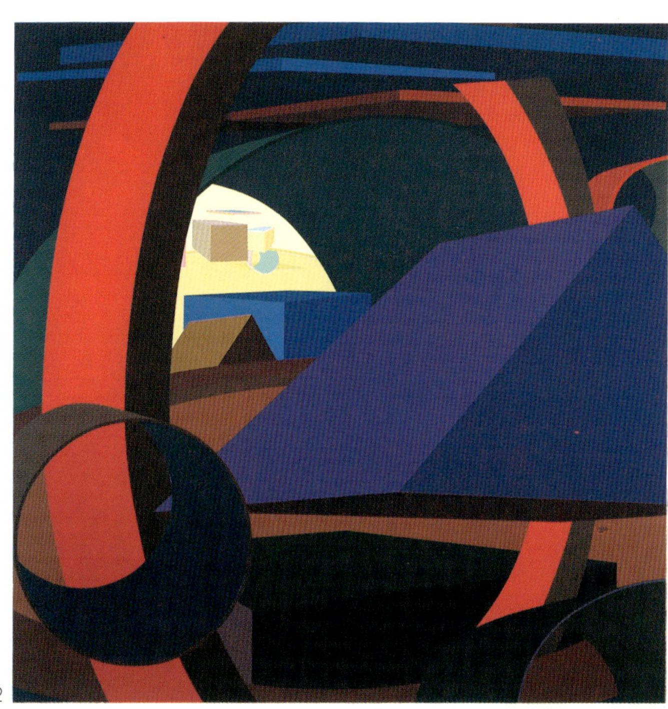

132

133. **Cygnus IV,** 1990.
Acrylic on canvas, 60×84 in. (152.4×213.4 cm).
André Emmerich Gallery, New York.

134. **Scand II,** 1989.
Acrylic on canvas, 96×144 in. (243.8×365.8 cm).
André Emmerich Gallery, New York.

135. **Q.C. XIV,** 1990.
Acrylic on canvas, 108×108 in. (274.3×274.3 cm).
André Emmerich Gallery, New York.

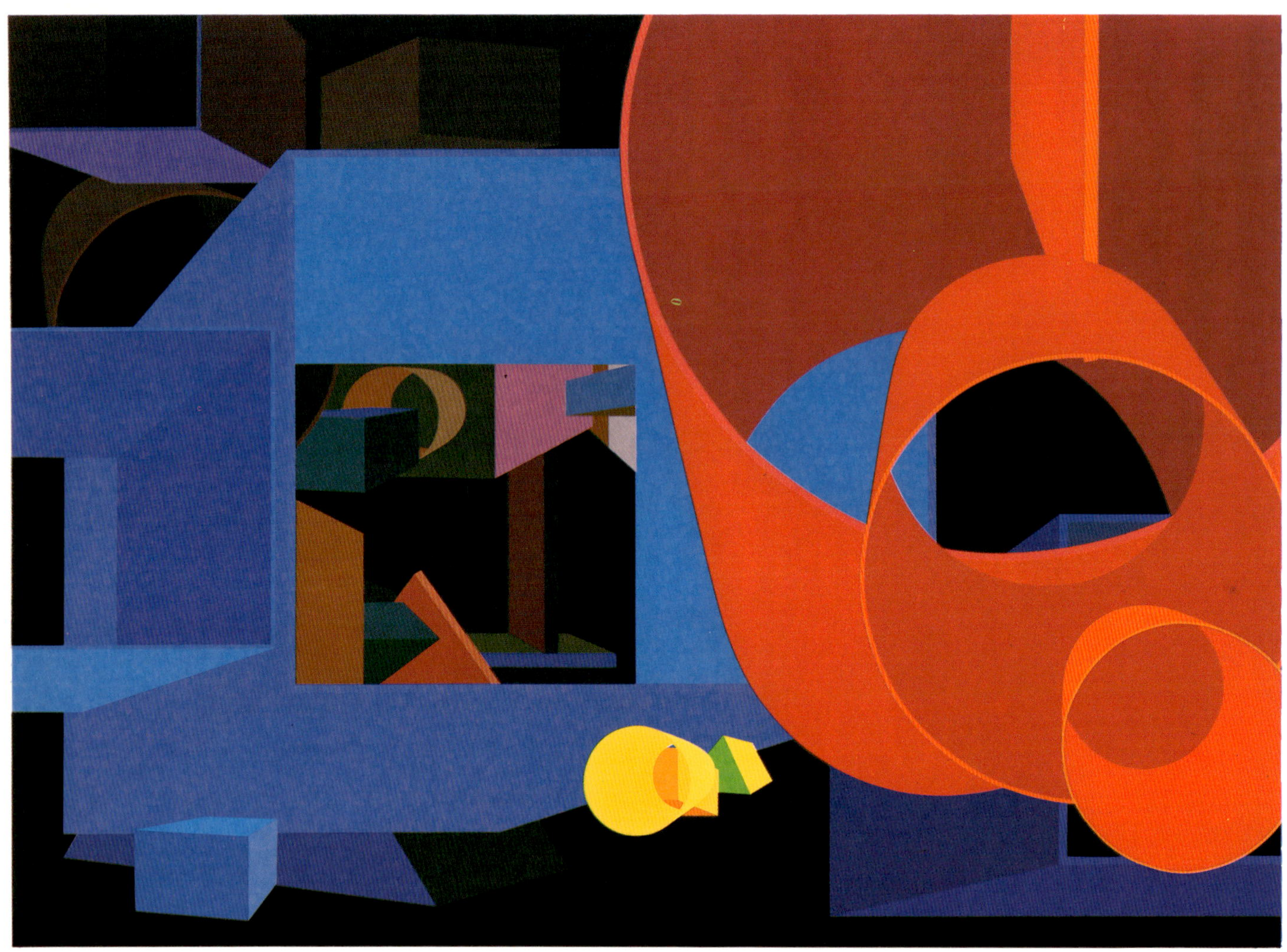

133

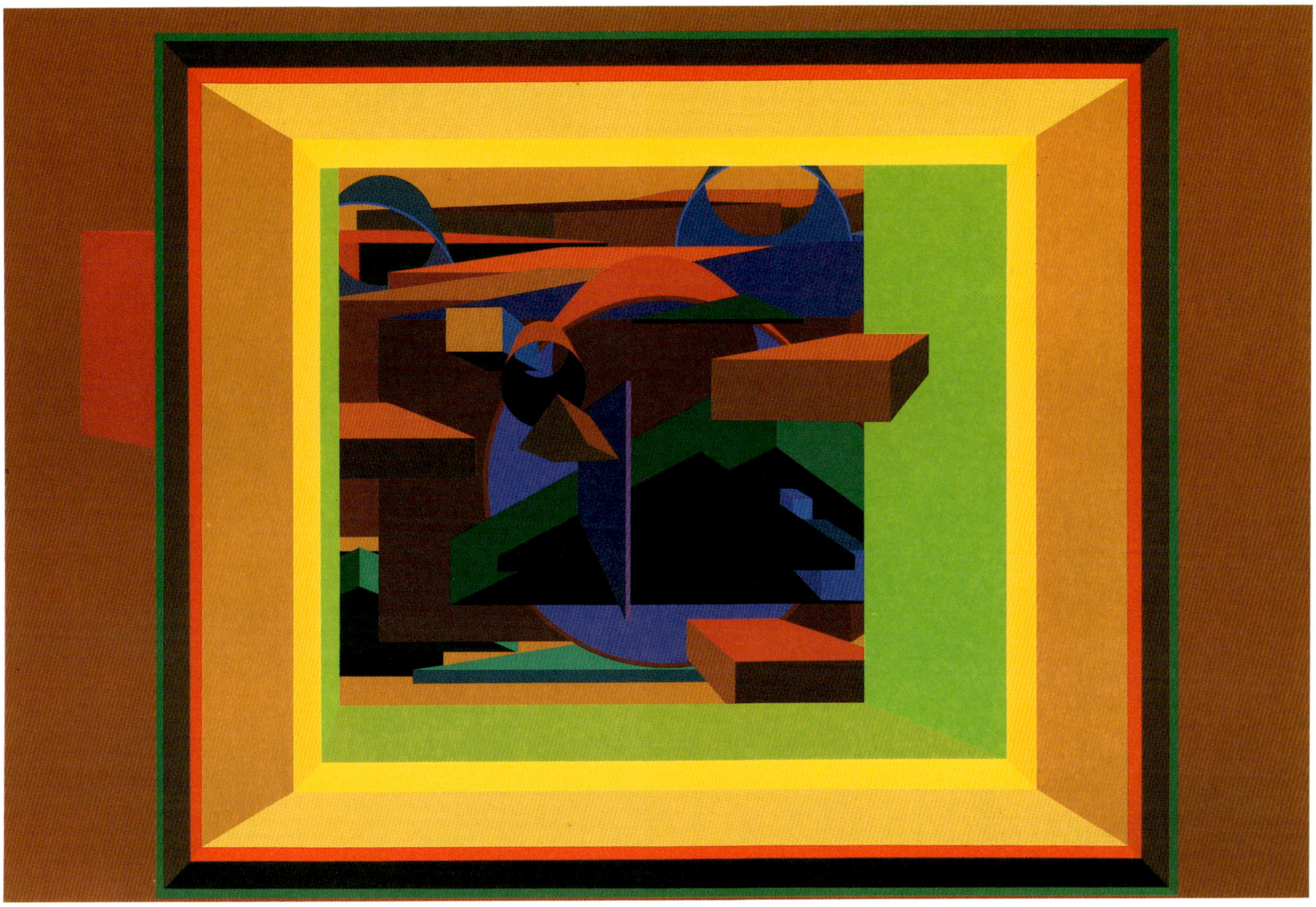

134

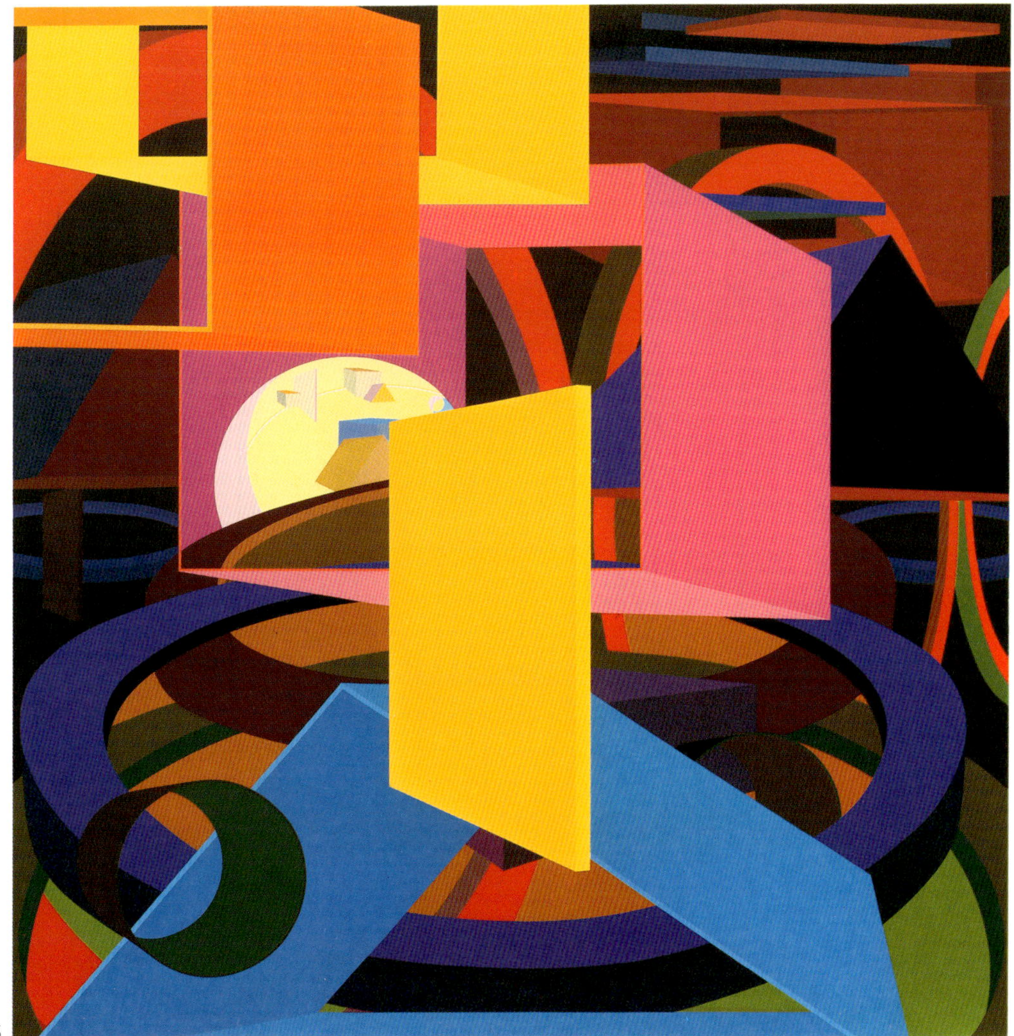

135

136. **Geocentric IV,** 1990.
Acrylic on canvas, 96×144 in. (243.8×365.8 cm).
André Emmerich Gallery, New York.

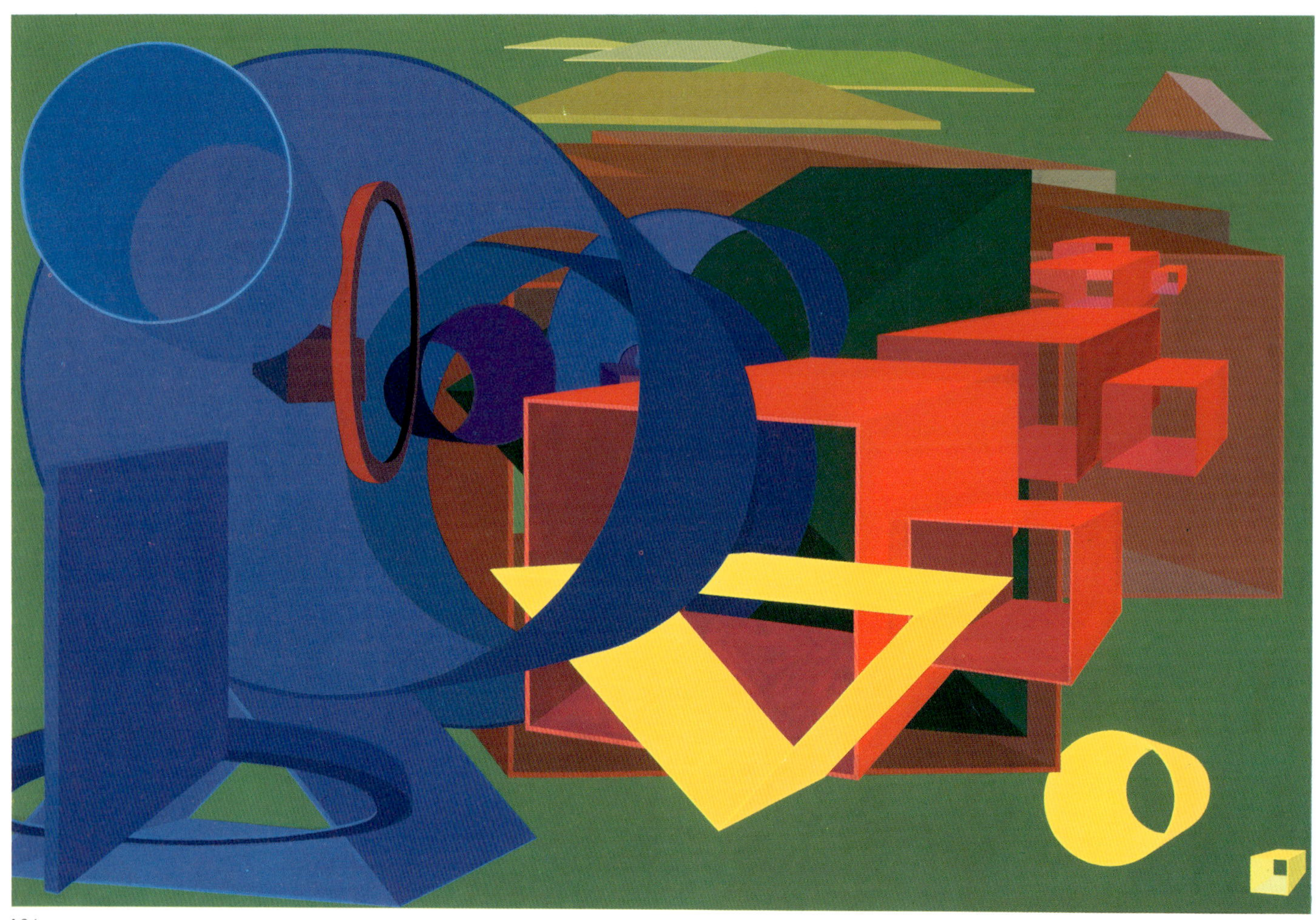

136

137. **H: If I told you, would you Know? II,** 1990.
Acrylic on canvas, 168×156 in. (426.7×396 cm).
André Emmerich Gallery, New York.

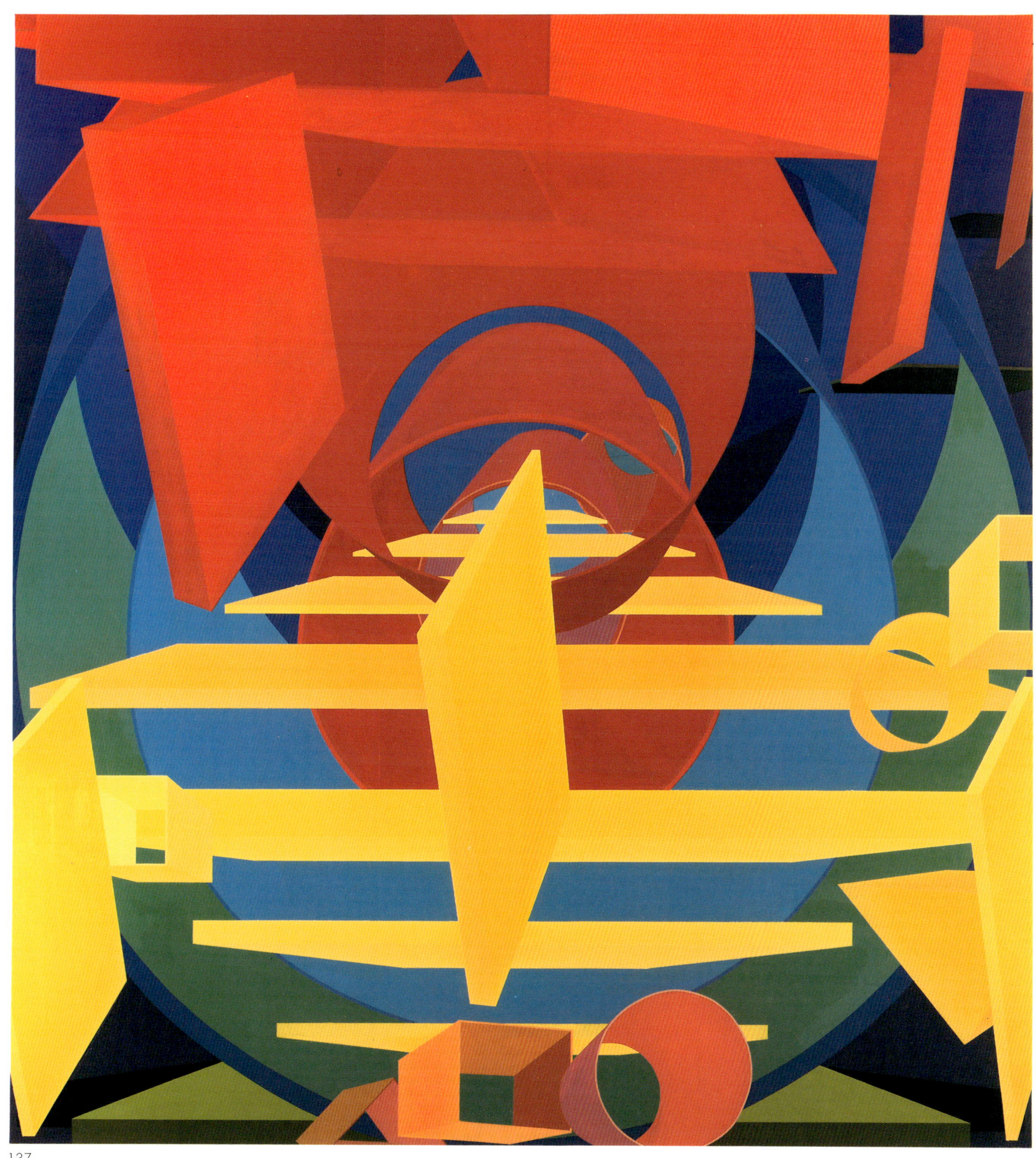

137

138. **H: If I told you, would you Know? I,** 1990.
Acrylic on canvas, 180×360 in. (457×914 cm).
André Emmerich Gallery, New York.

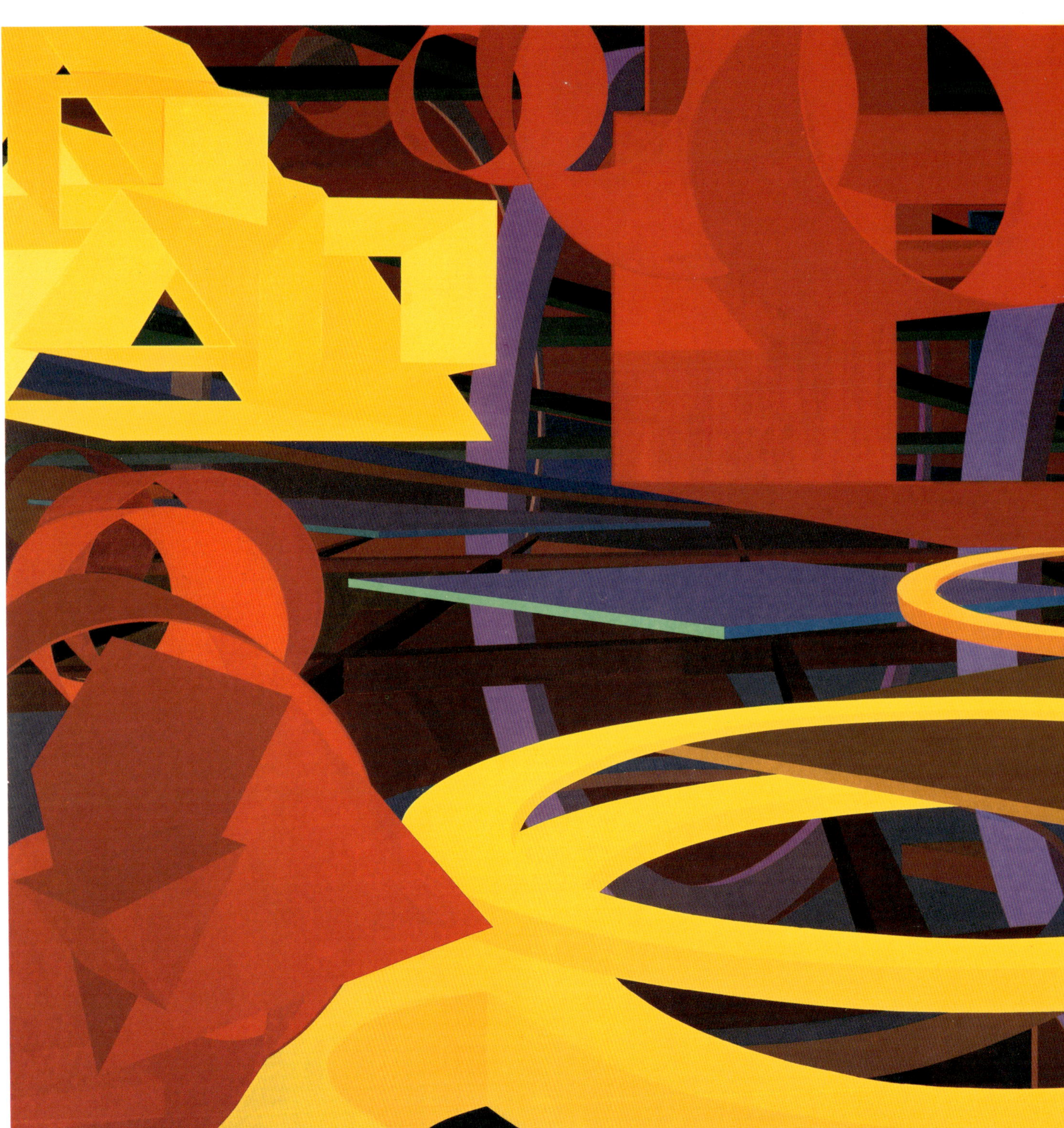

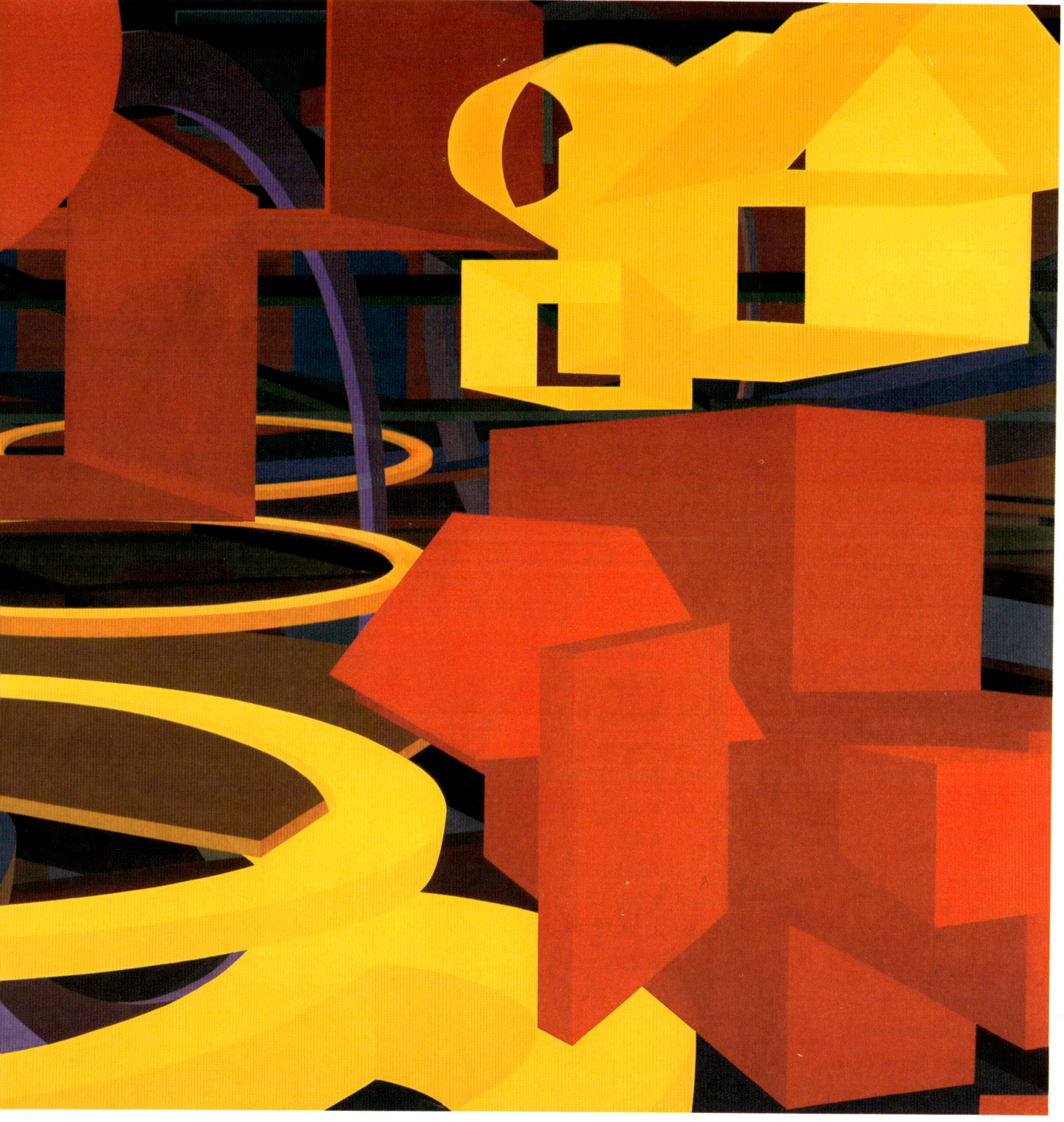